Work, Creativity, and Social Justice

WORK, CREATIVITY, AND SOCIAL JUSTICE

Elliott Jaques

International Universities Press, Inc.
New York

© Elliott Jaques 1970
First published 1970

Library of Congress Catalog Card Number: 72-128624

Printed in Great Britain

Preface

It may not seem immediately clear why these papers should have been published together. They deal with such apparently diverse matters as artistic creativity, industrial work, economics, psycho-analysis, law, groups, management, measurement, and science. But in fact they all have to do with one pattern of interconnected themes – that of work, creativity, and social justice.

Work and creativity do not follow from any special academic discipline. It is rather the other way round. We need a multiplicity of disciplines to help us understand the processes of work and creativity. We then avoid the pitfalls of viewpoints that are too restricted, and we gain some insight as to the true nature of these important human processes. They are psychological processes, with deep unconscious roots; they are part of economic life; they may occur in solitude or in the setting of groups or under management; they can be rewarded more equitably if measured, and they need to be considered together, since all work is creative and all creativity is work.

The connection of work and creativity with social justice arises from the fact that it is in a just environment that creativeness and the capacity for work find their optimum conditions for expression. Moreover, from the psychological point of view, work and creativity are limited and moulded by the same internal constraints that make lawful behaviour and social justice possible.

I would hope, therefore, that these essays will interest those who are intrigued by work and creativity and social justice in the widest sense; and that they will be experienced by my colleagues in art and literature, in economics, in psycho-analysis, in law, in management and administration, in sociology, in psychology, and in education, as a contribution to linking their own thought to that of others in other fields.

E.J.

Acknowledgements

A number of these papers have been printed or read before, and some of them appear here in an amended form. My thanks are due to the publishers for their permission to reprint:

'The Science of Society': Inaugural address on becoming Professor and Head of the School of Social Sciences, Brunel University; published in *Human Relations*, Vol. 19, No. 2, 1966.

'Death and the Mid-Life Crisis': *International Journal of Psycho-Analysis*, Vol. 46, Part 4, 1965.

'Disturbances in the Capacity to Work': *International Journal of Psycho-Analysis*, Vol. 41, Parts 4–5, 1960.

'Stress': *Journal of Psychosomatic Research*, 1966, Vol. 10, Pergamon Press (under title of 'Executive Organization and Individual Adjustment').

'Social Organization and Individual Adjustment': paper read to Royal Medico-Psychological Association, 6 July 1967 (under title 'Social Institutions and Individual Adjustment').

'Guilt, Conscience and Social Behaviour': read in the Winter

Lectures of the British Psycho-Analytical Society; 1967; published in the series by Ballière, Tindall and Cassell Ltd.

'Psycho-Analysis and the Current Economic Crisis': paper read as part of the Freud Centenary celebrations, and published in *Psycho-Analysis and Contemporary Thought*, No. 53 of the International Psycho-Analytical Library.

Contents

Contents

I

The Human Consequences of Industrialization

A massive change is taking place in the world, that is one of the outstanding features of the twentieth century. It is a change to a situation in which 90 per cent or more of the working population of industrialized nations are employed for a wage or salary in work organizations. This change, of the order of that from slavery to feudalism, is the accompaniment of industrialization. Max Weber might have called it the bureaucratization of society; Karl Marx, the process of proletarianization.

Up until the nineteenth and twentieth centuries the majority of the working population were in one form or another self-employed: either in one-family agricultural holdings, or in small family business, or on genuine piecework, or as itinerant or seasonal labour, or in that special part-of-the-family called being in service. Only very few people, perhaps no more than 10 or 20 per cent, were employed for a wage or salary in employment organizations – mainly in government, or in the army, or in the Church.

With world-wide industrialization, however, the whole situation is dramatically changing. There is a wholesale movement from the situation of self-employment to that of being employed in employment organizations for a wage or salary; and the organizations themselves are rapidly becoming more and more vast; great industrial complexes, commercial organizations, industrialized agriculture, local authorities, social services, the health service, educational organizations. This process of change has been completed in the so-called industrially advanced nations. But it is to be seen still taking place all over the rest of the world – a social process best described as herding everyone into a vast employment complex that constitutes a new zone of society – the zone lying between the nation and the state on the one hand and the family and the individual on the other. I propose to call this zone the *Intermediate Zone*.

The impact of this change on the individual and on family life has been studied and vividly portrayed by Miller and Swanson.[1] They have been able to show that much of the self-reliance and family cohesiveness that goes with possession of a small family holding or business is undermined. Family ties are weakened, values alter in the direction of a lessening of social concern. The changes are profound.

Despite the fact that this change is shaking the whole foundation of society, little is known about the properties of the employment organizations which make up the intermediate zone in which nearly everyone now works. In particular, no standards have been established as to the limits within which these employment organizations must be managed if they are to contribute to a socially healthy society, rather than contributing, as they do now, to great disturbances of our society.

One of the difficulties is that too narrow an approach is adopted in considering these organizations. Instead of recognizing that together they constitute an immensely significant intermediate zone influencing the whole of society, we tend to consider each organization separately in terms only of its economic efficiency.

This approach, however, merely scratches at the surface of the problem. It comes from those inside the organizations who are trying to make them run better in the sense of their giving less trouble, or of being more efficient or productive.

Within this limited frame of reference – the world of per-

[1] *The Changing American Parent* (New York: Wiley, 1958).

sonnel work, business economics, management consultancy and work study – all kinds of *ad hoc* procedures have the appearance of being reasonable and realistic: piecework, bonus schemes and productivity bargains that supposedly reward people for working harder, but which in fact are spurious and hollow methods; Whitley Councils, joint consultation, advisory committees, and similar institutions and procedures that are supposed to give more or less opportunity for participation, but which turn out to be empty procedures as far as any substantial influence on policy-making is concerned; procedures for assessing performance and for deciding progression and promotion, which are mostly inadequate even when systematically provided for, and which can never be effectively carried through because the relationships between superiors and subordinates are obscured and confused; and even arguments in favour of maintaining a state of moderate unemployment in society in order to avoid 'overheating the economy', a metaphor whose crudeness conceals its denial of the realities of human needs.

This narrow approach, with its mere palliatives, will not do. We are not dealing with individual enterprises. We are dealing with a vast sector of society – a sector in which people have their most direct relationship with their society. How people are treated at work has a profound influence upon their attitude towards their society, and upon society itself. Criteria such as the productivity or the efficiency of the individual enterprise cannot be allowed to be of primary concern when the shape of society itself is at issue.

Nor will a sentimental approach based on the notion that men of goodwill ought somehow to be considerate towards each other be of any greater help; nor an egalitarian approach which says that all men ought to be equal and therefore ought to be paid equally; nor a power-bargaining approach which says that men ought to be able to combine to use their power to get what they want.

What is required today, and urgently required, is not endless preoccupation with so-called management studies, and payment schemes, and palliatives for trying to make work organizations run better, but a hard look at what these organizations in the intermediate zone are really like, and how they can be managed, if we are to be able to use them in a manner that will contribute to the good society.

It is at this point, however, that we encounter the major problem with which I am here concerned. If we are not to use efficiency as our criterion for assessing employment organizations, what criteria are we to use? We have had to rely on the brilliance of insight of philosophers, of religious and revolutionary leaders, of moralists, of political theorists, for our conceptions of the nature of the best forms of social, economic, and political organization. But all these theories suffer from two major drawbacks: first, they are based upon over-simplified and incomplete conceptions of the nature of the human beings for whom societies are being planned; and second, the conceptions of human behaviour remain untested and untestable, so that the advantages of the various political ideologies remain a matter of opinion and political debate.

What is required is to find a more objective basis for our judgments. I am going to suggest that that basis may well be discovered in the findings of psycho-analysis. Instead of having to resort to general philosophical ideas of 'the good', we can turn to more precise formulations of the nature of man based upon direct observation. By doing so we can inquire into the characteristics of our social organizations in terms of how much they may or may not reinforce and encourage the psychologically healthy parts of human personality and mitigate human destructiveness.

Such an approach implies two propositions: first, that generalizations about normal human behaviour are possible; and second, that it is possible to describe social institutions in such a manner as to be able to display their psychological effects upon their members. I propose now to explore both these propositions. In doing so I shall assume a third, without being able to demonstrate it; namely, that if we construct our social institutions both in accord with the work to be done and in accord with the nature of human beings, then those institutions will function best. Such organization, paying due regard both to work and to human nature, may be termed requisite organization: requisite in the dictionary sense of 'being required by the nature of things'.

In pursuing my argument, let me first describe some features of the nature of employment organizations. Then I shall turn to consider the psychological implications of these organizations from the psycho-analytical point of view.

The Executive Hierarchy

The type of the organization in which most of us are employed has not been identified sufficiently clearly to be named. It is variously referred to as a 'family tree', or a 'pyramid', or a 'company', or most commonly simply as 'the organization'. These vague references will not suffice. They in no way satisfy our need for precision and clarity. In order to make it possible to consider the nature of these organizations in which people are employed, we shall need a name by which to refer to them. I propose to use the phrase 'executive hierarchies' – executive in the sense of having been established in order to get things done and hierarchy because they are constructed in a manner which gives some people authority over others. Most people will be familiar with this kind of organization, since most of us are employed in them.

Let me make it clear that I am considering only the organizations in which people are employed. I am not here considering the governing bodies of these organizations: variously referred to as Boards, or Boards of Directors, or Boards of Governors, acting on behalf of shareholders, or the government, or co-operators, or whichever association of people brought the organization into being in the first place.

Regardless of how or why these employment organizations are established, they all take on the same form of hierarchical structure. The larger they are, generally the more levels they have, ranging from two levels in very small shops or offices, to seven and eight levels in those very large organizations which employ tens or hundreds of thousands of people.

Clearly, there will be important differences between the large and the small executive hierarchies, differences for example in the content of work and in the degree of anonymity in relation to the total organization. But there are certain crucial common features of employment in executive hierarchies, that is to say of employment in the intermediate zone of society, and it is some of these common features to which I shall turn.

Once the intermediate zone of society is established, practically the only way in which you can work to gain a livelihood is by finding employment in an executive organization. In order to work, in order to live, you have to get a job – and getting a job means taking up a position in an executive hierarchy. If you cannot find a job – that is, if you cannot find an organization that will employ you – then, by and large, you cannot work. For it is open to only a very few to be able to start a business of their own, or to get a smallholding on which they can hope to live.

Second, once you get a job, you will find yourself in one of the most significant of modern human relationships – that obtaining between a superior and a subordinate. This relationship is variously called having an immediate manager, or a boss, or a supervisor, or a departmental head, or a foreman, or an administrator. Whatever its title, the relationship is the same, and it is a relationship with a highly-charged emotional content.

In the first place, the superior has the authority to assign tasks to his subordinates, to determine what work they shall have to do. But at the same time, he himself remains accountable for the quality of the work that his subordinates do. He thus not only has authority over them, but he is also dependent upon them. Once he hands out work he must be able to rely upon his subordinates to carry it out.

Because the superior is held accountable for the work of his subordinates, he must have the authority to assess the quality of their work, and to influence the reward they receive and their progress. In the final analysis, if the superior is realistically to be held accountable, then he must be able to have subordinates who, though they might not be completely acceptable, are at least not unacceptable to him. Therefore, there must be provision for removal or transfer of subordinates who really prove to be unacceptable to a superior.

Here then is a situation of great psychological subtlety and complexity. There is the interplay and interaction of authority and accountability, of mutual dependence, of assessment of ability, of judgments about personal potentialities, of acceptability and dismissal, of recognition and reward. The superior's career as well as the subordinate's career, their economic security, and their recognition and self-esteem are wrapped up in it.

Not only is the superior-subordinate relationship a psychologically complex one, it is both tremendously occupying and exceedingly widespread in industrial societies. It is occupying in that it takes up the largest part of the waking hours of those of us who are employed in executive hierarchies. It is exceedingly common in that each and every executive organization in the intermediate zone has only one superior-subordinate relationship less than the total number of people it employs; that is to say, if an organization employs ten thousand people, it brings into being 9,999 superior-subordinate relationships.

The third point I want to make is that the direction of each enterprise in the intermediate zone, and the policies by which it is run, are supposedly the responsibility of the Board and not of the employees. Yet the reality is that there is a complex power situation involving the interests of the shareholders, the interests of the consumers, and the interests of the employees. Each of these groupings can close any enterprise down. The power of the shareholders is expressed through the Board. The power of the consumer is expressed through sales representatives who visit them, or through public relations or market research institutions. By and large, however, there are no satisfactory institutions through which the power of employees can be exercised in a constitutional manner to influence policy. This fact is expressed in the political importance attaching to the urgency of developing means of so-called participation by employees.

The fourth point concerns reward. There is little need to do more than refer to the current situation with regard to the means of determining wages and salaries, to demonstrate what difficulties lie in this region. Note what happens.

The self-employed person earns what he can. He is independent and he must accept the risks as well as the advantages of this independence. His income level is dependent upon the public response to his own efforts.

For the employed person the situation is entirely different. His income level is determined by forces that seem to be entirely outside his own control or reckoning. What he does know is how his reward compares with others. That is what counts for most. Underlying these comparisons there is a demonstrable sense of fair pay that seems to tie in very accurately with the level of responsibility carried. People at the same level of responsibility feel fairly rewarded if they are receiving the same level of pay as others at the same level, more than those at lower levels, and less than those at higher levels.

Now consider what happens when under industrialization the intermediate zone of society is well established and encompasses 90 per cent or more of all people at work. Cross-comparisons are made right across the board – teachers with factory workers, Civil Servants with bank staffs, social workers with secretaries, nurses with book-keepers, postmen with bus drivers, engineers with accountants, physicists with airline pilots, and so on. The demand arises for equitable treatment for everyone working in the intermediate zone. And equitable treatment means comparable treatment for all.

In short, with industrialization and the development of the intermediate zone of society, whether or not a person works is dependent upon his being able to find a job; second, millions of superior-subordinate relationships are formed, and the type of job a person has depends upon how he is judged by his superior or potential superior; third, employing organizations are not required to establish institutions and procedures whereby employees can express their power in a constitutional manner and participate in making the policies within which they are expected to work; and fourth, employees compare their level of reward – their wages and salaries – with other groups whom they judge to be carrying equivalent levels of responsibility, regardless of differences in occupation: the intermediate zone is treated as a single vast economic field calling for equitable treatment for all.

Psychological Impact of the Intermediate Zone
Now what happens as a result of this way of living? It is an understatement to say that uncertainty about a job, having your future career influenced by being assessed by someone else, being dependent upon the work of others in order to discharge your own responsibilities, finding the nature of your employment organization changing without having a say, and not having any way of being sure of equitable and fair reward, are each a source of anxiety; in combination they are sources of chronic tension.

But it is not enough merely to say that anxiety is generated. Such matters are not to be taken for granted. If people were different from what they are, they might thrive upon being able to leave everything in the hands of someone else. Indeed such an outlook characterizes the lotus-land fantasies of men – the only trouble with such fantasies being that they do not match the realities of the nature of man.

The disturbance that is stirred by this employment situation in the intermediate zone is two-fold. First, there is the reality-based sense of uncertainty and insecurity; and second, the stirring of unconscious psychotic anxieties, the unresolved left-overs of the emotionally turbulent situation of early infancy.

Work in the intermediate zone is insecure, performance is never perfectly judged, reward is inequitable, opportunity to participate is minimal. These circumstances run counter to the normal nature of man, as I shall try to show in a moment. If we had sufficient constitutional and economic knowledge we could overcome these problems without too much difficulty. But we do not have that knowledge as yet – we are only beginning gradually to acquire it.

To make matters worse – and here lies the most difficult problem – the stirring of unconscious psychotic anxieties in the group situation sets up one of the most formidable barriers to learning and to change. I am not saying the *only* barrier; I am saying a very formidable barrier.

The employment situation I have described arouses intense feelings of persecution, and in doing so stirs up an unconscious reliving of the unresolved persecutory anxieties first experienced in infancy. It is these stirrings of unconscious anxieties and their accompanying defence mechanisms that add peculiarly in-tractable difficulties because they become projected into the social situation where they produce incalculable complications.

We owe it to the insights of Melanie Klein into the un-conscious mental life of children that we can follow through the complex processes of the very primitive anxieties which she termed paranoid, or persecutory, anxiety. What happens, briefly, is that to the extent that his primitive infant conflicts remain unresolved, a person is unable to control his unconscious loving and hating impulses. Two factors contribute to the primitive difficulties: first, the intensity of the impulses themselves; and second, the environmental situation – that is to say, inadequacies and inconsistencies in care and handling by the mother which arouse frustration and rage alternating with gratification and love. The resulting ambivalence is intolerable – it is emotionally traumatic to hate and to try to destroy what you love – it is equally traumatic to love your persecutors.

Ambivalence is resolved by splitting. The object is either perceived as a persecutor and hated; or it is perceived as good and loved. But there is no mixing. Of course the price to be paid for splitting is loss of reality by means of denial: denial of opposing feelings, so that hate and persecution cannot be mitigated by love.

Along with splitting of feelings, and denial, goes a third major feature of the paranoid-schizoid position, that of projection and projective identification. This unconscious mechanism supports splitting and denial by attributing the person's own hate to others, so that the sense of persecution is intensified. Similarly, love is projected, and the good part of the object thus gains in good qualities and becomes ideally good and loving. The end result is not difficult to envisage – intense idealization oscillating with intense persecution. This pattern firmly established is extraordinarily resistant to change.

Evidence that this unconscious persecutory situation is stimulated in people by the situation in the intermediate zone is not difficult to find. Splitting occurs in the taking of sides: all bosses are grasping and bad; all employees are greedy and irresponsible and lazy; everyone on your own side is good, everyone on the other side is bad. A particularly rigid and harsh black and white outlook dominates the inter-group relationships, despite the fact that the very same people may have a much more flexible attitude based on mutual respect when they meet each other as real individuals in the work situation as against the artificialities of the group situation where they must represent the views of others.

Along with this splitting and projective identification goes rampant denial, and evasion of reality. Gimmicks abound, reminiscent of the philosopher's stone and of alchemy. So-called productivity bargains are solemnly made, despite the fact that productivity cannot be measured, and even if it were possible to measure it, it would still not be possible to ascribe any increase to the activities of any particular work-group. Bargaining procedures are used which require greed and selfishness as sources of power; and yet greed, selfishness and the use of power are denied, at the same time that the dedicated and restrained are punished economically. The idea of management development has become the fashion, yet there is no generally agreed definition of what a manager is. Job evaluation is supposed to be a solution: but no one apparently notices that, when you really look into it, it is simply power bargaining in another guise.

These pseudo-solutions and procedures are to be found everywhere. The point about them is not so much that they are ineffectual, but that they are believed to be realistic and are treated as if they were so. This uncritical approach is the product of unconscious denial on a mass scale. It blocks all attempts to come to grips with reality. Clarity of definition and conceptual precision are often avoided. Everyone is entitled to mean what he wants to mean. The turbulent social situation has come to serve a widespread pathological function: that of acting as a reservoir in which to pile up and store inner unconscious psychological conflict and persecutory anxieties.

The mass unconscious collusion to deny reality and enhance conflict combined with what is in any case an intellectually difficult problem, almost precludes any rational solution to the management of the intermediate zone of society. And yet if the problem is not resolved, and resolved by the turn of the century, social chaos on a massive scale will be the result.

The Nature of Man

The problem then is how to break through the unconscious anxieties about effective social institutions in the intermediate zone. At least four rights must be firmly established for the employed 90 per cent of the working population: the right to employment at full capacity; the right of appeal against the judgements of superiors; the right to participate in policy-making; and the right to equitable reward.

It might be considered that these rights were self-evident. But self-evident truths are arguable. They are not always evident to everyone. They are articles of faith. They are therefore open to question. And in the world of business and commerce, or government, or the provision of social services, where financial resources are always in short supply, self-evident truths are too easily set aside if they threaten to add to the burden of expense. Arguments in favour of establishing fair and equitable conditions are thus readily pushed aside as being unrealistic, or 'soft', or at best of being totally uneconomic.

It occurred to me, however, that we might bring the argument on to much firmer ground if we could know what social conditions reinforce normal human behaviour and diminish the projection of psychotic anxieties into society. Such knowledge requires that we should know what, if anything, is normal behaviour – or even if there are general criteria of normality. Here is a difficult question that we might resolve by referring to certain findings implicit in psycho-analysis. For analysis does not deal only with psychopathology. It deals also with the normal personality – although this fact may be far less evident. Every time an analyst interprets his patient's behaviour, the intepretation is made against a conception of what the patient would be like if he or she were not subject to the unconscious play of unresolved early conflict. As the analysis progresses and conflict is reduced, types of behaviour are noted that are accepted as more normal. And finally as the analysis reaches the point of possible termination, the so-called criteria of termination are used by the analyst in judging when a stopping point is appropriate.

We may note further that many of these criteria of termination are general; as, for example, sexual potency, the capacity to comprehend verbal communication, control of murderous impulses, capacity to love and to recognize the needs and abilities of others, capacity to utilize abilities to the full in work, and so on. Such criteria are accepted as applying to everyone, not on moral or ethical or any *a priori* grounds, but as a result of repeated observation that individuals have these characteristics when they are freed from unconscious unresolved primitive conflict.

From the point of view of establishing the nature of requisite organization in the employment organizations of the intermediate zone, I would like to pick out the following features of personality consistent with the termination of an analysis – our so-called normal personality characteristics.

First, the normal person seeks not only to work, but to work at a level of responsibility that taxes his capacity to the full. Man is a problem-solving animal and must make continuous use of his mental and physical apparatus.

Not to be able to work at full capacity is restrictive, depressing, and finally persecuting. The avoidance of work at full capacity, or the acceptance of underemployment, is symptomatic of emotional disturbance.

Second, the normal person is independent in several important senses. He seeks to establish for himself the goals for which he is working, or at least to take part in establishing them if he is working in a group. He may not always appear to be in that state of mind, since if the objects of the nation, or the work group, or other associations in which he is involved, are sufficiently satisfactory to him, he does little. If, however, they are unsatisfactory, he feels the demand in him to have the right to try to alter those objects.

This independence is not inconsistent with a normal capacity to be involved in group consensus; that is to say, in taking part with others in arriving at a generally acceptable object and adhering to it, even though it may not completely satisfy him.

Another way in which this independence shows itself is in a rejection of subjecting himself to the final judgement of any one individual alone. Under circumstances where judgements are to be made – whether in the assessment of his performance at work, or of entitlements in the community, or of his behaviour in law – he does not accept the judgement of one person, whether manager, or official or judge. He demands recourse not only to a review of any such judgement if he is not satisfied with it, but to public review in a lawful setting.

In short, normal man is law-abiding and law-demanding in the sense of conforming to social consensus and due process of law, and in the sense of requiring independence from total control from any other individual acting privately.

The individual who gives himself up to the judgements of others and to the objects of others is observed to have the psychopathology of passivity and masochism. He is observed to attempt to relinquish his own personality to the analyst in the transference situation. Independence of view and of behaviour is a *sine qua non* of successful treatment.

Third, normal man has a strong sense of equity and social

justice. He is committed to achieving what he judges to be his proper place in society, and to taking part in a social arrangement which provides that proper place for himself and for everyone else. He is aware of the differences between himself and others, and can judge in what respects others may be more or less competent than himself.

In the absence of this sense of differences, of equity and of justice, what we see is the individual disturbed by omnipotence or by impotence and self-depreciation. Freed from such pathology, the individual seeks to participate in a society which provides appropriate differential treatment to individuals in accord with their normal make-up. In the employment work situation, this normal propensity shows up as a readily demonstrable set of norms of fair differential payment related to differentials in level of work carried and differentials in individual capacity.

This normal man would, of course, have his own strong individuality – characteristics in which he would differ from other people, such as in his interests, his ambitions, his likes and dislikes, his capacities. But there are also these positive qualities that each fully analysed person would possess. They may sound exceedingly virtuous. In some respects they combine all the characteristics of the godly man as perceived by the major religions, Christian, Muslim, Jewish. They are the qualities of the Greek heroes, as well as those of the good and ethical men of the philosophers – of Aristotle, Plato, Kant and others concerned with ethics and morality. They are also the qualities of the reasonable man whom the lawyers use as the yardstick against which to judge whether a particular act was or was not culpable.

But what I would like to suggest is that what we find in the religions, in ethics, in politics, in law, is not really a description of a 'good' man – it is nothing more than an approximation to a description of what men are like when they are undisturbed both from within and from without. That is to say, the good man turns out to be nothing more than man in his normal social and psychological state. There is really nothing either good or bad about it. It is just what it is. With our strong deistic and magical tendencies, however, we have been inclined to attribute a form of godliness to our natural state.

Conversely, it is noteworthy that what is called sinful in

religion, unethical in philosophy, illegal in law, is also behaviour that would not occur in a society of normal men and
women living within social codes reinforcing that normal
behaviour. Unethical, sinful, immoral, illegal, are value-laden
terms to describe deviations from normal individual behaviour
in a normal social setting.

Requisite Organization

We may now pose our original problem more sharply. Modern
industrial society organizes its work in executive employment
hierarchies, built up from hundreds or thousands of dyodic
superior-subordinate relationships. Nearly everyone who works
is left no choice but to obtain work in these hierarchical systems.
The executive hierarchy has thus come profoundly to affect the
nature of society. Yet practically nothing has been known about
these social systems – they have hardly yet been identified
sufficiently to have come into the explicit awareness of society.

   Our brief consideration of some aspects of the nature of man
suggests that if executive hierarchies, with their in-built
superior-subordinate accountability and authority, are to function in a socially constructive manner, they must provide for at
least four major needs that are demonstrably features of any
normally functioning human being. The four needs of the person are: utilization of his full capacity in problem-solving at
work; involvement in setting the objectives or policies of any
group or institution in which he is joined; independence from
control by any individual without recourse to public process of
review of that control by others; possession of his appropriate
differential position in the group and cohesive response to an
all-round equitable distribution of status and reward.

   These needs demand that our industrialized society must
provide: abundant employment in society at large; opportunity
for all employees to participate in setting the policies of the
executive hierarchy in which they are working; the right of the
subordinate to appeal against the judgement of his superiors;
authority for the accountable superior to judge the performance
of his subordinates and to cause this judgement to affect their
progress; the right of everyone to equitable reward.

   In fact the situation in society is that marginal unemployment is endemic, so that it is difficult for anyone to find

employment that fully stretches his capacities; opportunity for participation exists practically nowhere; nor do individual appeal systems; and systems of equitable reward not only do not exist, the very idea is almost universally held to be uneconomic and impractical.

The result is that work in industrial society, instead of strengthening normal mental processes, is in fact contributing to the strengthening of psycho-pathological processes and to the eruption of violence. Passivity is encouraged and omnipotence provoked. Unnecessary frustration and insecurity are to a greater or lesser extent continuously experienced. Greed and envy are stirred by manifest inequity. Autocratic and unjust treatment is inevitable, even with the best of goodwill, in the absence of provision for participation and appeal. All the conditions are present for the revival of the primitive paranoid-schizoid situation.

Society is suffering from these effects. Projection, with accompanying idealization and persecution, is widespread and accepted as ordinary. Splitting and fragmentation follow, and the split society is the result. It is from this splitting based upon paranoid-schizoid mechanisms that the violence stems.

The industrial relations approach to overcoming these problems is grossly inadequate. The problem is wider than industry, or commerce, or the Civil Service. What is needed is a political science of the intermediate zone, with standards derived not from ethics or religion, but from the objective analysis of the nature of man. I have tried to illustrate the application of psycho-analysis to the discovery of these standards. These have been described elsewhere[1] the results of twenty years of work at the Glacier Metal Company. This work has, in my view, demonstrated how the analysis of the nature of work, of superior-subordinate relationships, of executive organization, of the role of elected representatives, can lead to the development of effective institutions for manage-

[1] See, for example, Wilfred Brown, *Exploration in Management*: Heinemann Educational Books Ltd, London; Penguin Books, Harmondsworth, Middlesex, England, 1965; Wilfred Brown and Elliott Jaques, *Glacier Project Papers*: Heinemann Educational Books Ltd, London 1965; Elliott Jaques *Equitable Payment*: Heinemann Educational Books Ltd, London 1961; and Penguin Books, Harmondsworth, Middlesex, England 1967.

ment and for participation, for appeals and for reward. The various institutions have so far been the subject of far too little attention by managers.

The difficulties in managing our executive hierarchies have led to their earning an increasingly bad name. They have in fact been autocratic, because of the absence of requisite organization. It is understandable, therefore, that students and those concerned with human welfare should adopt a rejective attitude.

But such negative attitudes are wide of the mark. The advantage of the executive hierarchy is that it has made large-scale technology possible. If we are to have this advantage we must recognize that the executive employment hierarchy is not in itself a force either for good or for bad in society; it is neither a healthy nor an unhealthy form of institution. The issue is whether or not we can learn how to establish on a constitutional basis a *modus operandi* for these organizations that will demand and permit the application of normal human qualities and endeavour. Given the development of requisite institutions, the emergence of the intermediate zone could contribute both to the mental health of the individual and to the strengthening of a healthy society.

2

The Science of Society

I

Although, in this scientific age, after 300 years of technical advance, we have come to recognize the revolutionary difference that a scientific approach can make in solving apparently intractable problems, we must yet ask why there is so little development in the use of scientific method in the government, in administration, and in the management of society and its institutions.

By government, administration, and management of society and its institutions, I am referring not to vague generalities, but specifically to the institutions that we ourselves take part in, or that affect us: our educational system and modes of teaching in schools; the structure and location of our cities and towns; our health service and administration of hospitals; how authority and responsibility are distributed in the relationship between government and nationalized industries; the organization and running of Civil Service departments, trade unions, and universities; the structure of responsibility for decisions in the management of industrial and commercial enterprises. In short I refer to all types of institution in our society.

Our current mode of administering and managing our institutions is mainly by custom and practice built upon unchecked assumptions and conventions. We modify, adapt, and develop these methods by means of intuitive judgement, opinion, guesswork, and rule-of-thumb, or by debating and arguing with each other within a framework of various types of political philosophy.

This empirical, rule-of-thumb approach does not work badly up to a point, so long as there is not too much disagreement about objectives and methods. But even at its best, modern social life cannot be said to be so satisfactorily arranged that the introduction of disciplined scientific thinking could not help to improve matters. Why, then, do we move so slowly and reluctantly in this direction? If we had at least a strong desire for a disciplined approach to the problems, there would be apparent in each of us the signs of resolute endeavour to forward research and thus increase our knowledge. It is the existence of the resolve and desire that I would question.

For let us make no mistake – it simply cannot be taken for granted that scientific knowledge, and its use to advance the satisfaction and wellbeing of mankind, are unreservedly accepted in our society. I do not, of course, refer to verbal acceptance. Nearly everyone will say he is in favour of science. It is like saying one is in favour of racial equality. There's no hardship in that! But being verbally in favour of science is a far cry from accepting the personal implications of the use of disciplined description of our own institutions and behaviour as a practical everyday guide to our own decisions and actions.

For now we must seek to understand not only the inanimate world around us, but also the social world of which we form a part. We must have the courage to seek disciplined descriptions and adequate models of ourselves, individually and in relation to each other; of the social institutions in which we take up roles – at work, at home, and at leisure; of the larger social environment of the nation and of the world, in which we co-operate and survive, or fight and die.

Disciplined description meets resistance, for it seems to challenge the freedom of the human spirit – the freedom of

ideas. What in fact is challenged is a spurious freedom, one not
worth preserving. It is the freedom to believe that, because we
think something, then it must be so – a kind of *cogito ergo est!*
We resent losing the freedom to have our own personal models:
prejudices about the effects of the death penalty; stereotypes
about shop stewards and business tycoons; fantasies about the
best way to overcome the problems of the adolescent; opinions
about whether comprehensive schools are best; illusions about
the existence of absolute principles and policies – not to mention
our anxiety about the possibility of losing relative position and
privilege.

Francis Bacon described this resistance as 'the rejection of
difficult things from impatience of research; sober things
because they narrow hope; the deeper things of nature from
superstition; the light of experience from arrogance and
pride . . .'[1].

Freud explained it as the unconscious impulse in each one of
us to seek the primitive state in which everything is magically
pleasurable, in preference to the pain and limitation, albeit
the maturity, of living under the constraint of the reality
principle.

II

Anxiety about freedom shows in countless ways. One of these
ways – and a most important one, widespread in its mani-
festations – is the cultivation of vagueness and confusion in
our own organizations. The slogan is: 'Let us leave it vague
so that individual creativeness can have a greater chance!'.
Even some social scientists favour this outlook, and express it in
the concept of informal organization; that is to say, in pur-
posely leaving unspecified the responsibility in certain areas of
organization, in which individual endeavour is allowed to
express itself in personal network, idiosyncratic to the persons
who happen to be in the organization at a given time. Perhaps
the best illustration is provided by so-called old-boy networks.

Many readers will be familiar with a recent expression of the

[1] Bacon, Francis (1620). *Novum Organum.* Trans. *The New Organon* (New
York: Liberal Arts Press, 1960).

reliance upon vagueness in the sections in the Robbins report[1] dealing with the government of universities. I choose this example because it is such an immediate issue to those connected with universities and it may thereby help to illustrate one of my main themes, which is that the point of social science is its application to our own institutions, so that it touches our own personal lives.

'Universities', the report states in discussing where ultimate authority lies, 'are no exception to the general rule that a great gulf lies between constitutions on paper and government in practice. A description of the function and composition of the statutory bodies is not necessarily an analysis of the real sources of initiative and power; these depend partly on the imponderables of specific circumstances and individual personalities, and are almost impossible to determine.' Later, in regard to major policy issues such as decisions about the size of the university and of the individual faculties, it says: 'Such policy-making is thus essentially in the hands of the senior academic staff', although it recognizes that this arrogated power of the senior professors often frustrates the reasonable expectations of the governors and the other members of staff to take a greater part in policy-making.

As a result of vaguely formulated constitutions of this kind, some of the most crucial issues for the development of university policy are left vague and unresolved. Through confusion of the question of *de jure* authority, which can be identified, with that of *de facto* power, which must always be a dynamic field of changing forces, the major question of where the nation can locate accountability for the policy of the individual university is left vague and unsettled. And we are all aware what stress and tension and pain can be engendered by this vagueness. There is accepted by default what the report recognizes as 'a system of government . . . which is based on an elaborate committee structure' – a structure which leaves the question of final accountability no clearer.

That this vagueness is something more than just an accident or oversight is demonstrated in a more explicit statement in the

[1] Ministry of Education. *Higher Education.* Report of the Committee on Higher Education (Chairman: Lord Robbins), Cmnd 2154 (London: HMSO, 1963).

report on the role of the Vice-Chancellor. Here it is stated: 'His
is a role which, probably fortunately, is seldom precisely spelt out
in written constitutions. Yet it would be difficult to overstate its
importance, particularly in a period of expansion, which calls
for imagination and continuous initiative.' What the report
fails to note in this praise of vagueness is its inconsistency with
the statement further down the same paragraph that 'governing
bodies should give serious attention to improving their organization' with regard to the variety and burden of work of the Vice-
Chancellor. Such improvement cannot be achieved for a role
which is imprecisely defined.

I have quoted at some length from the Robbins report, not
for the purpose of singling it out for criticism, but merely to
illustrate how readily we accept the hope that issues of great
moment will sort themselves out if only they are left sufficiently
vague. Even in such a scholarly report, with its generally
meticulous concern for fact, the emphasis is certainly not on the
urgent need for a practical and systematic attack upon the
problems mentioned. Nor is there even any evidence of regret
that a more comprehensive and systematic solution was not
available. No, somehow the interests of freedom – in this
case academic freedom – are felt to be better served by lack of
clarity.

III

We may ask, however, if our hanging on to descriptions we know
intuitively to be inaccurate or incomplete really matters. Is this
anxiety about what would happen if we tried to describe ourselves and our social environment more clearly of any great
significance? Do we need, after all, to have such clarity and
precision in our descriptions and our statements of policy, of
organization, of principle, of authority and responsibility, of
individual behaviour? Are we not in danger of becoming too
formal about these things? I do not believe that we are in such
a danger. The danger lies in leaving things too informal, too
vague.

These questions all have the same general implication: Are
we not in danger of carrying accurate description too far?

Where is it all to lead? We will be subjecting ethics, religion, everything, to scientific scrutiny – is nothing in all humanity to be left sacrosanct? It can only be said in reply that the healthy progress of humanity depends on our getting away from any and all unrealistic mental images of the world in which we live. For the alternative to having concepts and mental models based upon careful and minute description is not that of having no models at all; it is that of having formulations that are based upon biased conventions and unchecked assumptions. The resulting distorted models are important. Once thought of and expressed, they influence our own outlook and actions, and the outlook and actions of others.

In the ordering of our social affairs, we are weighed down by countless such distorting formulations. They impede our actions, or, worse, cause us to act in ways which preclude the resolution of the problems we wish to settle. For instance, in trade-union/management negotiations it is held that union leaders are accountable for representing management's views to the workers. Strikes are often alleged to occur, and to persist intractably, because of distorted or false representations of these views. I believe that this description is often correct. But to castigate the union leaders causes resentment and heightens tension, and will not overcome the difficulty. The solution to the problem depends upon both management and unions recognizing that it is in fact the responsibility of managements to convey their own views directly to their workers. It is not the job of union representatives to do so, since they are accountable to the workers who elected them and not to management.

Examples of false and misleading formulations, tailor-made for trouble, abound in their hundreds and thousands: judging the performance of individuals on the basis of a few simple quantifiable aspects of what they do, like judging a teacher on the number of students he has who pass examinations, or a chief executive on the profit for the year; the assumption that there is one single cause for every problem; the assumption that if all students pass their examinations, then standards must be dropping, or that if there is a high failure rate, then the quality of the intake must be low; the assumption that those who do mental work should have shorter hours than those who do

c

manual work. Ideas like these are to be found in every area of our social life, imprisoning our thoughts and actions and leading into muddle, argument, and unnecessary strife. They are a prime and dangerous enemy of freedom.

IV

Another explanation might be offered for the comparatively retarded development of the social sciences and psychology. Perhaps, it might be argued, scientific method cannot be applied to the study of really important social issues; they are too complex and we are too emotionally involved; moreover, one cannot experiment with serious issues concerning real people and institutions. This view is based upon a too narrow definition of scientific method with its picture of a cold, impartial, dry-as-dust scientist carrying out controlled, repeatable, and quantified experiments in an utterly detached impersonal manner. Such a definition is a definition of only a small part of science. Even in the natural sciences, as, for example, in astronomy with its massive achievements, experimentation is not always the keystone of scientific method. It is often necessary to wait for nature itself to produce the circumstances for observation and recording, to wait for what is sometimes termed an experiment of nature or an experiment of opportunity, such as an eclipse of the sun.

The problem of the social sciences and psychology is not that they cannot be scientific in the sense of using a disciplined scientific approach, but that they try to achieve academic respectability either by aping too rigidly the experimental sciences or by remaining theoretical and bookish. Neither being forced into a narrow scientific mould nor proliferating great theoretical systems will take the social sciences far. They are in their early stages and are in need of detailed teasing-out, observation, and description of our social institutions and behaviour. Indeed, it is one of the current central tasks in these sciences to encourage a proper attitude towards the value of simple observation of great matters, and to overcome the belittling and devaluation of work that is not either experimental or based on intellectual theorizing. As Charcot has put it, the task is to learn 'to stare at the facts over and over again, until they speak to you'.

Just think for a moment of the rate at which discoveries were made in mechanics and astronomy, in chemistry, in anatomy and physiology, and of the rapid advances in technology and medicine that became possible when men learned to give up being seduced by the intellectual grandeur of sweeping theories and came down from their academic towers to look at the world around them as it actually was; learned that enlightenment and true authority were to be gained from observing and describing the real natural environment.

For me, the most dramatic moment in the opening of this more humble road was when Vesalius, the father of anatomy, eschewed the niceness and the comfort of metaphysical theorizing about the structure of man himself, and set about the hard and practical task of dissecting the human corpse to see and minutely describe, at first hand, what there really was inside.

Bagehot described the need in his classic work, *The English Constitution*,[1] in the following terms:

> The literature which has accumulated upon it [the English Constitution] is huge. But an observer who looks at the living reality will wonder at the contrast to the paper description. He will see in the life much which is not in the books; and he will not find in the rough practice many refinements of the literary theory.

In so writing he was following in the tradition of Machiavelli, perhaps the first man to try to look in depth at social processes as they really were, to describe them, and to draw practical conclusions therefrom, untainted by political or religious ideology.

This step – the systematic observation of important issues – is a very difficult one in the social sciences. We are often too close ourselves to the material, too emotionally committed and involved. Yet, if we become too detached and uninvolved, the problems we study become unimportant and insignificant. The great issues are waiting to be tackled – freedom, the optimum forms of government, academic liberty, the nature of authority and accountability in management and administration, the nature of learning and the educational process, the problems of

[1] Bagehot, Walter (1867). *The English Constitution*.

ethics in relations among men, the use of punishment and the nature of discipline, the relationship between law and morality.

Systematic observation of these issues calls for a special attitude, an attitude of detached involvement, to be achieved only with intense mental toil. By mental toil I mean that creative act in which our conscious beliefs, principles, and concepts are held not as perfect and immutable, as hard-and-fast currency, but as flexible counters, always uncertain and incomplete, and always under scrutiny for modification in the light of the reality of experience – concepts, ideas, principles, models, constantly subjected to the modifying influence of common perception.

Systematic observation does not arise spontaneously. It comes from directed and enduring curiosity which is an essential part of a disciplined scientific approach. Inherent in this curiosity are ideas about what one is looking for or might find. It is these ideas that give direction to our interest and attention. Sometimes we have merely an intuitive and inexpressible feeling about something, sometimes perhaps a roughly formulated hunch; sometimes, if we are working in a well-developed field, we start with comprehensively stated hypotheses derived from previous work or from a system of theories and laws. Our concepts influence our observations, and our observations lead to changes in our concepts.

The objective of systematic observation is to perceive facts, so that we may group them into logically consistent concepts, which we can then use in communicating with each other. This process of concept formation is one of the central features of scientific advance. By concepts I mean verbalized and communicable ideas which define a particular collection of percepts. In the natural environment, concepts refer to what we ordinarily think of as things – chair, electron, plant cell. In the social environment, they refer to what we may equally refer to as things, though they are less tangible than physical things – like the concept of university, or role in a social system, or marriage. What makes the difference is that in the natural environment we build up our concepts from perceptions of tangible things, whereas in the social environment we are perceiving not the tangible bodies, but the social relationships among people. And determining the nature of social relationships is not always so easy. It starts at a more abstract level than that of observation in the natural environment.

In forming concepts, what we do is draw boundaries (for this is what definition means), saying that our concept includes this percept and that one, but not those others. I can illustrate this process of boundary definition of concepts by the concept of scientific method that I am using. The boundary encloses enduring curiosity, systematic observation, and described and published perceptions. It excludes random observation, unrecorded perceptions, uncommunicated work, and artistic creativeness.

We can draw these boundaries rather loosely and widely, or very tightly and precisely, depending upon the extent of our knowledge at any given time. Scientific endeavour takes great strides forward as its concepts take on the formal and organized quality given to precise boundary definition. We have only to think of the tremendous progress that became possible with the fixing of the boundaries and the naming of concepts like electron, blood circulation, vitamin, genes. The organized and bounded perception makes it possible for us to speak together with the assurance that we are referring to perceptions that we already share – things that we have each seen or heard or otherwise perceived; or that we can go out and seek to perceive in order to build up a shared perception. In the opposite vein, we have only to think of the confused and fruitless discussion, the source of endless conflict, that arises when one says that the social sciences can never be scientific, while another argues that they can be and are – but each is subsuming a different set of perceptions under the same name.

The tricky thing about concepts is that they can be made up out of imagination and used as though they have perceptual content. For example, the concept of industrial democracy can be shown not to have any perceptual content. It is a hollow concept. It refers to no agreed percepts in the real social world which can be observed and shared. The constant testing of concepts against real perception is necessary if muddle is to be avoided.

What we observe, of course, is not the concept, but perceptual qualities of things – length, colour, weight, sound – and qualities of relationships, like authority, love, power, jealousy, ambition.

To define these qualities accurately requires the act of measurement, as Bridgman, adapted by Brown[1] has shown: for example, that the quality of length is defined by the steps involved in the construction and use of a yardstick.

Once we achieve the boundary definition of concepts and an operational definition of qualities, our scientific endeavour becomes objective. For the objectivity of science lies not in its experiments, nor in the impartiality of the observer. It lies in the communicability of its observed facts. As Karl Popper[2] has said, 'What we call "scientific objectivity" is not a product of the individual scientist's impartiality, but a product of the social or public character of scientific method; and the individual scientist's impartiality is, so far as it exists, not the source but rather the result of this socially or institutionally organized objectivity of science.'

The objectivity of science, therefore, depends upon the art of using language. As part of the very process of becoming conscious, our concepts attach themselves to words. Here, then, is an art that scientists must at least aspire to cultivate. It requires first of all a protective attitude towards words, an attitude of concern for the precise and careful use of language, so that the currency of words is not debased by lazy usage. There is required a sense of when new words are necessary to fit new concepts, and when a tighter definition of existing language is more proper to the aim of expressing increasing conceptual precision and the clarity derived from measurement.

V

With our concepts we can construct conceptual models. They are mental models with which we try to describe the natural or social environment. For example, a mentally constructed model of the organizational structure of a university, a factory, a Civil Service department, a trade union, a political party, showing

---

[1] Brown, Wilfred. 'Organization and science.' In: Brown, Wilfred and Jaques, Elliott, *Glacier Project Papers* (London: Heinemann Educational Books, 1965).

[2] Popper, K. R. (1945). *The Open Society and its Enemies.* (2 vols.) (London: Routledge & Kegan Paul, 4th rev. edn., 1962).

the authority and accountability in each position, how decisions are arrived at, how the work actually goes on, the standards of performance, and setting out the required relationships between positions; or a system of factors presumed to be operating inside the individual, such as, for example, various unconscious factors, which are used to explain behaviour.

Models of the real situation can be examined for their internal consistency, and inconsistencies in the real situation may thereby be discovered – for example, inconsistencies between the accountability in a particular position and the authority allocated to it. Moreover, developments in cybernetics, computers, and applied mathematics give promise of expressing these models in more rigorously mathematical terms.

We can modify these models in our minds, and think up new models, in accord with changing perceptions. We can hypothesize what would happen if these changes were actually implemented in the situation modelled. It is at this point that experiment – if it is possible – is so useful, for the hypotheses, and the models on which they are based, can be systematically tested *ad lib*.

In the social sciences we cannot, of course, experiment with new institutions as we like, trying this and trying that, and rejecting what does not work. Our institutions are part of our on-going social life, and changes in them affect the lives of people. Every failure constitutes a social jolt. Nor can we make and remake individual human beings, merely casting aside our failures, for every one of us is entitled to endure.

But sometimes, when the moment is opportune, we may have the chance to test the new model and hypotheses in practice, either because we happen to be the responsible administrator or the person concerned, or because we have the opportunity to communicate with that administrator or person. Social science and psychology will find their major avenue of advance in applied and professional work, which provides a piecemeal testing in practice of hypotheses and models as the exigencies of real life allow, reinforced by such experiments as may be possible. But at no stage do we assume control over our personal and social environment in the same absolute sense in which we strive to dominate our physical environment. We must seek rather to gain systematic experience and knowledge, to provide a framework for our behaviour, to express our laws as legislation, and wisely to regulate our personal and our social lives.

I can exemplify my meaning by returning to the passages I quoted from the Robbins report: 'The real sources of initiative and power . . . depend partly upon the imponderables of specific circumstances and individual personalities and are almost impossible to determine.' No! We cannot accept this outlook. Systematic observation, perception, and description of what actually happens in each situation – who takes initiative, who decides what, who gets credit for good decisions or is called to account for bad ones – these are the processes that can give us the shareable information necessary for assembling accurate models of what goes on even in universities, and for constructing new models where necessary in order to create the conditions needed for greater definition of responsibility.

In the case of universities, some conceptual clarification would be required before adequate model-building could be achieved. For example: What are the main operational tasks of the university? Who is accountable for teaching programmes and to whom? What does 'academic freedom' mean? Who appoints whom and who assesses whose performance? As these concepts and relationships are clarified and defined in boundary terms so that we know what shared percepts are involved and can assume with some assurance that we understand each other, model-building and modification can take place in terms of structure and relationships – including the authority and responsibilities of councils and senates, various types of committee, heads of departments, members of departments and students, and the nature of the required relationships among them. Upon the model chosen depend such significant decisions as whether we appoint figureheads for rubber-stamping councils, or working members of councils with authority.

Such a process of perception, concept formation, and model-building is not dramatic. It moves step by step as new perceptions are recorded. But it denies the existence of the imponderable and the undefinable, so long as we have the will to ponder and describe in connection with our own organizations and behaviour.

VI

We may rightfully conclude that a true science of society and its institutions, and of human behaviour, is achievable. The fact that measurement is very little developed, and that the testing of predictions may have to rely rather more upon model-building and experiments of nature than upon controlled laboratory experiment, is no cause for pessimism or despair. Rigorous and disciplined scientific observation and description of ourselves and our social environment, with the construction and testing of models, and the development of a sound technology of society and the individual, ought to be capable of infinite elaboration.

There is, however, one difficulty that needs to be recognized. It is the difficulty of gaining access in depth to the data to be observed. By access in depth I do not mean statistical surveys of attitude or of population movements. I mean first-hand observation by means of work *in situ* with teachers and pupils, boards of directors, prisoners and prison staff, families, and tenants' associations, so that the details can be dissected and teased out of the structure of the situation: how relationships are mediated, how attitudes are influenced and changed, how policies are argued and fixed, in a live and telling manner. Unformulated and even unrecognized activities, policies, and motives can be identified and conceptualized, and accurate and comprehensive models constructed which do not suffer from the omission of the things that really count.

In the natural sciences, the route of access to deeper-lying or more distant data is through instrumentation – microscopes, spectroscopes, radio-active isotopes, and flights into space. But one does not have to ask the permission of the materials one is observing, and it does not matter if a certain amount of material is destroyed and thrown away in the process.

In the social sciences and psychology, because we are dealing with human beings, systematic study cannot even begin without some co-operation from the people involved. What is needed is a particular attitude in each of us, an attitude favourable not to vagueness but to knowledge, to discovery and clarification rather than to hidebound custom, practice, and tradition. It contains the resolution to understand oneself and one's own institutions. To the extent that any given society seeks enlightenment about its institutions will the science of society grow, and only to that extent.

Access to data in the social sciences should be sought only with the constructive aim of advancing social technology. Such an aim entails a professional collaborative relationship between the scientist and people who are determined to undertake the difficult task of doing what they are doing and understanding what they are doing at the same time. At its simplest level, the relationship involves discussion with subjects of the significance for them of their performance in a new test. At a more complex level, it is a full-scale collaborative relationship that may extend through long periods of time between a professional consultant and those – be it an individual, a marital couple, a trade union, a school, or other institution – who are seeking the insight and understanding they hope he will help them to acquire.

Within a professional working relationship of this kind between social scientists and people in roles collaborating to dispel vagueness, access to data and opportunity for observation not only are possible, they are demanded by the individual or by the organization. They are a part of the process of analysis whereby progress is expected. Unlike the natural scientist, therefore, the social scientist must have at least some competence in carrying a professional role. It is one of the prime working tools enabling him to carry out the fundamental scientific process of observation. And if it might be thought that scientific objectivity is lost because of this collaborative relationship, then that is only to say that the social sciences share this problem with modern physics which, with the discovery of the principles of relativity and uncertainty, is also affected by the relationship between the observer and his field.

Given a proper relationship with those of us who take part in their field of study, the social scientist and the psychologist can report their perceptions directly to us, and get some verification then and there, on the spot, of the soundness of their observation. The reporting and checking of results are constant characteristics, for example, of work in psychotherapy, and of social consulting work. In both cases, the client judges and responds to every interpretation or report. Although there may be technical difficulties involved in assessing the validity of these judgements, at least the judgements are available, in contrast to the field of study of the physicist which cannot speak to him at all.

It is in this possible collaboration between the social scientist or psychologist and people who seek a more disciplined approach to overcoming social problems that the social sciences have a potential advantage over the natural sciences. For, while the field of observation of the physicist cannot withdraw, crying 'Leave me vague', neither can it engage with him in a collaborative attack upon the problem to be studied. I would like to illustrate certain implications of this collaboration by reference to the design of education in the new School of Social Sciences at Brunel University.[1]

VII

The Brunel School of Social Sciences will offer education to students seeking either of two major types of career:

(*a*) administrators and managers: to take up leadership roles in government, social services, and education, and in industry and commerce;

(*b*) professional social scientists – both psychologists and social consultants: to work with administrators and managers in the adaptation of institutions and the creation of sound policies; to assist with the adaptation of individuals; and to carry out research and development.

These two categories of student will be educated together in a common core course extending throughout the undergraduate and postgraduate years. This common course will seek to give them a live and practical understanding of the nature of human behaviour and of social institutions: the behaviour of individuals, and the influence of behaviour on taking up positions in social systems; how structure and changes in structure affect the way institutions operate; the economics of social systems, and the interaction of economic factors and individual and

[1] This programme has been running for four years now (1969), and its feasibility seems fairly well assured.

group behaviour; law and the constructive or restrictive policy limitations upon and within institutions; the means by which institutions are managed.

The teaching will encompass the nature of specific institutions such as: industrial enterprises; Parliament and the Civil Service; schools and other educational establishments; public corporations, etc.; and different theories of behaviour, thus giving the student opportunity to study a wide variety of models of social institutions and psychological models of behaviour.

Relevant teaching in social and political history, philosophy, and jurisprudence and law will be threaded through the course to give a broad foundation to the understanding of social institutions and behaviour, and of how they adapt and change.

A grounding will be given in scientific method and the nature of conceptualization, both to teach the nature of science and to teach how the human mind organizes perception. Language and the basic principles of mathematics will be included to help students to appreciate the value of appropriate and rigorously formulated concepts, to describe and express the result of their work in these terms, and to forward their thinking in terms of conceptual models.

In addition to the common core courses, each teaching department will provide elective courses to enable students to specialize in fields of their own interest.

By means of this educational plan, future administrators and managers, and professional psychologists and social consultants can be educated side by side, and can thus learn from the start how to work together – educationists with educational psychologists, industrial managers with industrial psychologists and consultants, policy-makers with social-analysts, and so on. The insight of the potential administrator will be deepened, and the outlook of the professional may be broadened, as a result.

If the educational programme is successful, administrators and managers, and social scientists and psychologists, having shared the same basic education, will have the knowledge and the resolve to collaborate with vigour in furthering observation and understanding of the social institutions and the individuals with whom they themselves are concerned. It is this kind of collaboration that could, for example, tackle problems like that of authority and power in universities, in industry, in commerce.

But can the same basic training, it might be asked, be of equal value to future men of action and future men of science? From the point of view of the administrator and the manager, the application of the type of social science and psychology I have described is a practical matter. The man of action will do his work better by being able to observe, define, and make explicit his organization, his policies, and his procedures. If he is by nature a good administrator or manager, this explicitness will help him to become more decisive through the increase of self-assurance he will gain once he has an accurate working model of his organization based on greater clarity of definition and common understanding of such concepts as leadership, performance, consultation, boards, and committees.

From the point of view of the professional psychologist and social consultant, there is the opportunity of learning, early on, how to collaborate with administrators and managers; of laying the basis for the collaborative endeavour that will, if all goes well, develop later. Moreover, they can be helped to gain a human and practical outlook in their work, through greater sensitivity to the needs and outlook of those who may use the results of their creativeness.

VIII

There are two other basic policies of the School of Social Sciences that will reinforce the academic programme in educating students with the kind of outlook I have tried to describe. They are, first, that the School will try to practise what it teaches, and, second, that the School – like the rest of Brunel University – will use the sandwich mode of education.[1]

The organization and administration of the School will, to the extent possible within university policy, be based upon a conscious and explicit application of the theories and concepts that are taught about institutions. The School itself and the university can thus be used as one case study for teaching. The use of the School as a teaching case study will enable the student to have a sharp personal awareness of his own position in an

[1] Sometimes termed the integrative or the co-operative mode of education.

institution. This awareness is of special importance, since it prevents the social sciences and psychology from becoming something that is good for others but to be avoided by oneself.

This exercise in administration will be real and living. As opportunity and time allow, it is hoped to scrutinize, define, and formulate explicit models within the School for such matters as: our educational policies and administrative procedures, academic freedom, the assessment of performance of our staff and students (including the function of examinations), the role of the student, and the functions of different teaching methods. By so doing, we may contribute not only to the education of our students and the management of our own affairs, but also to the general body of knowledge with which we are concerned.

With regard to the second policy – the sandwich mode of education – it is a fortunate fact that Brunel as an institution is committed to this principle. It will, I believe, prove to be of prime importance in the social sciences and psychology. It can provide the equivalent of clinical work for the medical student, or of being articled for the law student. It can give the student the opportunity to observe his own reactions and behaviour in role in an organization. And it may give him a quality of working contact with others during his education, which is essential to the development of a professional outlook.

It is the first-hand experience of industry or commerce or the Civil Service, or of professional psychological or social science work in education, in prisons, or in the health or other governmental services, that will help to build a storehouse of first-hand percepts to give content to and bring alive the concepts taught in class.

IX

In the School I hope we shall be able to provide an education which may help to overcome some of the difficulties I have discussed: that of society's cultivation of vagueness, the failure to get through to a fundamental scientific approach based on observation, the need for bounded definition of concepts and quantitative definition of qualities, and for the elimination of confusing and unsystematic language.

I hope, further, that we may imbue our students with a sense of cultural tradition and heritage; with a desire for precise observation of data and definition of concepts and for a matching precision of language; with a concern for human beings and for society that will fortify the will for mental toil and appropriate detachment; and with an awareness of the need to understand their own behaviour and institutions, and not to escape this task by preoccupying themselves with other people.

In all this endeavour there is a stimlating challenge, not only in teaching but in research and development, to fulfil a primary function of the university as a place where knowledge is created. The possible field of exploration is wide: a psychology of real people and their feelings, skills, intellect, capacity, conflicts, conscious and unconscious strivings; their relationships in work, in family, in love, in groups, and in society at large; and a social science of real institutions at work in every sphere of social life.

The testing of the School will emerge from application of its work – in the performance of its graduates and the practical value of its research to society. That is the fair test of responsible academic freedom.

3

Death and the
Mid-Life Crisis

I

In the course of the development of the individual there are
critical phases which have the character of change points, or
periods of rapid transition. Less familiar perhaps, though
nonetheless real, are the crises which occur around the age of
thirty-five – which I shall term the mid-life crisis – and at full
maturity around the age of sixty-five. It is the mid-life crisis
with which I shall deal in this paper.

When I say that the mid-life crisis occurs around the age of
thirty-five, I mean that it takes place in the middle-thirties, that
the process of transition runs on for some years, and that the
exact period will vary among individuals. The transition is often
obscured in women by the proximity of the onset of changes
connected with the menopause. In the case of men, the change
has from time to time been referred to as the male climacteric,
because of the reduction in the intensity of sexual behaviour
which often occurs at that time.

Crisis in Genius

I first became aware of this period as a critical stage in development when I noticed a marked tendency towards crisis in the creative work of great men in their middle and late thirties. It is clearly expressed by Richard Church in his autobiography *The Voyage Home*:

> There seems to be a biological reason for men and women, when they reach the middle thirties, finding themselves beset with misgivings, agonizing inquiries, and a loss of zest. Is it that state which the medieval schoolmen called *accidie*, the cardinal sin of spiritual sloth? I believe it is.

This crisis may express itself in three different ways: the creative career may simply come to an end, either in a drying-up of creative work, or in actual death; the creative capacity may begin to show and express itself for the first time; or a decisive change in the quality and content of creativeness may take place.

Perhaps the most striking phenomenon is what happens to the death rate among creative artists. I had got the impression that the age of thirty-seven seemed to figure rather prominently in the death of individuals of this category. This impression was upheld by taking a random sample of some 310 painters, composers, poets, writers, and sculptors, of undoubted greatness or of genius. The death rate shows a sudden jump between thirty-five and thirty-nine, at which period it is much above the normal death rate. The group includes Mozart, Raphael, Chopin, Rimbaud, Purcell, Baudelaire, Watteau. ... There is then a big drop below the normal death rate between the ages of forty and forty-four, followed by a return to the normal death rate pattern in the late forties. The closer one keeps to genius in the sample, the more striking and clearcut is this spiking of the death rate in mid-life.

The change in creativity which occurs during this period can be seen in the lives of countless artists. Bach, for example, was mainly an organist until his cantorship at Leipzig at thirty-eight, at which time he began his colossal achievements as a composer. Rossini's life is described in the following terms:

> His comparative silence during the period 1832–68 (i.e. from forty to his death at seventy-four) makes his biography like the narrative of two lives – swift triumph, and a long life of seclusion.

D

Racine had thirteen years of continuous success culminating in *Phèdre* at the age of thirty-eight; he then produced nothing for some twelve years. The characteristic work of Goldsmith, Constable, and Goya emerged between the ages of thirty-five and thirty-eight. By the age of forty-three Ben Jonson had produced all the plays worthy of his genius, although he lived to be sixty-four. At thirty-three Gauguin gave up his job in a bank, and by thirty-nine had established himself in his creative career as a painter. Donatello's work after thirty-nine is described by a critic as showing a marked change in style, in which he departed from the statuesque balance of his earlier work and turned to the creation of an almost instantaneous expression of life.

Goethe, between the ages of thirty-seven and thirty-nine, underwent a profound change in outlook, associated with his trip to Italy. As many of his biographers have pointed out, the importance of this journey and this period in his life cannot be exaggerated. He himself regarded it as the climax to his life. Never before had he gained such complete understanding of his genius and mission as a poet. His work then began to reflect the classical spirit of Greek tragedy and of the Renaissance.

Michelangelo carried out a series of masterpieces until he was forty: his 'David' was finished at twenty-nine, the decoration of the roof of the Sistine Chapel at thirty-seven, and his 'Moses' between thirty-seven and forty. During the next fifteen years little is known of any artistic work. There was a creative lull until, at fifty-five, he began to work on the great Medici monument and then later on 'The Last Judgement' and frescoes in the Pauline Chapel.

Let me make it clear that I am not suggesting that the careers of most creative persons either begin or end during the mid-life crisis. There are few creative geniuses who live and work into maturity, in whom the quality of greatness cannot be discerned in early adulthood in the form either of created works or of the potential for creating them: Beethoven, Shakespeare, Goethe, Couperin, Ibsen, Balzac, Voltaire, Verdi, Handel, Goya, Dürer, to name but a very few at random. But there are equally few in whom a decisive change cannot be seen in the quality of their work – in whose work the effects of their having gone through a mid-life crisis cannot be discerned. The reactions range all the way from severe and dramatic crisis to a smoother and less troubled transition – just as reactions to the phase of adolescent crisis may range from severe disturbance and break-down to relatively ordered readjustment to mental and sexual adulthood – but the effects of the change are there to be discerned. What then are the main features of this change?

There are two features which seem to me of outstanding importance. One of these has to do with the mode of work; the second has to do with the content of the work. Let me consider each of these in turn. I shall use the phrase 'early adulthood' for the pre-mid-life phase, and 'mature adulthood' for the post-mid-life phase.

Change in Mode of Work
I can best describe the change in mode of work which I have in mind by describing the extreme of its manifestation. The creativity of the twenties and the early thirties tends to be a hot-from-the-fire creativity. It is intense and spontaneous, and comes out ready-made. The spontaneous effusions of Mozart, Keats, Shelley, Rimbaud, are the prototype. Most of the work seems to go on unconsciously. The conscious production is rapid, the pace of creation often being dictated by the limits of the artist's capacity physically to record the words or music he is expressing.

A vivid description of early adult type of work is given in Gittings's biography of Keats:

> Keats all this year had been living on spiritual capital. He had used and spent every experience almost as soon as it had come into his possession, every sight, person, book, emotion or thought had been converted spontaneously into poetry. Could he or any other poet have lasted at such a rate? . . . He could write no more by these methods. He realized this himself when he wished to compose as he said 'without fever'. He could not keep this high pulse beating and endure.

By contrast, the creativity of the late thirties and after is a sculpted creativity. The inspiration may be hot and intense. The unconscious work is no less than before. But there is a big step between the first effusion of inspiration and the finished created product. The inspiration itself may come more slowly. Even if there are sudden bursts of inspiration, they are only the beginning of the work process. The initial inspiration must first be externalized in its elemental state. Then begins the process of forming and fashioning the external product, by means of working and reworking the externalized material. I use the term sculpting because the nature of the sculptor's material – it is the sculptor working in stone of whom I am thinking – forces him into this kind of relationship with the product of his creative imagination. There occurs a process of interplay between unconscious intuitive work and inspiration, and the considered perception of the externally emergent creation and the reaction to it.

In her note 'A Character Trait of Freud's', Riviere[1] describes Freud's exhorting her in connection with some psycho-analytic idea which had occurred to her:

> Write it, write it, put it down in black and white . . . get it out, produce it, make something of it – *outside you*, that is; give it an existence independently of you.

This externalizing process is part of the essence of work in mature adulthood, when, as in the case of Freud, the initially externalized material is not itself the end product, or nearly the end product, but is rather the starting point, the object of further working over, modification, elaboration, sometimes for periods of years.

In distinguishing between the precipitate creativity of early adulthood and the sculpted creativity of mature adulthood, I do not want to give the impression of drawing a hard and fast line between the two phases. There are of course times when a creative person in mature adulthood will be subject to bursts of inspiration and rapid-fire creative production. Equally there will be found instances of mature and sculpted creative work done in early adulthood. The 'David' of Michelangelo is, I think, the supreme example of the latter.

But the instances where work in early adulthood has the sculpted and worked-over quality are rare. Sometimes, as in scientific work, there may be the appearance of sculpted work. Young physicists in their twenties, for example, may produce startling discoveries which are the result of continuous hard work and experimentation. But these discoveries result from the

---

[1] Riviere, J. 'A Character Trait of Freud's.' In: *Psycho-Analysis and Contemporary Thought*, ed. J. D. Sutherland (London: Hogarth, 1958).

application of modern theories about the structure of matter – theories which themselves have been the product of the sculpted work of mature adulthood of such geniuses as Thomson and Einstein.

Equally, genuinely creative work in mature adulthood may sometimes not appear to be externally worked over and sculpted, and yet actually be so. What seems to be rapid and unworked-over creation is commonly the reworking of themes which have been worked upon before, or which may have been slowly emerging over the years in previous works. We need look no farther than the work of Freud for a prime example of this process of books written rapidly, which are nevertheless the coming to fruition of ideas which have been worked upon, fashioned, reformulated, left incomplete and full of loose ends, and then reformulated once again in a surging forward through the emergence of new ideas for overcoming previous difficulties.

The reality of the distinction comes out in the fact that certain materials are more readily applicable to the precipitate creativity of early adulthood than are others. Thus, for example, musical composition, lyrical poetry, are much more amenable to rapid creative production than are sculpting in stone or painting in oils. It is noteworthy, therefore, that whereas there are very many poets and composers who achieve greatness in early adulthood – indeed in their early twenties or their late teens – there are very few sculptors or painters in oils who do so. With oil paint and stone, the working relationship to the materials themselves is of importance, and demands that the creative process should go through the stage of initial externalization and working-over of the externalized product. The written word and musical notation do not of necessity have this same plastic external objective quality. They can be sculpted and worked over, but they can also readily be treated merely as a vehicle for the immediate recording of unconsciously articulated products which are brought forward whole and complete – or nearly so.

Quality and Content of Creativity
The change in mode of work, then, between early and mature adulthood, is a change from precipitate to sculpted creativity. Let me now consider for a moment the change in the quality and

content of the creativity. The change I have in mind is the emergence of a tragic and philosophical content which then moves on to serenity in the creativity of mature adulthood, in contrast to a more characteristically lyrical and descriptive content to the work of early adulthood. This distinction is a commonly held one, and may perhaps be considered sufficiently self-evident to require little explication or argument. It is implied, of course, in my choice of the adjectives 'early' and 'mature' to qualify the two phases of adulthood which I am discussing.

The change may be seen in the more human, tragic and less fictitious and stage quality of Dickens's writing from *David Copperfield* (which he wrote at thirty-seven) onwards. It may be seen also in the transition in Shakespeare from the historical plays and comedies to the tragedies. When he was about thirty-one, in the midst of writing his lyrical comedies, he produced *Romeo and Juliet*. The great series of tragedies and Roman plays, however, began to appear a few years later; *Julius Caesar, Hamlet, Othello, King Lear,* and *Macbeth* are believed to have been written most probably between the ages of thirty-five and forty.

There are many familiar features of the change in question. Late adolescent and early adult idealism and optimism accompanied by split-off and projected hate, are given up and supplanted by a more contemplative pessimism. There is a shift from radical desire and impatience to a more reflective and tolerant conservatism. Beliefs in the inherent goodness of man are replaced by a recognition and acceptance of the fact that inherent goodness is accompanied by hate and destructive forces within, which contribute to man's own misery and tragedy. To the extent that hate, destruction, and death are found explicitly in early adult creativeness, they enter in the form of the satanic or the macabre, as in Poe and in Baudelaire, and not as worked-through and resolved anxieties.

The spirit of early adult creativeness is summed up in Shelley's *Prometheus Unbound*. In her notes on this work, Shelley's wife has written:

> The prominent feature of Shelley's theory of the destiny of the human species is that evil is not inherent in the system of the Creation, but an accident that might be expelled ... God made Earth and Man perfect, till he by his fall 'brought death into the

world, and all our woe'. Shelley believed that mankind had only to will that there should be no evil in the world and there would be none. . . . He was attached to this idea with fervent enthusiasm.

This early adult idealism is built upon the use of unconscious denial and manic defences as normal processes of defence against two fundamental features of human life – the inevitableness of eventual death, and the existence of hate and destructive impulses inside each person. I shall try to show that the explicit recognition of these two features, and the bringing of them into focus, is the quintessence of successful weathering of the mid-life crisis and the achievement of mature adulthood.

It is when death and human destructiveness – that is to say, both death and the death instinct – are taken into account, that the quality and content of creativity change to the tragic, reflective, and philosophical. The depressive position must be worked through once again, at a qualitatively different level. The misery and despair of suffering and chaos unconsciously brought about by oneself are encountered and must be surmounted for life to be endured and for creativity to continue. Nemesis is the key, and tragedy the theme, of its recognition.

The successful outcome of mature creative work lies thus in constructive resignation both to the imperfections of men and to shortcomings in one's own work. It is this constructive resignation that then imparts serenity to life and work.

The Divine Comedy

I have taken these examples from creative genius because I believe the essence of the mid-life crisis is revealed in its most full and rounded form in the lives of the great. It will have become manifest that the crisis is a depressive crisis, in contrast to the adolescent crisis, which tends to be a paranoid-schizoid one. In adolescence, the predominant outcome of serious breakdown is schizophrenic illness; in mid-life the predominant outcome is depression, or the consequences of defence against depressive anxiety as reflected in manic defences, hypochondriasis, obsessional mechanisms, or superficiality and character deterioration. Working through the mid-life crisis calls for a reworking through of the infantile depression, but with mature insight into death and destructive impulses to be taken into account.

'This theme of working through depression is magnificently expressed in *The Divine Comedy*. This masterpiece of all time was begun by Dante following his banishment from Florence at the age of thirty-seven. In the opening stanzas he creates his setting in words of great power and tremendous psychological depth. He begins:

> In the middle of the journey of our life, I came to myself within a dark wood where the straight way was lost. Ah, how hard it is to tell of that wood, savage and harsh and dense, the thought of which renews my fear. So bitter is it that death is hardly more.

These words have been variously interpreted; for example, as an allegorical reference to the entrance to Hell, or as a reflection of the poet's state of mind on being forced into exile, homeless and hungry for justice. They may, however, be interpreted at a deeper level as the opening scene of a vivid and perfect description of the emotional crisis of the mid-life phase, a crisis which would have gripped the mind and soul of the poet whatever his religious outlook, or however settled or unsettled his external affairs. The evidence for this conclusion exists in the fact that during the years of his early thirties which preceded his exile, he had already begun his transformation from the idyllic outlook of the *Vita Nuova* (age twenty-seven–twenty-nine) through a conversion to 'philosophy' which he allegorized in the *Convivio* written when he was between thirty-six and thirty-eight years of age.

Even taken quite literally, *The Divine Comedy* is a description of the poet's first full and worked-through conscious encounter with death. He is led through hell and purgatory by his master Virgil, eventually to find his own way, guided by his beloved Beatrice, into paradise. His final rapturous and mystical encounter with the being of God, represented to him in strange and abstract terms, was not mere rapture, not simply a being overwhelmed by a mystical oceanic feeling. It was a much more highly organized experience. It was expressly a vision of supreme love and knowledge, with control of impulse and of will, which promulgates the mature life of greater ease and contemplation which follows upon the working-through of primitive anxiety and guilt, and the return to the primal good object.

Dante explicitly connects his experience of greater mental

integration, and the overcoming of confusion, with the early infantile relation to the primal good object. As he nears the end of the 33rd Canto of 'Paradiso', the climax of his whole grand scheme, he explains:

> Now my speech will come more short even of what I remember than an infant's who yet bathes his tongue at the breast.

But the relationship with the primal good object is one in which reparation has been made, Purgatorio has been traversed, loving impulses have come into the ascendant, and the cruelty and harshness of the super-ego expressed in the inferno have been relieved. Bitterness has given way to composure.

In Dante, the result of this deep resolution is not the reinforcing of manic defence and denial which characterizes mystical experience fused with magic omnipotence; but rather the giving up of manic defence, and consequent strengthening of character and resolve, under the dominion of love. As Croce has observed:

> What is not found in the 'Paradiso', for it is foreign to the spirit of Dante, is flight from the world, absolute refuge in God, asceticism. He does not seek to fly from the world, but to instruct it, correct it, and reform it . . . he knew the world and its doings and passions.

Awareness of Personal Death

Although I have thus far taken my examples from the extremes of genius, my main theme is that the mid-life crisis is a reaction which not only occurs in creative genius, but manifests itself in some form in everyone. What then is the psychological nature of this reaction to the mid-life situation, and how is it to be explained?

The simple fact of the situation is the arrival at the mid-point of life. What is simple from the point of view of chronology, however, is not simple psychologically. The individual has stopped growing up, and has begun to grow old. A new set of external circumstances has to be met. The first phase of adult life has been lived. Family and occupation have become established (or ought to have become established unless the individual's adjustment has gone seriously awry); parents have grown old, and children are at the threshold of adulthood.

Youth and childhood are past and gone, and demand to be
mourned. The achievement of mature and independent adulthood presents itself as the main psychological task. The paradox
is that of entering the prime of life, the stage of fulfilment, but at
the same time the prime and fulfilment are dated. Death lies
beyond.

I believe, and shall try to demonstrate, that it is this fact of
the entry upon the psychological scene of the reality and inevitability of one's own eventual personal death, that is the
central and crucial feature of the mid-life phase – the feature
which precipitates the critical nature of the period. Death – at
the conscious level – instead of being a general conception, or an
event experienced in terms of the loss of someone else, becomes a
personal matter, one's own death, one's own real and actual
mortality. As Freud[1] has so accurately described the matter:

> We were prepared to maintain that death was the necessary out-
> come of life. . . . In reality, however, we were accustomed to
> behave as if it were otherwise. We displayed an unmistakable
> tendency to 'shelve' death, to eliminate it from life. We tried to
> hush it up. . . . That is our own death, of course. . . . No one
> believes in his own death. . . . In the unconscious everyone is
> convinced of his own immortality.

This attitude towards life and death, written by Freud in
another context, aptly expresses the situation which we all
encounter in mid-life. The reality of our own personal death
forces itself upon our attention and can no longer so readily be
shelved. A thirty-six-year-old patient, who had been in analysis
for seven years and was in the course of working through a deep
depressive reaction which heralded the final phase of his
analysis some eighteen months later, expressed the matter with
great clarity. 'Up till now,' he said, 'life has seemed an endless
upward slope, with nothing but the distant horizon in view.
Now suddenly I seem to have reached the crest of the hill, and
there stretching ahead is the downward slope with the end of
the road in sight – far enough away it's true – but there is
death observably present at the end.'

From that point on this patient's plans and ambitions took on
a different hue. For the first time in his life he saw his future as

[1] Freud, S. (1915). 'Thoughts for the times on war and death.' *S.E.*, **14**.

circumscribed. He began his adjustment to the fact that he would not be able to accomplish in the span of a single lifetime everything he had desired to do. He could achieve only a finite amount. Much would have to remain unfinished and unrealized.

This perspective on the finitude of life was accompanied by a greater solidity and robustness in his outlook, and introduced a new quality of earthly resignation. It reflected a diminishing of his unconscious wish for immortality. Such ideas are commonly lived out in terms of denial of mourning and death, or in terms of ideas of immortality, from notions of reincarnation and life after death to notions of longevity like those expressed by the success-ful twenty-eight-year-old novelist who writes in his diary, 'I shall be the most serious of men, and I shall live longer than any man'.

Unconscious Meaning of Death
How each one reacts to the mid-life encounter with the reality of his own eventual death – whether he can face this reality, or whether he denies it – will be markedly influenced by his infantile unconscious relation to death – a relationship which depends upon the stage and nature of the working-through of the infantile depressive position, as Melanie Klein discovered and vividly described.[1] Let me paraphrase her conclusions.

The infant's relation with life and death occurs in the setting of his survival being dependent on his external objects, and on the balance of power of the life and death instincts which qualify his perception of those objects and his capacity to depend upon them and use them. In the depressive position in infancy, under conditions of prevailing love, the good and bad objects can in some measure be synthesized, the ego becomes more integrated, and hope for the re-establishment of the good object is ex-perienced; the accompanying overcoming of grief and regaining of security is the infantile equivalent of the notion of life.

Under conditions of prevailing persecution, however, the working-through of the depressive position will be to a greater or lesser extent inhibited; reparation and synthesis fail; and the

---

[1] Klein, M. (1940). 'Mourning and its relation to manic-depressive states.' In: *Contributions to Psycho-Analysis.*
—— (1955). 'On identification.' In: *New Directions in Psycho-Analysis* (London: Tavistock; New York: Basic Books).

inner world is unconsciously felt to contain the persecuting and annihilating devoured and destroyed bad breast, the ego itself feeling in bits. The chaotic internal situation thus experienced is the infantile equivalent of the notion of death.

Ideas of immortality arise as a response to these anxieties, and as a defence against them. Unconscious fantasies of immortality are the counterpart of the infantile fantasies of the indestructible and hence immortal aspect of the idealized and bountiful primal object. These fantasies are just as persecuting as the chaotic internal situation they are calculated to mitigate. They contain omnipotent sadistic triumph, and increase guilt and persecution as a result. And they lead to feelings of intolerable helplessness through dependence upon the perfect object which becomes demanding of an equal perfection in behaviour.

Does the unconscious, then, have a conception of death? The views of Melanie Klein and those of Freud may seem not to correspond. Klein assumes an unconscious awareness of death. Freud assumes that the unconscious rejects all such awareness. Neither of these views, taken at face value, is likely to prove correct. Nor would I expect that either of their authors would hold to a literal interpretation of their views. The unconscious is not aware of death *per se*. But there are unconscious experiences akin to those which later appear in consciousness as notions of death. Let me illustrate such experiences.

A forty-seven-year-old woman patient, suffering from claustrophobia and a variety of severe psychosomatic illnesses, recounted a dream in which she was lying in a coffin. She had been sliced into small chunks, and was dead. But there was a spider's-web-thin thread of nerve running through every chunk and connected to her brain. As a result she could experience everything. She knew she was dead. She could not move or make any sound. She could only lie in the claustrophobic dark and silence of the coffin.

I have selected this particular dream because I think it typifies the unconscious fear and experience of death. It is not in fact death in the sense in which consciously we think about it, but an unconscious fantasy of immobilization and helplessness, in which the self is subject to violent fragmentation, while yet retaining the capacity to experience the persecution and torment to which it is being subjected. When these fantasies of suspended persecution and torture are of pathological intensity, they are characteristic of many mental conditions: catatonic states, stupors, phobias, obsessions, frozen anxiety, simple depression.

A Case of Denial of Death

In the early adult phase, before the mid-life encounter with death, the full-scale reworking-through of the depressive position does not as yet necessarily arise as a part of normal development. It can be postponed. It is not a pressing issue. It can be put to one side, until circumstances demand more forcibly that it be faced.

In the ordinary course of events, life is full and active. Physiologically, full potency has been reached, and activity – social, physical, economic, sexual – is to the fore. It is a time for doing, and the doing is flavoured and supported to a greater or lesser degree – depending on the emotional adjustment of the individual – by the activity and denial as part of the manic defence.

The early adult phase is one, therefore, in which successful activity can in fact obscure or conceal the operation of strong manic defences. But the depressive anxiety that is thus warded off will be encountered in due course. The mid-life crisis thrusts it forward with great intensity, and it can no longer be pushed aside if life is not to be impoverished.

This relationship between adjustment based upon activity in the early adult phase, and its failure in mid-life if the infantile depressive position is not unconsciously (or consciously, in analysis) worked through again, may be illustrated in the case of a patient, Mr N, who had led a successful life by everyday standards up to the time he came into analysis. He was an active man, a 'do-er'. He had been successful in his career through intelligent application and hard work, was married with three children, had many good friends, and all seemed to be going very well.

The idealized content of this picture had been maintained by an active carrying on of life, without allowing time for reflection. His view was that he had not come to analysis for himself, but rather for a kind of tutorial purpose – he would bring his case history to me and we would have a clinical seminar in which we would conduct a psycho-analytic evaluation of the case material he had presented.

As might be expected, Mr N had great difficulty in coping with ambivalence. He was unconsciously frightened of any resentment, envy, jealousy, or other hostile feelings towards me, maintaining an attitude of idealized love for me and tolerant good nature towards every attempt on my part to analyse the impulses of destructiveness and the feelings of persecution which he was counteracting by this idealization.

When he finally did break through this inability to cope with ambivalence – indeed a pretty complete unfamiliarity with the experience – it emerged that, in all his relationships, his idealization was inevitably followed by disappointment – a disappointment arising out of failure to get the quality of love he was greedily expecting in return, and nursed by the envy of those whom he idealized.

It was out of the analysis of material of this kind that we were able to get at the reflection in the analysis of his early adult mode of adjustment. He admitted that he was ill, and that unconscious awareness of his illness undoubtedly was the main reason for his seeking analysis. Being active, and over concerned for others, were soporifics, to which he had become addicted. Indeed, he confessed, he had resented my analysis taking this defensive addition away from him. He had secretly entertained ideas of stopping his analysis 'because all this thinking about myself, instead of doing things, is no good. Now I realize that I have been piling up my rage against you inside myself, like I've done with everyone else.'

Thus it was that during the first year of his analysis, the patient lived out many of the techniques which had characterized his early adult adjustment. It was with the onset of the Christmas holiday that the unconscious depressive anxiety, which was the main cause of his disturbance in mid-life, came out in full force. It is this material that illustrates the importance of the depressive position and unconscious feelings about death in relation to the mid-life crisis.

He had shown definite signs before the holiday of feelings of being abandoned, saying that not only would he not see me, but his friends were to be away as well. Three days before the end of the holiday, he telephoned me and, in a depressed and tearful voice, asked if he could come to see me. I arranged a session that same evening.

When he came to see me, he was at first afraid to lie on the couch. He said that he wanted just to talk to me, to be comforted and reassured. He then proceeded to tell me how, from the beginning of the holiday, a black gloom had settled upon him. He yearned for his mother to be alive, so that he could be with her and be held and loved by her. 'I just felt completely deserted and lost,' he said. 'I sat for hour after hour, unable to move or to do any work. I wanted to die. My thoughts were filled with suicide. Then I became terrified of my state of mind. That's why I phoned you. I just had never conceived it as even remotely possible that I could lose my self-control like this.' Things were made absolutely unbearable, he then explained, when one of his children had become nearly murderously aggressive towards his wife a few days before. His world seemed to have gone to pieces.

This material, and other associations, suggested that his wife stood for the bad aspect of his mother, and his son for the sadistic murderous part of himself. In his fear of dying, he was re-experiencing his own unconscious fantasies of tearing his mother to pieces, and he then felt abandoned and lost. As I interpreted on these lines, he interjected that the worst thing was the feeling of having gone to pieces himself. 'I can't stand it,' he said, 'I feel as though I'm going to die.'

I then recalled to him a dream he had had just before the holiday, which we had not had time to analyse, and which contained material of importance in the understanding of his infantile perception of being dead. In this dream he was a small boy sitting crying on the kerb in his home town. He had dropped a bottle of milk. It lay in jagged shattered bits in the gutter. The good fresh milk ran away, dirtied by contact with the muck in the gutter. One of his associations to the dream was that he had broken the bottle by his own ineptness. It was no use moaning and crying over the spilt milk, since it was himself, after all, who had caused the damage.

I related his dream to his feeling of being abandoned by me. I was the bottle of milk – containing good milk – which he destroyed in his murderous rage because I abandoned him and went dry. He unconsciously felt the Christmas holiday as losing me, as he felt he had lost his mother and the good breast, because of his ineptness – his violence and lack of control – and his spoiling me internally with his anal muck. He then felt internally persecuted and torn to pieces by the jagged bits of the bottle, representing the breast, myself, and the analysis; as Klein[1] has expressed it, 'the breast taken in with hatred becomes the representative of the death instinct within'.

I would conclude that he had unconsciously attempted to avoid depression by paranoid-schizoid techniques of splitting and deflecting his murderous impulses away from me, through his son against his wife. These techniques had now begun to fail, however, because of previous analytical work with respect to his splitting and denial. Whereas he had been able to deny what in fact turned out to be a pretty bad situation in his home, by perceiving it merely as the product of his own projections, he now became filled with guilt, anxiety, and despair, as he began to appreciate more that in reality the relationships at home were genuinely intolerable and dangerous, and were not just a projection of his own internal chaos and confusion.

During the succeeding months, we were able to elaborate more fully his attitude towards death as an experience of going to pieces.

A connection between his phobic attitude to death and his escape into activity was manifested, for instance, in his recalling one day a slogan that had always meant so much to him – 'Do or die'. But now it came to him that he had always used his own personal abbreviation of the slogan – simply 'Do'. The possibility of dying just did not consciously exist for him.

On one occasion he demonstrated at first hand how his fear of death had caused him always to retreat from mourning. A friend of his died. The patient was the strong and efficient one, who made all the necessary arrangements, while friends and family stood about helplessly, bathed in tears and paralysed with sorrow. He experienced no feeling – just clear-headedness and a sense of action for the arrangements which had to be made. He had always been the same, had done the same when his father and his mother had died. More than that, however, when

---

[1] Klein, M. (1935). 'A contribution to the psychogenesis of manic-depressive states.' In: *Contributions to Psycho-Analysis* (London: Hogarth, 1948). P. 313.

I interpreted his warding off of depression by means of denial of feeling and refuge in action, he recalled an event which revealed the unconscious chaos and confusion stirred within him by death. He remembered how, when a cousin of his had suddenly collapsed and died a few years before, he had run back and forth from the body to the telephone to call for a doctor, oblivious of the fact that a small group of people had gathered about the body, and not realizing that everyone but himself was perfectly aware that his cousin was quite dead, and had been for some time before he arrived upon the scene.

The chaos and confusion in the patient in connection with death, I would ascribe to his unconscious infantile fantasies equivalent to death – the fantasies of the destroyed and persecuting breast, and of his ego being cut to pieces.

Mainly, I think, because of the love he got from his father, probably reinforcing his own innate good impulses and what he has had described to him as good breast-feeding in the first five weeks with his mother, he had been able to achieve a partial working-through of the infantile depressive position, and to develop his good intellectual capacities. The partial character of his working-through was shown in the extent of his manic denial and activity, and his excessive use of splitting, introjection and projection, and projective and introjective identification.

During the period of early adulthood – the twenties and early thirties – the paranoid-schizoid and manic defence techniques were sufficiently effective. By means of his apparent general success and obsessional generosity, he was able to live out the role of the good mother established within, to nurture the good part of himself projected into others, to deny the real situation of envy and greed and destructiveness expressed by him as his noxiousness, and to deny the real impoverishment of his emotional life, and lack of genuine love and affection in his behaviour as both husband and father.

With the onset of mature adulthood in his mid-thirties, his defensive techniques began to lose their potency. He had lost his youth, and the prospect of middle-age and of eventual death stimulated a repetition and a reworking-through of the infantile depressive position. The unconscious feelings of persecution and annihilation which death represented to him were reawakened.

He had lost his youth. And with both his parents dead,

E

nobody now stood between himself and the grave. On the contrary, he had become the barrier between his children and their perception of death. Acceptance of these facts required constructive resignation and detachment. Unconsciously such an outlook requires the capacity to maintain the internal good object, and to achieve a resigned attitude to shortcomings and destructive impulses in oneself, and imperfections in the internal good object. My patient's unconscious fantasies of intolerable noxiousness, his anxieties of having polluted and destroyed his good primal object so that he was lost and abandoned and belonged nowhere, and his unconscious fantasies of the badness of his internalized mother as well as his father, precluded such detachment and resignation. The psychological defences which had supported his adjustment in early adult life – an adjustment of a limited kind, of course, with a great core of emotional impoverishment – failed him at the mid-life period when, to the persecutory world in which he unconsciously lived, were added his anxieties about impending middle and old age, and death. If he had had a less well established good internal object, and had been innately less constructive and loving, he might have continued his mature adult life along lines similar to his early adult type of adjustment; but if he had, I think his mid-life crisis would have been the beginning of a deterioration in his character, and bouts of depression and psychosomatic illness, due to the depth and chronicity of his denial and self-deception, and his distorted view of external reality.

As it has worked out, however, the positive factors in his personality make-up enabled him to utilize his analysis, for which he developed a deep sense of value and appreciation. The overcoming of splitting and fragmentation first began to show in a session in which, as out of nowhere, he saw two jagged edged right-angled triangles. They moved together, and joined to make a perfect square. I recalled the dream with the broken bits of bottle to him. He replied, 'It's odd you should mention that; I was just thinking of it. It feels like the bits of glass are coming together.'

Evasion of Awareness of Death

One case history does not of course prove a general thesis. It can only illustrate a theme, and the theme in this instance is the notion that the circumstances met by this patient at the mid-life phase are representative of a general pattern of psychological change at this stage of life. The extent to which these changes are tied up with physiological changes is a question I am not able to tackle. One can readily conjecture, however, that the connection must be an important one. Is libido, the life-creating impulse represented in sexual drive, diminishing; and the death instinct coming relatively more into the ascendant?

The sense of the agedness of parents, coupled with the maturing of children into adults, contributes strongly to the sense of ageing – the sense that it is one's own turn next to grow old and die. This feeling about the age of parents is very strong – even in patients whose parents died years before there is the awareness at the mid-life period that their parents would then have been reaching old age.

In the early adult phase of life, contemplativeness, detachment, and resignation are not essential components of pleasure, enjoyment and success. Manically determined activity and warding off of depression may therefore – as in the case of Mr N – lead to a limited success and pleasure. Splitting and projection techniques can find expression in what are regarded as perfectly normal patterns of passionate support for idealized causes, and equally passionate opposition to whatever may be felt as bad or reactionary.

With the awareness of the onset of the last half of life, unconscious depressive anxieties are aroused, and the repetition and continuation of the working-through of the infantile depressive position are required. Just as in infancy – to quote Klein[1] again (1940, p. 314) – 'satisfactory relations to people depend upon the infant's having succeeded against the chaos inside him (the depressive position) and having securely established his "good" internal objects', so in mid-life the establishment of a satisfactory adjustment to the conscious contemplation of one's own death depends upon the same process, for otherwise death itself is equated with the depressive chaos, confusion, and persecution, as it was in infancy.

When the prevailing balance between love and hate tends more towards the side of hate, when there is instinctual defusion,

[1] Klein, M. (1940). 'Mourning and its relation to manic-depressive states.' In *Contributions to Psycho-Analysis* (London: Hogarth, 1948). P. 314.

there is an overspill of destructiveness in any or all of its various forms – self-destruction, envy, grandiose omnipotence, cruelty, narcissism, greed – and the world is seen as having these persecuting qualities as well. Love and hate are split apart; destruction is no longer mitigated by tenderness. There is little or no protection from catastrophic unconscious fantasies of annihilating one's good objects. Reparation and sublimation, the processes which underly creativeness, are inhibited and fail. And in the deep unconscious world there is a gruesome sense of invasion and habitation by the psychic objects which have been annihilated.

In primitive terms, the process of sculpting is experienced partly as a projective identification, in which the fear of dying is split off and projected into the created object (representing the creative breast). Under the dominance of destructiveness the created object, like the breast, is felt to

> remove the good or valuable element in the fear of dying, and to force the worthless residue back into the infant. The infant who started with a fear that he was dying ends up by containing a nameless dread (Bion).[1]

The conception of death is denuded of its meaning, and the process of sculpted creativity is stopped. It is the experience of a patient who, having created a work of art by spontaneous effusion, found that 'it goes dead on me; I don't want to have anything more to do with it; I can never work on it further once it is outside, so I can never refine it; it completely loses its meaning for me – it's like a strange and foreign thing that has nothing to do with me'.

The ensuing inner chaos and despair is unconsciously fantasied in terms akin to an inferno: '*I came to myself within a dark wood . . . savage and harsh and dense*'. If this state of mind is not surmounted, hate and death must be denied, pushed aside, warded off, rejected. They are replaced by unconscious fantasies of omnipotence, magic immortality, religious mysticism, the counterpart of infant fantasies of being indestructible and under the protective care of some idealized and bountiful figure.

A person who reaches mid-life, either without having success-

---

[1] Bion, W. *Learning from Experience* (London: Heinemann; New York: Basic Books, 1962).

fully established himself in marital and occupational life, or having established himself by means of manic activity and denial with consequent emotional impoverishment, is badly prepared for meeting the demands of middle age, and getting enjoyment out of his maturity. In such cases, the mid-life crisis, and the adult encounter with the conception of life to be lived in the setting of an approaching personal death, will likely be experienced as a period of psychological disturbance and depressive breakdown. Or breakdown may be avoided by means of a strengthening of manic defences, with a warning off of depression and persecution about ageing and death, but with an accumulation of persecutory anxiety to be faced when the inevitability of ageing and death eventually demands recognition.

The compulsive attempts, in many men and women reaching middle age, to remain young, the hypochondriacal concern over health and appearance, the emergence of sexual promiscuity in order to prove youth and potency, the hollowness and lack of genuine enjoyment of life, and the frequency of religious concern, are familiar patterns. They are attempts at a race against time. And in addition to the impoverishment of emotional life contained in the foregoing activities, real character deterioration is always possible. Retreat from psychic reality encourages intellectual dishonesty, and a weakening of moral fibre and of courage. Increase in arrogance, and ruthlessness concealing pangs of envy – or self-effacing humbleness and weakness concealing fantasies of omnipotence – are symptomatic of such change.

These defensive fantasies are just as persecuting, however, as the chaotic and hopeless internal situation they are meant to mitigate. They lead to attempts at easy success, at a continuation on a false note of the early adult lyricism and precipitate creation – that is, creation which, by avoiding contemplation, now seeks not to express but to avoid contact with the infantile experience of hate and of death. Instead of creative enhancement by the introduction of the genuinely tragic, there is emotional impoverishment – a recoil away from creative development. As Freud incisively remarked: 'Life loses in interest, when the highest stake in the game, life itself, may not be risked.' Here is the Achilles heel of much young genius.

Working through the Depressive Position

When, by contrast, the prevailing balance between love and hate is on the side of love, there is instinctual fusion, in which hate can be mitigated by love, and the mid-life encounter with death and hate takes on a different hue. Revived are the deep unconscious memories of hate, not denied but mitigated by love; of death and destruction mitigated by reparation and the will to life; of good things injured and damaged by hate, revived again and healed by loving grief; of spoiling envy mitigated by admiration and by gratitude; of confidence and hope, not through denial, but through the deep inner sense that the torment of grief and loss, of guilt and persecution, can be endured and overcome if faced by loving reparation.

Under constructive circumstances, the created object in mid-life is experienced unconsciously in terms of the good breast which would in Bion's[1] terms

> moderate the fear component in the fear of dying that had been projected into it and the infant in due course would re-introject a now tolerable and consequently growth stimulating part of its personality.

In the sculpting mode of work the externally created object, instead of being experienced as having impoverished the personality, is unconsciously re-introjected, and stimulates further unconscious creativeness. The created object is experienced as life-giving. The transformation of the fear component in the fear of dying into a constructive experience is forwarded. The thought of death can be carried in thinking, and not predominantly in projective identification, so that the conception of death can begin to find its conscious realization. The reality-testing of death can be carried out in thinking, separated partly from the process of creating an external object. At the same time the continuing partial identification of the creative sculpting with the projection and reintrojection of the feat of dying gives a stimulus to the sculpting process because of its success in forwarding the working-through of the infantile projective identification with a good breast.

Thus in mid-life we are able to encounter the onset of the

[1] Bion, W. *Learning from Experience* (London: Heinemann; New York: Basic Books, 1962).

tragedy of personal death with the sense of grief appropriate to it. We can live with it, without an overwhelming sense of persecution. The infantile depressive position can be further worked through unconsciously, supported by the greater strength of reality-testing available to the nearly mature individual. In so reworking through the depressive position, we unconsciously regain the primitive sense of wholeness – of the goodness of ourselves and of our objects – a goodness which is sufficient but not idealized, not subject to hollow perfection. The consequent feeling of limited but reliable security is the equivalent of the infantile notion of life.

These more balanced conditions do not, however, presuppose an easy passage through the mid-life crisis. It is essentially a period of purgatory – of anguish and depression. So speaks Virgil:

> Down to Avernus the descent is light. But thence thy journey to retrace, there lies the labour, there the mighty toil by few achieved.

Working through again the infantile experience of loss and of grief, gives an increase in confidence in one's capacity to love and mourn what has been lost and what is past, rather than to hate and feel persecuted by it. We can begin to mourn our own eventual death. Creativeness takes on new depths and shades of feeling. There is the possibility, however, of furthering the resolution of the depressive position at a much deeper level. Such a working-through is possible if the primal object is sufficiently well established in its own right and neither excessively idealized nor devalued. Under such circumstances there is a minimum of infantile dependence upon the good object, and a detachment which allows confidence and hope to be established, security in the preservation and development of the ego, a capacity to tolerate one's shortcomings and destructiveness, and withal, the possibility of enjoyment of mature adult life and old age.

Given such an internal situation, the last half of life can be lived with conscious knowledge of eventual death, and acceptance of this knowledge, as an integral part of living. Mourning for the dead self can begin, alongside the mourning and re-establishment of the lost objects and the lost childhood and youth. The sense of life's continuity may be strengthened. The gain is in the deepening of awareness, understanding and self-realization. Genuine values can be cultivated – of wisdom, fortitude and courage, deeper capacity for love and affection and human insight, and hopefulness and enjoyment – qualities whose genuineness stems from integration based upon the more immediate and self-conscious awareness and acceptance not only of one's own shortcomings but of one's destructive impulses, and from the greater capacity for sublimation which accompanies true resignation and detachment.

Sculpted Creativity
Out of the working-through of the depressive position, there is further strengthening of the capacity to accept and tolerate conflict and ambivalence. One's work need no longer be experienced as perfect. It can be worked and reworked, but it will be accepted as having shortcomings. The sculpting process can be carried on far enough so that the work is good enough. There is no need for obsessional attempts at perfection, because inevitable imperfection is no longer felt as bitter persecuting failure. Out of this mature resignation comes the serenity in the work of genius, true serenity, serenity which transcends imperfection by accepting it.

Because of the greater integration within the internal world, and a deepening of the sense of reality, a freer interaction can occur between the internal and the external worlds. Sculpted creativity expresses this freedom with its flow of inspiration from inside to outside and back, constantly repeated, again, and yet again. There is a quality of depth in mature creativity which stems from constructive resignation and detachment. Death is not infantile persecution and chaos. Life and the world go on, and we can live on in our children, our loved objects, our works, if not in immortality.

The sculpting process in creativity is facilitated because the preparation for the final phase in reality-testing has begun – the reality-testing of the end of life. For everyone, the on-coming years of the forties are the years when new starts are coming to an end. This feeling can be observed to arise in a particularly poignant way by the mid-forties. This sense of there being no more changing is anticipated in the mid-life crisis. What is begun has to be finished. Important things that the individual would have liked to achieve, would have desired to become, would have longed to have, will not be realized. The awareness of on-coming frustration is especially intense. That is why, for example, the issue of resignation is of such importance. It is resignation in the sense of conscious and unconscious acceptance of inevitable frustration on the grand scale of life as a whole.

This reality-testing is the more severe the greater is the creative ability of the individual, for the time scale of creative work increases dramatically with ability. Thus the experience is particularly painful in genius, capable of achieving vastly more than it is possible to achieve in the remaining years, and therefore frustrated by the immense vision of things to be done which will not be done. And because the route forward has become a cul-de-sac, attention begins its Proustian process of turning to the past, working it over consciously in the present, and weaving it into the concretely limited future. This consonance of past and present is a feature of much mature adult sculpting work.

The positive creativeness and the tone of serenity which accompany the successful endurance of this frustration, are characteristic of the mature production of Beethoven, Goethe, Virgil, Dante, and other giants. It is the spirit of the 'Paradiso', which ends in words of strong and quiet confidence:

> But now my desire and will, like a wheel that spins with even motion, were revolved by the Love that moves the sun and other stars.

It is this spirit, on a lesser scale, which overcomes the crisis of middle life, and lives through to the enjoyment of mature creativeness and work in full awareness of death which lies beyond – resigned but not defeated. It is a spirit that is one criterion of the successful working-through of the depressive position in psycho-analysis.

4

Theses on Work and Creativity

[1] The critical difference between employment work, creative work, and running a business lies in whether there is any external reference for the work, and in the character of the external reference, i.e. it lies in the manner in which the object of the work is determined.

[2] In employment work, the object is set in defined terms by means of an instruction from an employer, who inspects the final product and who must be satisfied if the employment is to continue.

[3] In creative work, the object is not at all externally prescribed. It derives from the internal world and is produced for an internal audience, it reflects an impulse of the artist to express something which he himself is moved for unconscious reasons to express; there is no external task in either concrete or symbolic terms to be completed; the finished product must satisfy the artist and, if he is successful, will touch depths in the minds of others, evoke a response, and establish new standards. The creative artist requires that his external audience should also work.

[4] In running a business, one of the main tasks lies in discovering the object of the work by discovering consumer needs which may be satisfied. This work of discovering what needs may be satisfied at a profit (i.e. understanding the market) is the hallmark of successful business. There is an external reference for the work but it is not given by instruction; to discover it requires a particular kind of sensitivity to the needs of others.

[5] Creative work is therefore wholly symbolic; the finished product is symbolic; and the work itself touches upon and derives from the deepest layers of the mind, unaided by any objective and concrete point of reference. In employment work, there is always an external framework to guide and assess the symbolic work; hence symbolic work does not touch so deeply or so completely upon the unconscious processes. Running a business is intermediate; there is an external framework, but it requires symbolic work to discover it; and failure to conform to it results in a gradual loss of business, and not in an external direct criticism as from an employer.

[6] The main differences in the psychology and the psychopathology of the three types of work can, I think, be derived from this starting-point.

Employment Work

[7] The general theme to be pursued is that of the connection between employment work (and other types of work as well) and the work of mourning; the relation to the object in work is characterized by temporary states of mourning, during which it is feared that the work is resulting in failure, and the object destroyed instead of being created.

[8] In the course of the work process, inner reality and external reality are connected by means of testing symbol formation against an object emerging in external reality and judged by someone else in terms of externally established standards.

[9] If the work is successfully completed, inner reality and external reality are slightly better understood, inner reality is slightly less chaotic, the lost primary object is experienced symbolically inside as good, and hope and confidence are increased in the capacity to create an object on which real and

demonstrable value is placed, and, symbolically, in the capacity for reparation.

[10] The most primitive phantasies of the relation to the primary object are awakened because the labour of creating a work is carried on for the purpose of gaining a livelihood; that is to say, the value of the labour is directly reflected in the standard of living achieved.

Relation to the Object

[11] A task is set by a manager in terms of: 'do that task'. If he is an effective manager the work is well organized, in the sense of reasonable tasks being set, proper value placed upon the work, and a fair assessment made of the capacity of the individual.

[12] The *quid pro quo* is that the employer will pay a livelihood for the work done – that is to say the doing of the work has material value.

[13] The expected result is always prescribed.

[14] Certain limits to the ways in which the work can be done are also always prescribed by the employer; that is to say, there are governing rules and regulations, in the form of limits on time and cost, methods, procedures to be followed, etc., which the person doing the work is expected to *know*.

[15] The task is always set in symbolic terms; that is to say, the work to be done may simply be described in words, or by a drawing, or by what the thing to be made must be able to do; at its most concrete, it will be set in terms of a quasi-symbolic equation – that is to say, 'make another just like this'.

[16] That is to say, the task is set in the symbolic terms of a goal or objective, the essence of a job of work being that the finished product does not exist but must be created.

[17] The work process starts with an object that has neither been created nor destroyed; but in the course of the work, either may occur. Unconsciously it is an absent or missing object to be created in order to receive material reward; that is to say, a breast or genital to be restored or repaired.

[18] Work represents a challenge in relation to the object. The life-giving forces are to be tested, as they are tested in

connection with the testing of potency and creativity in making a baby.

[19] The relation to the object may be complicated by the extent to which the relation to the employer giving the instruction, unconsciously represents the mother or father demanding that the object be created – that is to say, the lost object restored, and a baby created. This instruction may be experienced as a loving demand, as an intrusion, or as a threat, to be responded to by a show of loving and life-giving potency, by rejection, or by placation.

[20] If the depressive position has been sufficiently worked through, the work situation presents the opportunity to work through once again in fantasy the reparative relation to the lost and destroyed primary good object, restore it to the good mother, and have it received with proper valuation, while at the same time strengthening the tie to reality by symbolically matching the fantasy process by a concomitant real activity resulting in success and value in the external world.

[21] The relation to the internal objects must be sufficiently good to make it possible to accept the external standards and restrictions set by the employer – the standards for the completed work, and the prescribed limits within which the work is to be carried out; that is to say, the super-ego must be experienced as basically helpful and not attacking, for the standards and limits to be experienced as helpful in the sense of limiting and structuring the task rather than as restrictive and persecuting.

The Function of Knowledge

[22] The employee must be able to visualize more or less completely the finished work he is to create.

[23] Within the limits set, and materials and facilities provided, he must find the best way to complete the job.

[24] He must *know* the prescribed limits.

[25] He must have enough familiarity with work of that type to *know* some possible ways of doing it and to *know* some of the consequences likely to arise from various courses of action.

[26]   He will however, never *know* completely in advance the very best way to do any particular job, since every job differs in some respect from every other, and therefore he must exercise *discretion* in doing his work.

[27]   He must visualize (in symbolic terms) various ways of doing the job in terms of, 'if I do this, then that is likely to happen', and bring both *knowledge* and *symbolic work* to bear upon the problem.

[28]   Bringing knowledge to bear implies judgement in the sense of *jus-dicare* (to speak the law); that is to say, juxtaposing relevant knowledge so as to get limits to the process of symbol formation.

[29]   Knowledge can be regarded as an ego-bounding or ego-limiting function, and is thus similar to super-ego function.

[30]   It may prove useful to consider the super-ego as one part of an ego-boundary region (a kind of circum-ego), a region which comprises at least the following content:

- (*a*) super-ego function: prescribing general norms of conduct;
- (*b*) reality-tested knowledge of the social standards and physical properties of the external world;
- (*c*) non-reality tested working hypotheses, or beliefs, about the properties of the external world;
- (*d*) currently perceived external standards and limits, which constitute the externally set framework for the job in hand.

[31]   Knowledge is thus limiting – it states what can and cannot be done; to the extent that it is accurate knowledge it is confining in a helpful way, because it limits symbolic and real action within the bounds of what is possible in reality.

[32]   As Ezra Pound has expressed it – 'The tradition is a beauty which we preserve, and not a set of fetters to bind us.'

[33]   The effective functioning of the ego-boundary (and of knowledge) will depend upon the degree to which: the super-ego has been assimilated by the ego; the super-ego is integrated; and the super-ego and other regions of the ego-boundary are integrated with each other and with the ego.

[34] A harsh, unassimilated and unintegrated super-ego will disturb the functioning of knowledge to the extent that the super-ego relation determines the quality of the relation between ego function and the ego-boundary; knowledge, and thus reality, will be experienced as harsh, unduly restrictive and frustrating.

Symbol Formation and Symbolic Work

[35] The use of discretion in work implies the capacity to work the task through in one's mind, before actually tackling it.

[36] Symbolic work implies new symbol formation, however minute, for the purpose of following through in thought the likely consequences of various courses of action, and making discretionary choice of the best way to do the job.

[37] This process of symbolic work may be facilitated by trial actions in reality, in which only a small loss is sustained if the symbolic work does not match up to reality.

[38] Under conditions of integration and assimilation of the super-ego and ego (that is to say, with fusion in the ascendant), symbol formation can proceed in conjunction with and supported by knowledge, and without resort to denial of reality.

[39] The process of symbol formation will further be facilitated to the extent that the symbolic requirements of the task fit in with the line of symbol formation which would be naturally and spontaneously follows.

[40] It is this combination of knowledge and free symbol formation (and the interaction of conscious perception and unconscious processes implied in freedom of symbol formation) which I think describes the ancient Greek conception of 'nous' – mind comprising both heart and soul, intellect and feeling, thought and impulse. Yeats expresses it as:

> God guard me from those thoughts men think
> In the mind alone;
> He that sings a lasting song
> Thinks in a marrow-bone.

[41] Symbolic work, however, stirs the deepest anxieties of fragmentation and annihilation, because of the necessity to

separate the elements in a situation, consider them apart from each other in order to select the relevant ones.

[42]   This symbolic separating and choosing, if carried too far, has all the elements of splitting and fragmentation, and is fertile ground for the displacement of unconscious aggression.

[43]   Moreover, the essence of symbolic work is that it is carried out in the complete isolation and loneliness of the internal world; thus, only if the inner world is integrated will symbolic work of this kind not represent a threat of chaos and confusion, and be carried through to the point of decision.

[44]   The difference between differentiating and splitting depends upon the presence in essence of simultaneous integration.

[45]   At some point in the process of symbolic work, and trial, the decision must be made to undertake the real external task, armed with the symbolic work that has been done. It is the point at which reality testing begins.

[46]   Decision is from de-caedere – to cut apart; it implies embarking on the chosen path in the sense of cutting away from the other possibilities (or deciding not to look for others), and pursuing the chosen path in external reality.

[47]   A decision cannot be said to have been taken unless accompanied by real commitment in action.

[48]   The point of decision is the most likely to arouse anxiety: it symbolizes cutting and giving birth; it is the point of no return; it implies the loss of the other possible courses of action which have to be given up; it is the moment of success or failure.

[49]   Anxiety is increased by the fact that symbolic work can never be completed, not only because by the very nature of its being symbolic it cannot be completed in outside reality, but because there are always limits of time to be faced, and lack of information about what the real situation is will hold once external work has begun.

[50]   The art of successful work is to keep the process of symbolic work going just long enough, and with just the right amount of detailed sorting out. A nice balance is required between too early closure and obsessional spinning out.

[51] The achievement of this balance requires that the concomitant unconscious processes symbolized in the work task (of working through the reparative relation to the primal object and creating a child) are not dominated by hopelessness and fear, accompanied by obsessional or manic defences, or paranoid-schizoid regression.

External Working

[52] At the decision stage, the die is cast, and external work begins in which inner symbolic work and use of knowledge interact with the perception of the emerging real object.

[53] From this stage, to turn back and try another path would entail the *real loss* of the external work already done.

[54] The developing real object is kept in constant conjunction with the symbolical completed object, and compared with it, and constant fine adjustments are made to the plan of action by means of symbolic work, and to the emerging work by means of action carried on in the light of the symbolic work.

[55] Reality testing begins at the stage of external work which follows decision.

[56] Completion of the external work calls for unconscious acceptance of the loss in reality of the primary object, and attachment of affect to the external object which is being created.

[57] The external object will rarely, if ever, be perfect, nor will the path chosen for creating it: if, however, the work process has been carried out under the dominance of libidinal impulses (at depth, with fusion predominating) and a good relation with the internal primal object, lost opportunities and the concomitant fear of having lost the object can be coped with by temporary states of mourning which include mourning for the lost primal object, and the ego strengthened as a result.

[58] The increase in ego strength derives from the fact that the ability to experience uncertainties, lost opportunities, or mistakes, and by microscopic mourning to live through the implied loss symbolically to the full realization of what might have been achieved, is the basis of that constructive self-criticism which leads to learning from one's own mistakes.

[59]   The completed work is compared with the standards explicit and implicit in the symbolically stated instruction.

Completion of the Task

[60]   The completed work is handed to the manager for his inspection and, if satisfactory, his approval and acceptance.

[61]   The employer pays for the value of the work as already established.

[62]   Reality testing is completed when the work is inspected by or on behalf of the employer.

[63]   If the work is satisfactory, contact with reality is reinforced by the reward in current livelihood which is gained when the primal good objects and the parents are established inside and not confused by introjective or projective identification with the external real job.

Summary

[64]   The process of normal work is one in which the individual must descend within the depths of his own internal conscious and unconscious world, and there, in lonely and isolated state, carry out the double task of unconscious reparation to the primal object and symbolic creation of an external object.

[65]   Having thus tested the balance of chaos and of integration within himself, he must then expose his state of mind to the test of scrutiny and assessment by himself and others through the medium of the product of his mind and skill as represented in his external work.

[66]   In the course of the work, temporary states of mourning are experienced in connection with difficulties in advancing the work of creating the object, with lost opportunities, and with mistakes.

Psychopathology of Work

[67]   The processes described above may break down at any or all of the stages outlined. We may consider first of all how psychological disturbance may cause breakdown in work even in objectively good working conditions.

[68]   Given the ordinary conditions in neurosis of a too harsh

super-ego; anxiety about aggression; hopelessness and lack of confidence in the capacity to repair and restore the primal object; fear of depression and persecution; fear of chaos and confusion in the inner world; insufficient differentiation of the conscious from the unconscious parts of the mind, and of inner from outer reality, and excessive projective and introjective identification; (and underneath all, states of defusion of the life and death instinct, and a deeply repressed primal bad and persecuting object split off from the deeply repressed idealized primal good object); then the following pathology occurs.

Relation to the Object

[69]   The relation to the object in work is disturbed by excess of projective and introjective identification; the object of the work is insufficiently distinguished from the internal objects.

[70]   The absence of the object to be created stirs depressive anxiety; hopelessness and despair govern work, and the confidence in capacity to do the job is lacking.

[71]   Unconsciously the anxiety is that, under the predominance of oral, anal and urethral sadism, the object will be attacked while it is being created, and a bad product, equated with the destroyed internal object, destroyed or uncreated babies, and with bad excreta, will be the result.

[72]   The rejection of the bad product by the employer representing the persecuting and castrating parents and objects, and the withdrawal of livelihood, is anticipated.

[73]   The situation is at the same time experienced internally as an attack on the internal good object and on the ego which is attempting to repair and restore that object.

[74]   The job of work, and the manager who allocates it, are intensified as persecutors, through projection of bad objects and destructive impulses.

[75]   Fear of persecution increases hatred of the work and of the employer, and reinforces deeper-lying doubts in the ability to mobilize full capacity in doing the job.

[76]   Pathological envy and jealousy are aroused – envy of the employer who has work to give, and jealousy of him for giving work to others; nepotism will intensify these feelings. The

process of constructing a symbolic representation of the object to be made is interfered with by anxiety and by the displacement into the symbol formation of aggression directed against the internal object; there results an incomplete or distorted picture of the job to be done.

Function of Knowledge

[77]   The start of the job is further hampered by external standards and knowledge being perceived as hampering and restricting, through identification of the total functioning of the ego-boundary region with the harshness and severity of the super-ego which forms a part of that region.

[78]   Knowledge and helpful limiting regulations are therefore rejected, because they are unconsciously experienced as imprisoning, persecuting, and as castrating in the sense of denying freedom for magical thought and omnipotence; hatred is turned against the ego and its knowledge, and ego function accordingly weakened.

[79]   Contrariwise, the external persecutors may in turn be identified with, in order to gain control over internal persecutors and destructive impulses; there results a weakening of ego function, characterized by a rigid conformance to regulations and consequent unimaginativeness in work.

Symbolic Work and Symbol Formation

[80]   Symbolic work constitutes a decided psychological threat under conditions of neurosis.

[81]   The descent into the internal world under conditions of isolation and loneliness stirs the anxieties of descent into the inner chaos, and the fear either of not being able to return (that is to say, of remaining internally preoccupied and transfixed, or utterly confused), or of returning with some monstrous creation; the anxieties are a small-scale replica of the anxieties of pregnancy and labour, including the threat of loss and of mourning.

[82]   Thus, Aeneas is warned; 'Light is the descent to Avernus. Night and day the portals of Gloomy Dis stand wide: but to recall thy step and issue to the upper air – there is the trial and there the task!'

[83] These anxieties are increased by the real doubt and uncertainty which must be experienced in genuine work, in the process of symbolically differentiating the various elements and possible courses of action, picking over them, and selecting the preferred path: real doubt is equated with unconscious confusion and reinforces it.

[84] Differentiation under the predominance of destructive impulses is symbolically equated with, and unconsciously becomes, splitting and fragmentation: unconscious guilt and persecutory anxiety are increased, and the process of symbolic work is experienced as inner confusion.

The Point of Decision

[85] The moment of decision precipitates anxiety: the experience of failure is anticipated; reality testing must inevitably be faced under the conditions of work for an employer; unconsciously the moment is that of facing the prospect of failure to repair and restore the good object; desperation is at its height; and there is disruption of the capacity to make the cut away from other possible paths of action.

[86] The result is an inability to hold the necessary balance between excessive and insufficient symbolic work; the imbalance is expressed as indecisiveness and dithering, or as omnipotent and premature action.

External Working

[87] Finally, the carrying out of the external work is undercut by depressive anxiety.

[88] Imperfections in the object and/or the method chosen to create it (and these are in fact likely to be excessive) are seen as evidence of the dominance of destructive impulses and inability to repair and restore; guilt is heightened.

[89] The basic response to failure or threatened failure becomes, 'if only I had done so and so', or, 'I could kick myself' – a sense of paranoid stupidity reinforcing anxiety about self-destructiveness.

[90] Depressive reiteration of the badness of the self-militates against constructive self-criticism, since it is based upon hatred

of the self, obsessional inability to give up the lost opportunity, and use of the lost opportunity sadistically to attack the self (and the primal object) by demonstrating its ineptitude.

[91]   But, as in all mourning, the greatest danger is the turning of hatred outwards; against the object and the employer who demanded that the object be made: both are perceived by projective identification as persecuting, and failure is perceived as the natural objective, since by failure the object and the parental substitute can be destroyed.

[92]   Aggression against the work is increased by the mobilization of envy towards the employer who is to get the object, expressed as envious spoiling of the work and spoiling of the employer by letting him down.

[93]   The theme becomes, 'Why should I do good work for them', and internal mourning and external creative work are both brought to a standstill – intensified by the withdrawal of livelihood, which serves unconsciously to stimulate further the aggression associated with the lost primal good object.

Defences Against Anxiety in Work

[94]   The main defences against depressive anxiety – manic and obsessional defences, and regression to the paranoid-schizoid position – are brought to bear in a neurotic relation to work, and impress their features upon the character of the work done.

[95]   In each case the process of free symbol formation is interrupted or inhibited: the pleasure of symbolic work, which is life-giving, is lost; boredom, unconsciously experienced as death, is never far away; and the loss of the symbolic activity in turn demands to be mourned.

Manic Defence

[96]   Under the dominance of omnipotence and triumph, an 'I'll show them' attitude comes into work.

[97]   Excessive ambition and drive may be manifested, with denial of effect, single-minded adherence to work to the exclusion of other spheres of living, and general impoverishment of emotional life.

[98] Sadistic destructiveness finds an outlet in triumph-seeking competitiveness.

[99] Hatred and contempt are directed towards both the employer and the task.

[100] Symbolic work may be dominated by magical omnipotence; leading to grandiosity of plans, a carelessness for detail, and, usually, premature closure of the symbolic work process (or there may occur grandiose elaboration).

[101] Success is reacted to by depressive anxiety, because it is experienced as triumph.

[102] Failure is experienced as persecuting annihilation.

Obsessional Defence

[103] Symbol formation becomes stultified rather than free, because of rigid adherence to existing symbols and their use for ritualistic purposes.

[104] Development is restricted and ambition is inhibited.

[105] The unconscious goal is to maintain a state of bliss by means of living in an unchanging world, in relation to an ideal good and unchanging object which makes no demands for reparation because it has never changed.

[106] There is some denial of reality (but not psychotic, because of the predominating contact with reality and knowledge of change) by means of a ritualistic compromise in which activity is gripped in an obsessionally fixed frame (vide the Platonic notion of the unchanging ideal world as against the changing sensible world).

[107] The result is impoverishment of thought because of obsessionally ruminative play with symbols partially supplanting symbol formation, by means of which the destructive impulses and persecuting object are controlled.

[108] The resulting work is stultified, excessively detailed, and unimaginative, the process of symbolic work is carried too far, and indecisiveness is the keynote.

[109] The reaction to the result of the work is omnipotent denial and excessive appreciation of the detailing, and/or obsessional reiteration of the 'if only' feeling.

Paranoid-Schizoid Regression

[110]   Regression is characterized by two main elements in work; confusion and stupidity, and cunning and deceit.

[111]   The relation to the object, which is experienced as annihilated, is one of hatred and persecutory anxiety.

[112]   The process of symbol formation becomes intensely threatening because of the close tie with inner chaos and confusion, and is replaced by symbolic equation under the impact of destructive impulses and fear of annihilation, with excessive projective and introjective identification with the object.

[113]   Inhibition of thought occurs, symbols are destroyed, and work and the organization of work become confused and characterized externally by stupidity, and internally by magically omnipotent creativity and day-dreaming.

[114]   In conjunction with manic defence systems, slyness and cunning are used in relation to the object, bad work is concealed or glossed over, regulations are secretly breached, and untrustworthiness and delinquent irresponsibility result.

[115]   Failure is reacted to as confirming the persecutory situation, hatred and destructiveness against the object are reinforced, self-criticism is precluded by omnipotent triumph, and fears of persecutory retaliation are increased.

Concluding Theses

[116]   *These anxieties are increased under the impact of bad management,* that is to say when work, payment and capacity are not in equilibrium; as for example:

(a) underpayment mobilizes paranoid fears of exploitation, and envy and rivalry;

(b) under-employment arouses fears of rejection by the good object and of castration, and reinforces anxieties of not being able to use reparative skills at full stretch;

(c) overpayment plus over-employment supports manic grandiosity and denial of fear of failure, stimulates the sense of being idealized and overvalued, and gives rise to dependent toadying mixed with secret contempt.

[117]   The neurotic individual may seek precisely such conditions of external disequilibrium, unconsciously knowing his

ambitions (whether grandiose or self-depreciative) to be out of line with his unconscious knowledge of his true capacity, level of work, and equitable payment for that work.

[118] The non-neurotic individual commonly uses splitting to deal with externally foisted disequilibrium: he retains as good a relation as possible with the immediate object (his work and his on-the-spot manager), puts his destructive impulses and objects into the larger surrounding and more anonymous situation of the company, the 'boss' and politics, and by means of projective identification uses social systems to reinforce his defences against persecutory and depressive anxiety and to protect his relation to his work. (See Chapter 13, page 209.)

[119] These unconscious mechanisms do not exclude the possibility of actual exploitation by employers; exploitation and the impulse to exploitation do occur, especially as part of the use of slyness and cunning in the mechanism of paranoid-schizoid regression in managers in the attempt to avoid depressive anxiety in their own work.

[120] The psychologically constructive job of managers lies not in the provision of counselling and welfare services, but in arranging for work to be done efficiently in the sense of ensuring the employment of individuals at a level of work consistent with their capacity, and administering payment in accord with the equitable work-payment scale.

[121] Such arrangements are not a substitute for psychological treatment; they are preventive in the sense of eliminating an important external source of envy, destructiveness, and despair.

5

Disturbances in the Capacity to Work

In its most general sense, work as conceived by Freud[1] (and I am here concerned with work in the psychological sense only) is the mental energy or effort expended in striving to reach a goal or objective by means of the operation of the reality principle, and in the face of the demands of the pleasure principle.[2] If we examine this activity closely, however, a number of important features claim our attention.

The operation of the reality principle leads to delayed rather than immediate gratification. It requires the exercise of discretion (in the sense of judgement, and not the social sense of being discreet) in determining which courses of action will eventually lead to the best result. Discrimination and judgement must be used, and decisions made. Decision contains the un-

[1] Freud, S. (1911), 'Formulations on the Two Principles of Mental Functioning'. *S.E.P.*, **12**.

[2] This conception of work is followed by most psycho-analytical writers on the subject, as for example: Hendrick, Ives (1943), 'Work and the Pleasure Principle', *Psychoanal. Quart.*; Obendorf, C. P. (1951), 'The Psychopathology of Work'. *Bull. Menninger Clin.*; and Lantos, Barbara (1952), 'Metapsychological Considerations on the Concept of Work'. *Int. J. Psycho-Anal.*, **33**.

certainty of the wisdom of the choice, and calls for the capacity to tolerate uncertainty while awaiting the final outcome, and possible failure.

This uncertainty, however, it must be noted, has a special quality. The use of discretion depends upon unconscious as well as conscious mental functioning – the capacity for synthesis of unconscious ideas and intuitions and bringing them into consciousness. We may not be surprised to find, therefore, that at the core of this uncertainty lies anxiety – the anxiety aroused by having to depend for success upon the coherence and availability of unconscious mental life.

I was able to confirm this conclusion in social-analytic work in industry which I have reported elsewhere.[1] In the course of these studies, two major components of work were separated: first, the prescribed content – laws, customs, resources, instructions, rules and regulations, and material limitations – which allow no room for discretion but set the frame within which discretion is exercised; and second, the discretionary content, comprising all those aspects in which discretion and choice have to be exercised. The force of this distinction was brought home to me when it became clear that what is experienced as psychic effort in work – the intensity or weight of responsibility – is entirely concerned with the discretionary content of work. To conform to rules and regulations and other prescribed aspects of work requires knowledge; you either know or you do not; but it does not require the psychic effort of discretion and decision, with its attendant stirring of anxiety.

I was able to demonstrate that weight or level of responsibility is objectively measurable in terms of the maximum spans of time during which discretion must be exercised by a person on his own account. The longer the span of time, the more the unconscious material that must be made conscious, and the longer must uncertainty about the final outcome and the anxiety about one's judgement and discretion be tolerated. In short, the longer the path towards gratification chosen in accord with the reality principle, the greater is the experience of psychic effort or work.

We are led then to the following definition of work, and

[1] Jaques, Elliott, *Measurement of Responsibility* (London: Tavistock, and Harvard University Press, 1956).

formulation of the capacity to work. *Work* is the exercise of discretion within externally prescribed limits to achieve an object which can be reality-tested, while maintaining a continuous working-through of the attendant anxiety. The *capacity to work* depends upon the coherence of the unconscious, and upon the integration and strength of the ego and its capacity, in the face of anxiety and uncertainty, to sustain its functions, to maintain the reality principle, and to exert pressure to make the unconscious conscious.

The Main Components in Mental Activity

Work is never a simple process of striving towards an external objective. Combined in any act of work there is always a relation to the objective perceived as a symbol. In order to advance our analysis, I shall have to digress for a moment to establish a few conceptions and terms in connection with perception and symbol formation.

The perception of an object is determined by the interplay of the requisite content of the percept with two types of symbolic content which have been variously designated; for example, by Segal[1] as symbols and symbolic equations, and by Jones[2] as symbols and true symbols. Whatever the terms used for the two types of symbolic content – and many writers, including Milner[3] and Rycroft,[4] have emphasized the importance of the distinction – the central factor is that stressed by Klein[5] (and elaborated by Segal), namely, the degree of concreteness of the symbol, and the extent to which it coexists with the object or engulfs it. The degree of concreteness in turn depends upon the intensity and character of the splitting process which underlies the symbol formation. It is consistent with recent developments in Klein's

[1] Segal, Hanna (1957). 'Notes on Symbol Formation.' *Int. J. Psycho-Anal.*, **38**.

[2] Jones, Ernest. 'The Theory of Symbolism.' In: *Papers on Psycho-Analysis* (London: Ballière, Tindall and Cox, 1948).

[3] Milner, Marion (1952). 'Aspects of Symbolism in Comprehension of the Not-Self.' *Int. J. Psycho-Anal.*, **33**.

[4] Rycroft, Charles (1956). 'Symbolism and its Relation to Primary and Secondary Processes.' *Int. J. Psycho-Anal.*, **37**.

[5] Klein, M., 'On the Importance of Symbol Formation in the Development of the Ego'. In: *Contributions to Psycho-Analysis* (London: Hogarth, 1948).

conception of the paranoid-schizoid position (and indeed with unstated assumptions in her earlier work) to assume that it is when violent splitting with fragmentation of the object and the self is predominant that concrete rather than plastic symbol formation occurs. I propose to show that this assumption is useful and necessary not only in considering the problem of work, but in considering all mental processes, especially the fundamental process of perception, and shall use the following terms and schema.

The perception of an object is determined by the inter-connection of:

(*a*) the requisite content of the perception, resulting in a mental percept of the object itself;

(*b*) the symbolic content, in which the object is modified by protective identification, split-off parts of the self and internal objects being unconsciously perceived as in the external object or connected with it, and the object introjected in the modified form;

(*c*) what I propose to term the concretive content, in which the object is modified by the explosive projection into it of violently split and fragmented internal objects and parts of the self, loses its own identity and becomes a concrete symbol (or, in Segal's terms a symbolic equation); it is then violently introjected and experienced internally in concrete corporeal form in a split-off and and fragmented state within the body ego.[1]

This distinction between ordinary projection and introjection and the more concrete processes of violent projection and introjection is one consistently made by Klein in her earlier papers, in which she frequently uses the terms expulsion and

[1] This conception of concretism is connected with phenomena similar to those described by Goldstein under the heading of concrete as against abstract thinking, and by Piaget under the heading of syncretism. I believe that the processes of violent splitting and fragmentation, followed by explosive projection and violent introjection, with the accompanying very concrete forms of identification, offer an explanation of the dynamics of the phenomena observed by Goldstein in his patients with brain damage, and by Piaget in young children.

incorporation to refer to the more violent processes. Bion, in his papers on hallucinosis,[1] emphasizes the distinction, and retains these earlier terms.

Developmentally, violent splitting with fragmentation is associated with the earliest phases of the paranoid-schizoid position, when the rudimentary ego is under the impact of intense destructive impulses and instinctual defusion. At this stage, ordinary splitting fails as an ego defence because of the intensity of the anxiety aroused by the split-off persecuting primal object, and from the dangers of destroying the idealized split-off good object. As Klein[2] has recently shown, both aspects of the split primal object become experienced as persecutory, and contribute to the remorseless quality of the primitive super-ego.

Symbol formation with lessened concretism becomes possible at the transition stage between the paranoid-schizoid and depressive positions. The ego, with greater integration, is more able to contend with persecutory anxiety by means of less violent splitting and with lessened fragmentation. There results a growing confidence in the capacity to sustain the good objects split-off and segregated from the bad ones. The ensuing capacity to reduce anxiety by formation of symbols[3] in turn facilitates the onset of the depressive position. Contact with reality is strengthened, greater reality in perception comes to the fore, and a whole range of defences becomes available, especially reparation and sublimation and a more fully developed use of symbol formation.[4] Davidson has given a graphic account of this process in his clinical description of the treatment of a patient suffering from schizophrenia with mutism.[5] In passing, I would suggest that it is precisely because symbol formation is always based upon some splitting, that symbols tend towards being normative in mode – either good or bad.

[1] For example, Bion, W. R., 'On Hallucination.' *Int. J. Psycho-Anal.*, **39.**
[2] Klein, M. (1958). 'On the Development of Mental Functioning.' *Int. J. Psycho-Anal.*, **39.**
[3] Klein, M., 'On the Importance of Symbol Formation in the Development of the Ego.' op. cit.
[4] Segal, op. cit.
[5] Davidson, S. S., 'On Catatonic Stupor and Catatonic Excitement.' Unpublished paper read to the British Psycho-Analytical Society on 29 April 1959.

In separating out three main components of perceptual processes, and indeed of all mental activity – the requisite, symbolic, and concretive – I am doing so for the purpose of analysis only, and not to suggest that there are objective ego activities separated from symbolic and concrete contents and the conflicts and anxieties from which they arise. It is precisely the coexistence and interconnection of these components of mental activity which I wish to demonstrate in work: the relative quantity, balance, and content of the three components determining the degree of realism, the creativeness, the energy, and the direction in work, as well as the extent to which that work contributes to advances in psychic integration. The present formulation thus differs from that of Hartmann[1] who, in defining what he terms the conflict-free ego sphere, writes of 'that ensemble of functions which at any given time exert their effects outside the region of mental conflicts'. In contrast to Hartmann, I believe that the path from psycho-analysis to a general psychology cannot be traversed without taking into account the fundamental role of conflict in all mental functioning – a view which I hope may be supported by the present paper. In particular, I think that the understanding of normal psychological processes will be enhanced by teasing out from within them, and elaborating, the various types of splitting processes employed by the ego in dealing with conflict, and the vicissitudes of the resulting splits and fragmentations of the ego, objects, and impulses – a point frequently stressed by Klein.

The Process of Work

I now wish to turn to the process of work itself. Six main stages may be recognized:

(a) the achievement of a particular objective is undertaken, and a *relationship is established with the objective;*

(b) an *appropriate quantity of the mental apparatus must be allocated* to the task;

(c) an *integrative reticulum* must be constructed and elaborated, within which the work is organized;

(d) concentration upon the task, teasing out the contents of

[1] Hartmann, Heinz: *Ego Psychology and the Problem of Adoption* (London: Image, 1958).

those areas of the mind occupied upon it, and a scrutiny and searching for elements which will help in solving the problem; a process I shall designate by the terms *lysis* and *scanning*;

(e) *gathering*, *linking*, and *synthesis* of the elements which fit;
(f) *decision*, by which is designated a taking of action with significant committal of resources.

The processes I shall describe will refer throughout to the interplay of mental events between the conscious and unconscious areas of the mind. Although the focus of emphasis oscillates continually between the conscious and the unconscious – each one alternately becoming figure and then ground – neither the one nor the other process is ever inactive.

I shall outline the six stages of work sequence for purposes of presentation. In reality the various stages interact. The first integrative reticulum may be tentative – a hypothesis, or a mere hunch or feeling. Insufficient, or too much, mental capacity may be allocated. As lysis and synthesis proceed, and knowledge is collected, the integrative reticulum may be modified, and more or less mental capacity allocated; the libidinal relationship with the objective may be altered – ambivalence and the intensity of libidinal investment increasing or decreasing as the task and its difficulties are encountered and experienced.

Moreover, as lysis and linking proceed, trials may be essayed in external reality, but without extensive committal of resources, the knowledge and intuitions built up from these trials being fed back into the elements available for linking.

Relation with the Obje tive

An objective is an object-to-be – one which has to be brought into being, to be created. The objective may be worked for because of inner need and compulsion, for the personal satisfaction to be derived regardless of other gain. It may be an allocated task constituting part of a person's employment.

The amount of energy mustered for a task will depend upon both the desire to achieve the objective and obtain the attendant reward, and the symbolic meaning of the objective and attendant psychic gratification. Work is most satisfying when both these elements are consistent with each other, and relatively undisturbed by concretism.

If the depressive position has been sufficiently worked through the symbolic content of work will be connected mainly with reparation. The analytic literature contains many instances, for example, where the objective represents the creation of a baby and giving birth to it. At a deeper level is symbolized the reparation, restoring, and recreation of the primal good object, and revival of good impulses and good parts of the self. The objective in work is nicely suited for such a symbol, since it exists only as a partial schema requiring to be completed and brought to life by loving care and work. At the same time as the objective is symbolically identified with the good object undergoing reparation and restoration, the bad objects and bad impulses and parts of the self are symbolically identified with obstacles in the way of the work. The more the reality content of the work is consistent with the unconscious symbolic reparative activities, the greater will be the love for the task.

If the discrepancy between the reality and symbolic aspects is too great, lack of interest or hatred is aroused, and loss of incentive ensues. This hatred may be intensified by violent splitting and fragmentation, the incomplete objective being concretely introjected and identified with destroyed and persecuting internal objects. The objective itself then becomes increasingly persecutory through violent projection and concrete symbol formation. Moreover, the intensity of the concretism will determine the extent to which 'putting oneself into the job' becomes a matter of strong positive motivation and sound effort, or of confusion and inhibition. The negative effect is produced by the unconscious experience of losing parts of the self and internal objects into the task concretely perceived, combined with the experience of getting parts of the job lost inside oneself – in the same manner, for example, as when genital sexuality is inhibited by urethral and anal sadism. Fears of failure are then intensified through unconscious fears of uncontrolled destructive impulses.

Allocation of Mental Capacity
The amount of mental capacity allocated (i.e. the amount of occupation with the task) will be determined by the judgement

of the size of the task, given greater or lesser effect by the intensity of libidinal involvement and the amount of ambivalence. The accuracy of the judgement of size of task will be influenced by knowledge of that type of work. It will be distorted by violent splitting and fragmentation. The stronger the love for the real and the symbolic objective, the greater the psychic energy that will be made available for the task.

The allocation of mental capacity requires a genuine act of mental investment. More, it requires the segregation of the invested area from interference by other mental activities. It is an allocation in time as well as in amount. The intensity of absorption in the task is at stake. It is an estimate, and one which may require subsequent revision. The greater the time framework, ordinarily the greater is the area of the mental apparatus that is brought into play. To be preoccupied with other things means just what the word implies: so much of the mental apparatus has already been allocated that not enough is available for the task at hand. Segregation breaks down, and concentration on the task is disturbed. Capacity to work is impaired in neurosis by the absorption of mental capacity in internal conflict, which leaves relatively little capacity available for any other work.

Integrative Reticulum
The integrative reticulum is the mental schema of the completed object and the means of creating it, organized in such a manner that the gaps both in the mental picture of the object and in the methods of creating it are established. Consciously, it is a combination of any or all of concepts, theories, hypotheses, and working notions or hunches. Unconsciously, it is a constellation of ideas-in-feeling, memories-in-feeling, phantasies, and internal objects – brought together and synthesized to the extent necessary to direct behaviour, even if not sufficiently to become conscious.

The creation of an adequate reticulum requires sufficient ego-strength to achieve the necessary intensity of concentration upon the task. If ambivalence about the task is low, and if there is not excessive splitting of the conscious from the unconscious parts of the mind, then the greater the ego-strength and the greater the conscious mental concentration and effort applied to the task, the greater will be the concentration upon the task in the unconscious mind. That is to say, conscious mental effort has a continuous effect upon the mobilizing of unconscious mental activity and effort, and upon the content and direction of that activity.

Conversely, the strength of the ego-activity mobilized for the task, the capacity to concentrate upon the objective, and the coherence and synthesizing power of the resulting reticulum, depend in large measure upon the coherence in the organization of the unconscious mental processes. The degree of coherence in the unconscious is associated with the dominance of loving impulses over destructiveness, and the intactness of internal good objects – these conditions reducing the dependence of the ego upon violent splitting. When, however, there is insufficient coherence and violent splitting and fragmentation occur, a satisfactory integrative reticulum cannot be established. Indeed a schema of the objective constructed under such conditions will itself be split and fragmented and will thus facilitate further splitting and fragmentation: it acts as a disintegrating rather than an integrative reticulum inducing confusion and dis- organization in work.

The assumption of unconscious influences upon conscious mental processes requires no elaboration. The two assumptions, however – that of coherent structure and function in uncon- scious processes, and that of conscious effort in influencing the intensity, coherence, direction, and content of unconscious activity – may warrant a brief comment. The validity of these assumptions may be simply demonstrated. The successful accomplishment of any task requires the exercise of some or all of the functions which we describe as touch, or feel, or sense, or intuition, or insight. These functions are exercised in the main unconsciously, and are not simply preconscious. They can be brought into play by conscious orientation towards a parti- cular task. Once set going, they may operate, for instance, during sleep, throwing up a result that is consciously available, but without the problem-solving activities themselves becoming conscious. Such activities demand the assumption of coherence and dynamic organization in the unconscious, intimately con- nected with conscious activities.

Lysis and Scanning

By lysis, I refer to the process of separating and teasing out the contents of those areas of the mind occupied in the task – the products of conscious knowledge and of unconscious phantasies and feelings, awareness through experience, and intuition. By scanning, I refer to the process of mentally looking over and considering the teased-out materials. Both lysis and scanning are concerned with making the unconscious conscious.

Lysis and scanning require the capacity to loosen the elements organized within other sets of ideas, so that many relevant elements may be abstracted and used in the new context; e.g. certain ideas in a book; or the unconscious memory of a particular feature of the behaviour of another person, or of one's own childhood. At the same time the integrative reticulum itself must be loosened and prepared for the linking of new elements, the reticulum possibly needing to be modified in the process. Scanning may be external as well as internal. When insufficient material is discerned in the conscious and sensed in the unconscious mind, new information is sought in the outside world, by search and by research. When libidinal investment in the work is high, so are curiosity and the need for truth – and the desire to discover and use such knowledge as already exists – so that the work of others is prized and valued.

If the ego-strength is sufficient, the concentration of mental effort on the task within the frame of the integrative reticulum results in the loosening out and mobilization of thoughts and ideas relevant to the task. These elements do not come only from the conscious ego. If the unconscious ego is sufficiently oriented towards the task, it will be influenced into throwing forth elements associated with gaps in the reticulum. The more coherent is the organization of the unconscious ego, the greater is the influence upon it of the exertion of conscious mental concentration and effort; and the greater will be the release of elements from the unconscious to be made available for scanning and for possible use in achieving the objective.

In lysis and scanning, if the mental process is plastic, elements of thought are made available for synthesis within other thought processes, without destroying their mental context. At the symbolic level, this process goes on by means of a wide range of possible splits and fusions, but with the good and bad aspects of the splitting maintained intact. To the extent, however, that persecutory anxiety, violent splitting, and the ensuing concretism are at work, lysis and scanning are inhibited or lead to confusion, because lysis is experienced as fragmentation and disintegration. The mental process is concrete and inflexible, the bits and particles are not available for synthesis, and the integrative reticulum becomes unmodifiable.

Gathering, Linking, and Synthesis

As the process of lysis and scanning proceeds, those elements which fit together and into the schema are gathered together. The question of what constitutes fittingness is of the greatest importance, and warrants a separate treatment beyond the scope of the present paper.[1] The loosened elements are mentally tried out for fit into gaps in the reticulum, and those which fit are retained. The sensation is that of insight, of notions which click.

The gathering together of these elements, and their linking within the integrative reticulum constitutes the act of synthesis. To gather, meaning to draw together in a heap, comes from the same root as the word 'good'.[2] Linguistically, then, there is reason to connect the creative gathering and synthesizing processes in work, with the unconscious experience of establishing the good object.

Where the apposition and fit are *unconsciously* made, the sensation of insight is one of 'feel' – something clicks, but it is not quite clear what. It is the feeling that one could *do* it oneself, or *demonstrate* how to do it, but yet not be able to *explain* how. Effort and study are required to bring the experience into the preconscious by discovering verbal images which correspond to it, and thus to bring the elements forth into consciousness, as Freud[3] has described in *The Ego and the Id*. The existence of a coherent integrative reticulum spanning the conscious and the unconscious ego acts as a powerful agent enabling the

---

[1] It is a question which takes us, for example, into the role of insight and of trial-and-error in learning and in problem-solving.

[2] Both are from the Indo-European root 'gad' which means fit or suitable.

[3] Freud, S. *The Ego and the Id* (London: Hogarth, 1923).

unconscious thus to be made conscious. The necessary act of
attending to the task is experienced as mental strain.

When concretism is strong, however, linked objects are
experienced as persecuting, the act of synthesis – as shown by
Bion in another context[1] – representing the unconscious internal
re-enactment of the primal scene. The mental processes in work
are therefore attacked, and the integrative reticulum subjected
to tearing and destructive annihilation. The effect of the erotization of work is thus influenced by the strength of concretism:
if concretism is weak, symbolic erotization of the objective in
work may facilitate the work and reinforce sublimation; if it is
strong, work is disturbed and sublimation is inhibited because
of the concreteness of the erotization.

Decision and Action

When the mental process has proceeded sufficiently far, or when
time begins to run out, the moment of decision and committal is
reached. By the term 'decision', I wish to designate the taking of
action to create the object in whole or in part, with a significant
committal of resources, so that if the discretion and judgement
exercised have been adequate, success will be achieved, but if
they have been inadequate, failure will be experienced with
wastage of the resources committed.

By decision, therefore, I mean what the term implies –
'decaedere', a cutting apart – an act from which there is no
turning back. It is the point at which a person's confidence in his
mental capacity is put on trial, for the consequence of an act of
decision is reality testing. The results of the decision have to be
faced. It is the moment when anxieties about the task are
mobilized to the very greatest extent.

If, therefore, there is much violent splitting with fragmentation, catastrophe is unconsciously anticipated. This fear of
catastrophe is of the paranoid-schizoid type. It is the fear of
self-inflicted failure through self-imposed stupidity and self-
deception which occur whenever violent splitting and fragment-
tion, with their attendant confusion, are at work. It leads,
following actual failure, to self-recrimination of the 'if only I had
done so-and-so' type; and defence against this self-castigation
by projection of the blame only intensifies persecutory anxiety,

[1] Bion, W. R. (1958). 'Attacks on Linking.' *Int.J.Psycho-Anal.*, **40.**

and in no way repairs the damage. The potency of the destructive impulses is experienced as immediately present. Consequently, irreality and a retreat to the pleasure principle result. Evasion of reality testing may be achieved by obsessional indecisiveness and paralysis of action or, equally, by careless and grandiose 'decisiveness' based upon magically omnipotent phantasies and off-hand disregard of the result.

If, however, the objective in work is successfully achieved in reality, then reparation is reinforced, the bad objects and impulses are diminished by identification with the obstacles that have been overcome, and splitting is lessened. Integration in the ego is advanced, and the operation of the reality principle is strengthened.

But perhaps most important is the fate of the concrete components of the mental processes involved in the work. The very fact that a decision was made requires that some of the energy bound in maintaining the fragmentation is released, and with it some of the anxiety that had been tied up in the fixed and concrete symbolism. But the success of the objective work combined with the processes of symbol formation in creating an object in external reality, and reparation internally, mitigates hate and diminishes persecutory anxiety, increases the capacity to tolerate depressive anxiety and loss, and hence diminishes the need for violent splitting and fragmentation. Additional symbol formation occurs. And with the release and experience of anxiety there is relief as well, because of the experience, no matter how slight, of the capacity to tolerate that anxiety without disintegration, and to be creative in spite of it. I shall not, however, elaborate this point further. For Klein[1] has shown in detail in her paper on 'Mourning and its Relation to the Manic-Depressive States', how every experience of overcoming obstacles and anxiety – and this applies strongly in work – leads to a furthering of the working-through of the infantile depressive position, and a step forward in maturity and in the capacity for sublimation.

A Note on the Role of the Super-ego in Work
My omission of any reference to the role of the super-ego in work is no measure of its importance; for example, if it is not

[1] Klein, M., 'Mourning and its Relation to Manic Depressive States.' In: *Contributions to Psycho-Analysis* (London: Hogarth, 1948).

excessively persecutory, it plays a constructive role in facilitating sublimation, and forwarding work. But it is a subject which I cannot pursue on this occasion, other than to touch briefly upon one point.

When the super-ego develops in a setting of violent splitting and fragmentation it becomes harsh and persecuting in its relation to the ego, and is experienced as severely restrictive.[1] This circumstance is revived in work when concretism is strong. The prescribed limits – the rules and regulations – within which the work is to be carried out, are experienced as persecuting. And equally serious, knowledge itself becomes experienced as persecutory, because one of the important effects of knowledge is to restrict and limit the ego's field of choice of action, in the same way as does the super-ego. Unconsciously, then, knowledge is hated and is rejected, commonly by its being fragmented and repressed. The ensuing resentment against work is readily illustrated in the behaviour of delinquents and borderline psychotics who react to the demands of conforming to the prescribed content of work and the knowledge to be exercised, by omnipotence, carelessness, and hostile negligence. Equally familiar is the reaction formation of concrete acceptance of the knowledge one knows and over-dependence upon it, with resentment against new knowledge which threatens existing conceptions, theories, and frames of reference.

Psycho-analysis as Work

We may illustrate these processes and the effects of concretism under ordinary everyday conditions, by a brief reference to work which we all know – that of psycho-analysing a patient. The love and energy with which we pursue the treatment is dependent upon the consistency between the conscious objective of mental healing and the content and strength of our unconscious symbolical reparative drive. We must have undergone sufficient personal analysis to enable us to allocate the requisite mental capacity to the task without interference from other preoccupations – especially unconscious anxieties – which might distract our attention and weaken our concentration upon the patient's unconscious mind. In listening to

[1] Klein has elaborated this theme in her paper 'On the Development of Mental Functioning'. (1958), op. cit.

our patients, we each use an integrative reticulum, built up from an amalgam of previous material from the patient, and from the particular theories, concepts, and working notions we employ. This integrative reticulum determines our mental set or attitude and hence influences both the direction of our attention and the weight we place upon various aspects of the material that is forthcoming. It thus influences to an important extent what we each actually observe in our patients.

The clarity of our understanding of our patients will, moreover, depend upon the interaction between our objective perception of the patient and the exploration of the patient by projective and introjective identification through which we symbolically experience what it would be like if we were the patient, and if the patient were ourselves. It is likely, however, that the concretive content of the experience will always interfere with this symbolic process to a certain extent, the consequence being that one unconsciously feels oneself to be lost in the patient, and the patient confused inside oneself. This type of concrete projective and introjective identification occurs in counter-transference. If concretism is strong, our relationship with the patient may be distorted and disturbed.

The state of mind in lysis and scanning can be illustrated in the free-floating attention necessary for psycho-analytic interpretation. It is free-floating only in the limited sense of being free within a previously-established integrative reticulum of analytic theory and of knowledge about the patient. Lysis and scanning occur within this schema, elements of the patient's associations and behaviour being scrutinized and picked over in our search for what to interpret – the integrative reticulum acting as a kind of sieve. Then, by virtue of our own conscious and unconscious mental activity, various elements become linked in our minds, and a potential interpretation is gradually gathered up and consciously formed. At the same time, our sense of timing and tone and verbal formulation remains largely unconscious.

The moment of decision is that point when, having gathered together the material which we consider relevant to an interpretation, we not only feel that the time has come to make an interpretation, but we actually make it – we say it to the patient

– we commit ourselves. Having done so, we must then face in reality the effects and consequences of our interpretation.

It is probably the case that psycho-analytic work calls for more continuous concentration and mental work than any other. This fact, plus the fact that one's own anxieties are always subject to being aroused by those of the patient, makes us, as analysts, more readily vulnerable to disturbances in work by concretism. For instance, concentration might flag and attention wander, or the necessary continuous attention to minute detail in following the patient's associations might provoke a certain amount of confusion. In more extreme form, linking may be inhibited, and interpretation may be experienced as dangerous. Decisiveness in interpretation could be impaired.

A Clinical Illustration

I wish now to present some clinical material from the analysis of a patient who suffered a schizophrenic breakdown, and who in his fifth year of analysis was just getting back to work. I have chosen this case because it magnifies and highlights the effects of concretism by showing its operation in the setting of a large amount of violent splitting and fragmentation.

The patient, a twenty-eight-year-old man, had worked as a script-writer. The interaction of the various phases in work which I have described may be illustrated by material from a number of sessions at a time when he was trying to write a script for television. He came to one session in a half-triumphant half-despairing frame of mind. He thought he had written an excellent talk, but was convinced no one would buy it. 'If they did,' he boasted triumphantly, 'I would show them; I'd capture the audience!'

His attitude struck me as very similar to that of the previous day, when (as on some other occasions) we had analysed how he had attempted omnipotently to capture me with his talk, so as to get me to do exactly as he pleased – to analyse him, give him insulin treatment, let him stay with me in my house, sleep with my wife, and take over my friends and social life. I interpreted to him, therefore, that he wanted to use television to enter the homes of people and control them with his talk.

He roared with laughter at this connection, and gurgled with triumphant glee, 'I'd tell them! I'd get into millions of homes at once. The bastards – I'd shit all over them!'

In the light of his associations and previous material, I was able to interpret to him that the TV audience represented to him his own internal family broken into millions of bits – whom he projected into the viewing families. He was then able to gain control over them by gaining omnipotent control over the television, and entering into their homes. The entry was a forced entry, with his faeces, in which he greedily possessed and controlled everything – food, comfort, and parental sexuality. At a deeper level, it was unconsciously a forced entry into his mother's breast and body.

The producers who would turn down his programme were unconsciously his father who was envious of his potency, and who would try to prevent him from forcing entry into his mother and taking control of her. The persons who were libelled in the talk and whom he sought to destroy by so doing, represented his own sadistic and destructive super-ego; and it was this super-ego that was fragmented and projected into me and attacked, so that he felt me to be on their side and against him.

When he tried to write, therefore, he had neither a unified objective nor a coherent integrative reticulum. He was literally all over the place. He admitted that those passages of his talk which contained the more persecuted and libellous material tended to be badly written and confused – 'garbled' was the term he used. In effect, he could be said to be using a disintegrative framework rather than an integrative one for parts of his writing – attempting to smash his material in bits to disturb and confuse the fragmented internal objects and parts of himself projected into his audience rather than to satisfy that audience.

Under these conditions, the process of lysis was severely interfered with. He explained how, as he tried to write, he could not sort out his ideas. As he tried to find just the right words, the words and ideas seemed to break up in his mind. He could not think in words. He could only spell. A cat was not a cat, but a C–A–T. But even worse, he could not spell correctly, could not get the letters back together into words. Then he felt people laughing at him – his audience, producers, friends jeered and triumphed at his impotence.

Linking and synthesis became impossible for him at such a time, because he experienced himself so concretely inside the job standing for his mother's body. To link only increased his persecutory anxiety, because, for example, it was experienced as a bringing together of the cruel and sadistic penis with the already dangerous contents of his mother's body. Moreover, if he tried to look outside for additional information or knowledge, he became so utterly consumed by envy that he went almost blind with rage. On one occasion, he read a few pages of a favourite author to get just the right style for something he was writing. He then found himself unable to write. In his session on the same day, his associations took us to his unconscious envious and greedy eating of the words on the page – literally 'tearing them out of context' – and then feeling terrified and dominated by them internally, with the fear that they would appear in a spoilt but recognizable form in his own writing. The simultaneous idealization and incorporation of the other author and her work partly made matters worse by increasing his own feelings of inferiority, hopelessness, and despair.

Under these conditions, decision became terrifying and he would retire to bed, sometimes for days on end, and retreat into magical phantasies in which he believed for the time being that he was sorting out all his difficulties.

Working Capacity and Confidence
I should like finally to return to an earlier theme – that weight or heaviness of responsibility is connected with the length of time a person must exercise discretion on his own account. The longer the time-span the longer must the anxiety of uncertainty be faced – anxiety without which work cannot be said to have been done. The ability to maintain a continuous working-through of that anxiety, and to go on exercising discretion and making decisions, demands that the requisite and symbolic contents of the mental processes involved in work must predominate over the concretive processes – a state of affairs requiring the dominance of love over hate. It is these conditions which lead to confidence in one's own judgement and capacities. They reduce persecutory anxiety and violent splitting. They provide an unconscious sense of well-being and ease, and faith in the ability to restore and nurture the internal good objects. These feelings lie at the root of confidence in one's own creative impulses and sublimations and capacity to tolerate anxiety and uncertainty.

To the extent that these conditions are not fulfilled, confidence in work, and the capacity to do it, are diminished. Uncertainty replaces confidence, and increases anxiety and confusion. The longer the time-span of the discretion to be exercised, the greater will be the piling up of anxiety and uncertainty.

Under these conditions the processes of sublimation tend to be reversed. Plastic symbol formations break down and become increasingly fragmented and concretive in order to bind defused instinctual energy and to diminish persecutory anxiety. I believe that these are the basic processes underlying disturbed work.

This description applies equally to neurotic flight into excessive work. Such flight generally contains as a dominant feature the splitting-off and fragmentation of a part of the work-field with the result that the work tends to be soulless and lacking in humanity. The internal reflection of this work is a splitting-off and fragmentation of parts of the mind, so that psychic processes which might enrich the work-process are not available, and sublimation is inhibited. One of the paradoxical results of making a 'success' of such work is that concretism and fragmentation are thus reinforced, and an impoverishment of personality occurs.

Processes of disintegration and concretism are always present to some extent in the unconscious, and they are reinforced by the failure and anxiety they induce. These processes require constantly to be reversed, and daily work is one of the means by which this reversal occurs. Working – and especially working for a living – is therefore a fundamental activity in a person's testing and strengthening of his sanity.

Etymological Appendix

A number of the psychological processes described in this paper can be illustrated in the metaphoric content of the language of work which symbolizes these processes and the accompanying sensations, in concrete terms.

1   *Lysis* ('lysis' – to loosen) is the root of analysis to loosen apart. This notion of a loosening and separating out of mental elements at this stage in work occurs in many words connected with it: *discern, discriminate,* and *discretion* (all from 'dis-cernere', to separate apart), The term *skill* has the same reference (from 'skijl', to divide or separate), relating it to the ability to tease out and discern; so also have the words connected with solving a problem, *solve, resolve, solution* (from 'se-luere', to loosen apart, 'luere' being the Latin equivalent of the Greek 'lysis').

The loosening in the above sense is linguistically to be contrasted with fragmentation ('frangere', to fracture or break) which expresses a sharp and conclusive breaking apart.

As against words having to do with discretion and choice, *knowledge* ('gignoskein', a reduplicated form) has the meaning of being able automatically to reproduce previously established data without the anxiety of choice.

2   *Scanning* (from 'scandere', to climb or ascend) has the sense of rising above the loosened elements in the mind and examining them from on high. *Search* and *research* ('circare', to circle about) and *concentrate* ('con-centre', centre together) express the sense of mentally circling about the loosened elements, and bringing relevant ones together.

The mental circling about from above accords with the concept of a *plan* ('planus', a plain or plateau), that is, a clear area at the surface of the mind from which the elements below can be perceived, and on to which they can be raised. A *hypothesis* ('hypo-thesis', place below) is a construction placed among the elements in the deeper layers of the mind to help in sorting out those which are to be raised to the surface plain. The conception of *relevance* ('re-levare', to raise again) expresses this sense of lifting or raising up and out.

To concentrate gives additional information if we take it back to its Greek root ('kentron', a spike, goad, prick, centre) which carries the sense of goading or pricking together. This meaning falls into line with the act of *distinguishing* various elements ('distingere', to prick apart, or to separate by marking with a prick), as though, in the process of lysis, those mental elements which, on loosening, appear to be relevant are mentally marked for synthesis. In line with this conception is the verbal root of *disappointment* ('dis-ad-punctare', against marking by a prick), in which the process of mental marking of elements is frustrated and leads to failure.

3   *Gathering* and *good* are connected in that both derive from the Indo-European root 'gad', meaning fit or suitable; i.e. that which is good is that which comprises good and suitable parts gathered together into one whole. The *art* of bringing relevant material together ('ars', fit) is that of the act of fitting. This notion of fitting or fixing elements together appears in many of the terms related to this phase of work: making connections ('connectere', to bind or knit together), bringing into *context* ('contexere', to weave together) and *synthesizing* ('synthesis', place together).

The *exertion* necessary ('ex-serere', to fasten or bind out), has to do with the putting together in such a manner as to get it out into active use, i.e. into consciousness and then into use in reality, or to force it out ('ex-fortis', effort), by means of *effort*.

As against these words associated with a putting or weaving or binding together in an organized form, *confusion* ('con-fundere', to pour together) has the sense of mental elements running together in an unorganized fashion, without patterning or plan.

4 These processes of analysis and synthesis (loosening and bringing together) of the contents of thought, are accompanied by differentiation and integration of the mental apparatus itself. The *differentiation* ('dis-ferre', to carry apart) has to do with the capacity to bring different parts of the mental apparatus and different mental processes into play, without destroying mental integration. *Integration* ('integrare', renew, heal, or repair, which in turn is from 'in-tangere', untouch, unharm), carries this metaphoric sense of undestroyed or left intact even though differentiated; the deeper psychological significance of this emerges in the fact that 'intangere' (Indo-European root 'dak', to bite or tear, from whence, e.g. the Greek 'dakos', animal of which the bite is dangerous), refers also to unharmed by eating, or untasted, an unconscious etymological connection between mental integration and being undamaged by oral sadism.

5 The use of *decision* in the active sense of committed to action is given by its root ('de-caedere', to cut apart). The essence of a decision is that once it is taken, the person is cut off from the other courses of action he might have taken.

6 The relating of the sensation of *failure* in work to psychic mechanisms of self-deception is consistent with its derivation ('fallere', to be deceived – and deceive deriving from 'de-cipere', to take by causing to fall into a trap); in effect, the internal objects and split-off mental processes are trapped or ensnared as a defence against destructive impulses and persecutory anxiety.

Frustration ('frustrari', to disappoint, and 'frustrus', deceitful) carries a similar connotation of being disappointed through deceit. That is, frustration and failure caused by a person's own inability are experienced in terms of paranoid feelings of being deceitfully treated, a projection of the cunning and deceit characteristic of paranoid-schizoid defences which frequently contribute to failure.

6

Time and the Measurement of Human Attributes

In the course of attempts to measure the level of work assigned into roles, certain fundamental aspects of measurement, not only of work but of social and psychological processes in general, claim our attention. The first is the peculiar and special importance of the dimension of time in such measurement; the second has to do with the more general problem of relating data about human activities to quantitative scales, a problem which applied just as much to physical measurements in its early days. Furthermore, despite the common assumption to the contrary, there is nothing inherently less precise in social measurement than there is in physical measurement, as long as we proceed from simple observation of the processes in which we are interested.

Measurement in the Physical World
To illustrate some of the main points, I shall consider first of all some basic features of the measurement of temperature. To get at the essentials, it will be useful to have a fresh look at the problem as it appeared to scientists in the fifteenth century, before thermometers had been discovered. In those days the

H

concept of temperature as a potentially measurable quality hardly existed. The prevalent theory was that of heat as a fluid calor which could be transmitted from one substance to another; but whether all heat was the same, or whether heat of combustion, solar heat, and animal heat were different, was uncertain.

Imagine then the available data. First and foremost there is the sensation of heat; the sensation of one thing feeling warmer than another, or of things getting hotter and hotter. These sensations are the basic data. It is these sensations which allow us to know about the existence of something we call hot, or cold, or warm, or burning, or freezing. Along with these sensations go our observations of hotter and colder things: flames are hot; so is the sun; ice is cold; fresh water is cool; put a flame under it and it gets hot and eventually it boils; some animals, including humans, are warm to the touch, others, like snakes, are cold. We know that things get hotter and colder, because our senses tell us so.

Let us interject at this moment an observation on the similarities between that situation and our present-day experience of phenomena such as level of responsibility – we can sense when it is higher and when lower; or individual capacity – we can sense our own capacity to be increasing as we mature; or aggression, or love, or envy, or any of a hundred other social and human attributes which we 'know' to be greater and lesser, and to be changing in amount, but which we do not, as yet, know how to measure. So with the problem of heat and temperature up until the fifteenth century.

Returning again to the past, there is one other observation that is of outstanding importance; namely, that as calor is transmitted to air, the air not only gets warmer, but it also increases in volume. We can observe this phenomenon by warming the air trapped in a test-tube held upside down in a dish of water. If we hold the tube in our hand, or otherwise warm it, the level of water in the tube can be observed to go down; if we cool the base, say by holding a piece of ice against it, the water level can be seen to rise in the tube. Clearly, we may conclude, the air is expanding and contracting as it gets warmer and colder.

This observation, and its possible significance for measurement, are not, of course, available simply for the taking. We

have to be in a proper frame of mind to pay particular attention
to it. For it is merely one datum in the midst of a host of other
data and pseudo-data and questions which are in many ways
emotionally more attractive; for example: What is the nature
of calor? How is it transmitted from the sun through space?

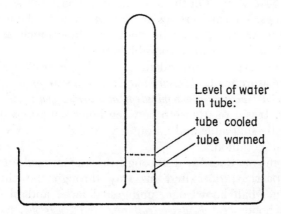

Level of water
in tube:

tube cooled
tube warmed

What are flames? Are there flames inside the human body?
What happens when water turns into steam, or into ice? These
are the fascinating questions. And surely they are more practical
and realistic than bothering with the problem of trying to
measure what after all is an insubstantial psychological sensation, namely hotter and colder.

But happily it is a characteristic of human scientific endeavour
that it does eventually cut through the distraction and obscurity
of popular thought to the things that matter. The significance of
the column of air in the test-tube gains force until someone
(the general opinion is that it was Galileo) thinks to graduate it.
He puts a mark in the tube at the level of the water when the
tube is held in the hand, and another at its level when the tube
is immersed in ice. And so the thermoscope is born. Not much
can be done with it, but it is a kind of scientific curiosity which
we can use to show what happens to a column of air when it is
warmed and cooled.

The thermoscope remained a scientific curiosity for some
hundred years. What would the view of a modern man be?
Would he dare claim to perceive the thermometer nascent in
that test-tube? To do so it would have to occur to him that the

column of water was going up and down *and* that it was getting colder and warmer, both *at the same rate*. Who could make such an assumption? And if he did, how could he prove it?

What data are available? On the one hand we have the column of water going up and down. We can all see that. It is directly observable. On the other hand we have our sensations, our feelings. We can perhaps agree that the test-tube is getting colder and warmer, but who knows by how much and how quickly? And how can we possibly agree?

Here we have the prime dilemma and the prime characteristic of all measurement. *Measurement is the process of ordering the psychological experience of magnitude to an external and readily observable scale.* It is a relationship between inner sensations that are not directly shareable and an outer yardstick which we can all observe in common.

Yet someone does break through these emotional and intellectual barriers, does find his way through the clutter of knowledge, half knowledge, undigested facts, and phantasies and falsehoods. *He decides to calibrate the thermoscope*: to divide the space between the body temperature mark at one end of the scale and the freezing point mark at the other end into one hundred points. With that one decisive act we have moved from thermoscope to thermometer.

It is not certain who took this step, but it was very likely Newton, for the instrument first appeared in England in Newton's circle at the height of his best work. The instrument was no longer in the form of an open-ended tube, but of a tube sealed off at both ends. And the liquid was no longer limited to water. Coloured alcohol and other non-freezing liquids were also used.

With the use of these first crude thermometers, the study of temperature was transformed. The movement of columns of various kinds of liquid (including soon after the liquid metal, mercury) could be systematically observed, recorded and compared as they were moved between different baths of sensibly different temperature.

From this point the problem of the development of the thermometer became a technical problem, firstly of discovering which liquids expanded and contracted with greatest constancy as they were heated and cooled (water, for example, was ruled out, for it was known that after contracting as it grew colder, it began to expand again just before it began to freeze), and secondly of stating a theoretical basis for the instrument. A major step forward was taken in the middle of the nineteenth century with the formulation of the laws of thermodynamics, and with the development of inert gas thermometers. Then another major step was achieved with the discovery of the behaviour of electric currents at different temperatures and the construction of the thermo-electric couple.

Thus it became possible to measure changes in temperature by means of changes in liquids, in gases, and in the flow of electricity. It can be fairly well established that equally calibrated distances represent equal changes in temperature. But it has taken some 300 years to get to this point.

Our brief sketch of the development of the thermometer allows us to illustrate several important points in measurement. One we have already mentioned; namely, that measurement involves the ordering of sensory impressions to an external scale. In effect, it is incorrect to say that we measure temperature. We do not. We measure the length, say, of a column of mercury, and we assume that this measurement corresponds to a particular sensation of warmth or coldness, as a result of the construction and calibration of an instrument called a thermometer. Our construction has been good enough so that we have not yet had the experience of the column of mercury getting observably shorter as the air gets sensibly warmer. Should such a happening occur but once, we should probably have to throw our thermometers away and start again!

Thus it is that it can not correctly be said that we measure temperature, but – as Bridgman has pointed out – it is our thermometers, our measuring instruments that give us our best mode of defining temperature. All qualities of things, like temperature, length, hardness, redness, are most accurately definable in terms of the operations we go through to measure them.

The next general point has to do with the scale. In the case of temperature it can be noted that we have related our data to a length scale. A length scale is one of three ways we have of representing an equal interval quantitative continuum in physical terms. That is to say, if we mark out equal intervals

and name them 0, 1, 2, 3, 4, 5, etc., then the distance from 0 to
2 is twice that from 0 to 1; from 2 to 6 (4 intervals) it is one half
that from 8 to 16 (9 intervals), from 0 to 10 it is twice that from
0 to 5, and so on for addition, subtraction, multiplication and
division.

The second physical scale with these properties is that of mass.
If we start with any given weight, and find other weights that
exactly balance it, we have a number of units from which we
can build up a system of weights equivalent to half, or twice, or
three times, etc., the standard, and establish a scale with the
same quantitative characteristics as the scale of length.

The third physical scale is that of time. The recording of time
is achieved by establishing an instrument which moves at regular
and equal intervals, such as a pendulum or the molecular
oscillations in a crystal. From these equal intervals we can build
up an equal interval quantitative scale like that of length or of
mass.

The problem of measurement, then, can be stated in terms of
finding a means of ordering changes in our sensations about the
properties of things or of people or of social relationships to
changes along the equal interval scales of length or of mass or
of time. Against this background, let us now consider some
problems of the measurement of qualities of social life, and the
particular relevance of a time-scale for such measurement.

Measurement in the Social World
Our starting-point is the measurement of level of work as
developed on the Glacier Project, in terms of time-span of
discretion. We need not go into detail about the method of
measurement; it has been fully described elsewhere.[1] But its
essential elements are as follows:

1. Managers assigning tasks to subordinates always, explicitly
   or implicitly, assign the maximum period of time allowed
   for the completion of the task; this maximum target completion time is an inherent part of the task.

[1] Jaques, Elliott. *Equitable Payment.* (London: Heinemann Educational
Books, 1961.)
———*Time-Span Handbook.* (London: Heinemann Educational Books,
1964.)

2. The maximum target completion time sets the framework within which the subordinate can exercise discretion in driving the task through to completion; it sets the time-span of discretion within which he works.
3. The longer the maximum target completion time assigned, the longer the time-span of discretion.

The reason for our taking an interest in the time-span of discretion was that its length was observed to accord with the sensation of level or weight of responsibility. The longer the time-span the greater the feeling of weight; the shorter the time-span the lighter the feeling of weight; increase the time-span and the feeling of weight increases; decrease the time-span and the feeling of weight decreases.

These observable relationships were supported by the unexpected finding that people at the same time-span feel entitled to by and large the same pay; the longer the time-span the higher the payment to which they feel entitled. However, there is the familiar phenomenon that if a manager finds that the responsibility he has assigned to a subordinate is too heavy, he can reduce it by dividing the larger tasks into two or three parts, giving him the first part, then the second part when he finishes the first, and so on. In effect the manager is involved in progressing the work for his subordinate on a shorter time-scale. Or contrariwise, it will be found that as a manager gains confidence in a new subordinate, he allows him greater freedom by allowing him longer tasks.

We have here the same conditions that we found in the case of the measurement of temperature. There is first of all the sensation, the psychological experience of weight and level of responsibility. And secondly, there is the objectively measurable datum that seems to vary in correspondence with variations in the sensation. Let us consider each in turn.

The psychological sensation of weight of responsibility is just as 'real' a sensation as the sensation of warmth. We have all experienced it. We know when we feel the weight is too heavy, and we feel worried, oppressed, and overburdened. Equally we know when the weight is becoming lighter, and when it has become too light; oppression and worry turn into relief, which turns into boredom and lack of interest if the weight of responsibility is too light.

That is to say, we are here dealing with an individual experience, sensed in terms of magnitude, of greater and lesser; we can equally sense variations in magnitude, in terms of feelings of weight of responsibility getting lighter and heavier.

The problem of measurement (or definition) of this sensed property of tasks – namely weight or level of responsibility – just as was the case in measuring the sensed heat of liquids or other bodies, is to find some objectively measurable datum that appears to vary, as did the length of a column of liquid, in concert with variations in our sensation. That datum was found in the assigned time-span of discretion.

Time-span of discretion is just as objective a datum as is mercury in a glass tube. In order to be able to observe it, we must get an explicit and definitive statement from the manager of the maximum target completion time for the tasks he has assigned to his subordinate. These target times – and his subordinate can be informed of them – are objective facts. They are the facts that then govern the behaviour of the subordinate in planning and carrying through his work.

Moreover, they are measurable data; they can be ordered to a time-scale. We are thus in a position to examine variations in the subjective sense of weight or level of responsibility, and concomitant variations in the objectively measurable time-span of discretion of the assigned responsibilities whose weight is experienced. The situation is the same as that of being able to examine variations in the sense of warmth, say, of liquids, and the thermometric readings of those liquids. Systematic observation can begin.

Time and Human Activity

It remains, of course, to establish rigorously – as in the case of thermometers – that equal intervals in time-span of discretion represent equal intervals in weight of responsibility. Moreover a general theory to explain the relationship is needed, and work on the subject is currently under way. This research has led to the occurrence of certain ideas of a general kind.

In the first place, it now seems obvious common sense that

level of work should be measurable in terms of time. For work is an activity that occurs in and through time. It is thus no more surprising that we should measure its level in terms of time, than that we should measure velocity or acceleration in terms of time.

This statement of the seemingly obvious leads on to other questions. Are there perhaps many human attributes that may turn out to be readily measurable in accord with a time-scale? One at least occurs immediately; namely, individual capacity or creativity. Capacity and creativity are problem-solving activities that occur through time. Might we not measure a person's capacity if we could find means for measuring his capacity to organize activities through time?

I believe that this line of endeavour is in fact likely to lead to the solution of the problem of measuring the magnitude of an individual's capacity to work. The larger the time-span he can manage, the greater his capacity. Conversely, the size of his capacity can be defined in terms of the maximum time-span over which he is capable of organizing and progressing his work.

Time-span of capacity ought to be observable, for example, in very small children. If we observe, for instance, the age at which a child becomes capable of foregoing immediate gratification in favour of promised enhanced gratification the next day, I think we might have a good indication of its potential capacity. The younger the age at which a child becomes able to achieve a one-day time-span, the higher his capacity is likely to be.

In full adulthood, we find individuals capable of undertaking tasks calling for a sequence of activities over periods of months and years, the higher positions in life calling for the longer time-spans. At the extreme, we have individuals whose whole lifetime is one great progressive development without satisfactory closure at any points along the way. In such cases we are dealing with genius; and we have available an operational definition of this quality – namely, a person whose capacity operates in a time-span longer than his own span of life, so that he dies with his talent inevitably incompletely fulfilled.

What other human qualities, individual or social, might also be defined and measured in terms of time-scale, I cannot readily suggest. But possibilities that come to mind are properties such as ego strength, ambition, tenacity, social cohesion. Whatever is the case, it may be useful to keep in mind that individual and social processes are processes – they are dynamic. They occur through time. Time-scale, therefore, may often hold the key to the problem of measurement, and measurement in the natural science sense.

7

Learning
for Uncertainty

In this chapter I want to concentrate upon one important factor in education – a factor whose existence has been much neglected but which exerts a weighty influence upon the dynamics of the classroom group, causing a restriction in the development of one crucial area in education – the area that relates education most closely to work and to creativity.

My argument runs as follows:

1. The communication and acquisition of knowledge, while an important part of education, cannot be its sole major object. There must also be the object of learning about the worry and uncertainty that accompany work and creative activity; that is to say, of learning how to work and how to learn, and of expanding one's capacity to use knowledge creatively in problem-solving. I shall refer to this activity by the phrase *creative application*.

2. But, despite all attempts to construct educational methods and examinations which grade creative application as well

as knowledge, our educational rewards tend to go to those students who shine at the acquisition of knowledge whether or not they can put this knowledge to work, and to the teachers who can transmit knowledge.

3. The problem is partly a technical one of further development of our educational and grading methods to incorporate the students' own initiative and creativity into the programme. But it is also partly an emotional problem tied up with the dynamics of the classroom group.

4. The teaching and absorbing of knowledge give both teacher and pupil a secure feeling of certainty – the pupil can reproduce what the teacher produces, and everyone can feel that knowledge thus shared is tangible and real.

5. But this sense of reality is ill-founded, since real-life problems are open-ended in the sense of not having correct answers but only answers that may be shown by subsequent experience to have been better or worse.

6. We all recoil – sometimes consciously but certainly unconsciously – from the more painful reality that open-ended problems are inevitably accompanied by worry and uncertainty, and never end with a reassuring sense of completeness. It is easier, therefore, for teachers and pupils to collude unconsciously to cling to a relationship based upon the security of knowledge and spurious certainty, than to allow the reality of uncertainty to intrude too far into the classroom.

7. Administrators, educators and parents are no more immune from unconscious anxiety about the uncertainties of reality than are teachers, so that the classroom dynamic is bolstered up from outside.

8. I shall give an indication of how open-ended learning and creative application can be introduced into education (once we learn to understand our anxieties about the uncertainty of reality), not to supplant the acquisition of knowledge but to counterpoint and spice it.

II

If we wish to find the central aim of our educational system, it is wiser to observe what we do than to listen to what we say we are trying to do. For in what we say we are trying to do there is much variety and difference of opinion: to convey information and knowledge; to stimulate the growth of personality; to create responsible citizens; to develop memory or intelligence or ability; to transmit culture; to facilitate socialization. In what we actually do there is less difference, for nearly everywhere it mostly ends up in examinations and in gradings which test the acquisition of knowledge and are produced as the tangible end product of the process.

One of the central aims of our educational process can be observed to be to learn whatever it is that passes examinations and gets high grades. Whatever else goes on in school, whatever else there may be in the relationship between teacher and pupil, the public reward for teacher as well as for pupil is the exam result, and the exam grades are the key to advancement.

Far and away the most outstanding characteristic of examination passing is the acquisition of the required knowledge. Acquisition of knowledge, therefore, becomes, *de facto*, the main activity of our education. High grades imply high acquisition, and the ability to absorb information; low grades show low acquisition, but do not necessarily tell us much about the ability to learn. There is however, a disjunction between performance as manifested in the acquisition of knowledge as rated by exam grades in school, and performance in adult life – a disjunction with which you will all be familiar enough. School grades do not necessarily predict University performance, nor do University grades correlate tidily with work performance and creativity, despite the fact that work and creating also call for learning.

In broad terms, it is not surprising that there is this disjunction. It is not to say that the acquisition of knowledge is unimportant. It is simply that in work – whether it is administrative, research, professional or creative – knowledge alone will not see you through. You are confronted not by examinations but by problems which have no absolutely correct answer. You have to use knowledge and judgement in interaction. And your performance is judged, and promotion gained, not in terms of your knowledge alone – that is largely taken for granted – but in terms of the quality of your judgement and your capacity to use your knowledge. Let us, therefore, compare the process of acquiring knowledge with the process of creative work, for if we can get clear enough about the differences we shall be able to uncover a significant feature in the dynamic of the classroom group.

III

The process of acquiring knowledge can be understood only if we can define what knowledge is. I do not, however, propose to enter into an epistemological disquisition. I think we may avoid that course by seeking a practical working definition in psychological terms.

A central characteristic of knowledge is that it is verbally formulated and therefore precisely reproducible. This characteristic is given in its etymology – knowledge – from gignoskein – a reduplicated form.

But what is it that is verbally formulated?

The raw data of experience are non-verbal, or perhaps more accurately, pre-verbal. I shall use the term percepts to refer to these new perceptions. We perceive – hear, see, feel . . . on a wide front, and only a small portion of our percepts are brought into that central focus of conscious attention that allows us to verbalize them. Indeed many of our raw percepts remain tantalizingly unidentifiable and unverbalized. Let me cite, for example, the complex of percepts that build up into our judgement of the performance and capacity of students. When we try to express our reasons for such judgements, our verbal justifications fall far short of what is required and we cannot teach what we have done. In effect, words fail us, but we may feel secure in our judgements nevertheless. It is not that these percepts will always remain unidentified. Experience, inquiry and research may help eventually to recognize and isolate them so that they can be verbalized. They then become part of knowledge and can be taught.

The process of verbalizing percepts requires that they be organized in accord with man-made rules to form concepts. In effect what we do is to agree among us that this percept and that, and any others like them, shall be included within a given concept which we identify and to which we allocate a word. The perceptions may be things, actions, or relationships. Definition consists of specifying the boundary line (drawing a boundary is what definition means) which delimits which data of perception fall within the concept and which fall outside it. Thus, a triangle is not a thing but a concept in the minds of men, and does not exist in nature. What does exist in nature is a perceivable shape which, in accord with man-made rules, we include within the defined boundary of the concept of a triangle. This distinction between the verbal construction – the concept – and the perceptual experience of specific data, is often found to be emotionally difficult to get hold of. Far too many University students, for example, graduate still believing that a triangle is a thing rather than a mathematical concept.

The point I wish to emphasize is that knowledge is man-made. That is why we can be so sure of it. We have made the rules, and set the limits. And it is these rules and limits which allow us to reduplicate it with such precision. In effect we know that two is two, and two plus two make four because we have decreed the formulation. What we know with certainty is the formulation. We can convey the rules to others. And we can thus set examinations to determine whether the rules have been learned and can be regurgitated. The constant danger, however, is that the word to some extent becomes the thing, and we dull and inhibit to the same extent our capacity to perceive.

The acquiring of formulated knowledge thus gives a secure feeling. It is identifiable, sure, and complete. When you know it, you know. You know because you can reduplicate it. And if you do not quite know it, you can work a bit more until you can reduplicate it.

Moreover, the acquiring of formulated knowledge is socially cohesive, and brings the security of group solidarity. You join up with others in the operation of shared rules. You increase your powers of communication. You can show your teacher what you know. And your teacher can show the outside world what you have been taught.

As the gestalt psychologists would express it, the acquisition of knowledge brings with it a sense of closure. You know when the task is complete.

It is this sense of sureness, of completeness, of reproducibility, that gives the psychological experience of the concept being the thing itself – a fact of experience as against a psychological fact. As Abercrombie[1] has emphasized, this sureness can block creative perception and inhibit flexibility in thought.

In examining for the acquisition of knowledge, objective examinations are the most relevant. But since there is always the desire to examine for more than the mere reproduction of knowledge, essay type exams may be used. But even with essay questions, the demands of objectivity and comparability require that they be marked in such a manner as to put a premium upon the factual content of the answers, with a small allowance for the creative content expressed in the way the reply is organized. The judgement of the individual marker must be kept to a minimum.

IV

When we turn to consider work and creativity, we enter a different sphere of mental activity. In work, the essence of the activity is the exercise of discretion. Indeed, as I have had the opportunity to learn in connection with work measurement, the psychological experience of effort in work lies solely in the exercise of discretion. This feature is the same whatever the type of work at issue; that is to say, whether we deal with so-called creative work, or research work, or administrative work, or manual work, or the work of teaching, the crucial factor has to do with the exercise of discretion. We may, therefore, for our present purposes drop the distinction between creativity and work, and speak of work alone. For the difference between them lies not in the exercise of discretion; it lies in the fact that in so-called creative work the person generally sets his own object

[1] Abercrombie, M. L. J. *The Anatomy of Judgement* (London: Hutchinson, 1960).

and task, whereas in other types of work his object or task is set for him.

In saying that discretion and judgement constitute the sole factor in the sense of effort in work, I do not mean to imply that knowledge is unimportant. Knowledge is essential for work. But it is essential in being one of the tools of work – like a saw, or a microscope; it is not the work itself. There may be work in deciding which fact or theory or procedure to muster and employ, but to the extent that you know your way, you do not have to work to find your way.

For example, as a teacher you know the length of time for given classes, you know specific material that has to be covered and by when, you know the type of exam to be set, you know which category of teaching method you are using – you do not have to start afresh in those things each day. But to help a particular child to advance in a particular subject in the face of difficulty – that is a problem that has to be faced afresh each time. You have to judge from day to day what is the best next step, and how best to handle the matter as you go along. If you knew what to do in the sense of there being an automatic formula to apply, it would be easy. But judging what is best done at any given moment is not easy. It takes work. And you can never be sure that you might not have achieved a better result if you had proceeded differently.

What is it then about the exercise of discretion and judgement that gives the sensation of work and of creativity? We are involved here with a sphere of psychological activity which, although extremely familiar, remains conceptually ill-defined. There is no satisfactory, commonly employed and accepted language for it. We speak about judgement, intuition, 'nous', skill, experience, know-how, scholarship, common sense, discretion, discrimination, hunch, and more crudely, expressions like 'using your loaf' and 'guesstimating'.

The sensation itself is one of uncertainty, of worry. We cannot put into words what it is that we are taking into account in doing what we are doing, and in that sense we do not know that what we are doing will get us where we want to go, will achieve the result we want to achieve. We judge that it will, we think it will, but we are not sure, and only time will tell.

Moreover, it is also of the essence of work that, having

ı

decided how to set about a task, and having completed it, you can never be sure that if you had decided to do it another way that you might not have done it better or more quickly. You just do not know. Once a task is done it is done. You cannot reduplicate the task and the conditions under which you did it. If you can, then it is no longer a task in the psychological sense; you have created knowledge, and you can lay down procedures for dealing with problems of that kind.

The mental processes involved in work, are unconscious. They are mental processes at the preconceptual stage – preconceptual thinking as opposed to conceptual thinking. It is thinking which uses unconscious preconceptions (as described by Bion)[1] rather than conscious conceptions. It is therefore unverbalizable, and because of that, it cannot be taught by direct formulated communication. It is the kind of experience ordinarily communicated by apprenticeship techniques – whether in manual work, or law, or medicine, or teaching – in which we say to the student, 'Watch what I do, and try to get the feel of it', or 'I wouldn't have done it that way, I would have done it this way'.

V

I would hope that this description of the difference between knowing and working, between the conscious use of concepts and the unconscious flow of preconcepts, is sufficient to point up gross differences, which will be familiar to educators, between education designed to transmit knowledge and education designed to encourage or stimulate creativeness and the capacity to work and to solve problems. The distinction between the two is currently most widely expressed by educational psychologists in terms of the educational processes concerned with convergent thinking on the one hand, and divergent thinking on the other. Paraphrasing Goetzels and Jackson, convergent thinking tends towards the usual and expected, towards retaining the known, learning the predetermined, and preserving what is; divergent thinking tends towards the novel and speculative, towards revising the known and explaining the undetermined. One favours

---

[1] Bion, W. R. *Learning from Experience* (London: Heinemann Medical Books, 1962).

certainty, the other favours risk. As these authors point out, in modern Western society our education tends to be concerned with convergent thinking, rather than with the encouragement of divergent thinking. It transmits knowledge and examines for it. It provides some opportunity for creative work and thought, but does not examine for it. And there is always the hope that some inspiration will rub off on to the pupil from the teacher.

And yet our aspiration is strong that education should do more – should inspire, should stimulate students to want to learn, should help to get them intellectually under way, to open their minds to be receptive to new knowledge and to new perceptions, should give them the experience of what it is like to work for data and to solve problems. Existing knowledge is constantly being made redundant as new knowledge is gained. Our students must learn how to go about revising this knowledge, adapting to change.

But consider what would be involved. I am not talking, for example, about improving laboratory methods for the teaching of science. For carrying out experiments that have already been done, however advantageous from the point of view of acquiring scientific knowledge, does not necessarily increase scientific imaginativeness or creativity. Nor am I talking about periodic opportunities for free expression, or for creative projects, organized in a manner peripheral to the syllabus in the sense of not counting for marks. What we are concerned with is the experience of learning to learn, learning about problem-solving and decision-making, or more precisely, learning about the uncertainty, worry and anxiety involved in problem-solving, in work, in creating.

VI

If learning to work and to be creative is what we want as one aspect of the education process, why is it so widely experienced as difficult to give it the place in the syallabus and in examinations that we protest it warrants? Here we come to the crunch. Is it because the problem is too difficult technically or intellectually? Perhaps it is a difficult technical problem and would take a good bit of creative work to overcome it. But I think that is not the whole story, nor even the starting-point. We have to ask just what evidence there is that we can tolerate a situation in the classroom which is worrying and anxiety provoking. It is my thesis that there is in fact a strong unconscious collusion, central to the dynamic of the classroom group, in which teachers and pupils are involved in keeping the educational process which counts, firmly tied to the transmission of knowledge with its certainty and group cohesion, and to hold at arm's length the individual effort and uncertainty of preconceptual learning.

Consider for a moment what would be involved.

In addition to classes as we have them now – with teaching, laboratory work, projects – there would have to be the opportunity for project work of a particular kind, calling for the creative applications of knowledge. It would be concerned with projects – I will call them creative application projects – of graded complexity, intensity, difficulty, which could be assigned to students in such a way that they would eventually find their own level – that is to say, the level that would put them at full stretch. The problems would have to be open-ended, in the sense of having no predetermined solution. They would have to be genuine problems, and not, for example, merely the collection of information for a project book. And the assessment of the quality of the performance would be a matter of the judgement of the teacher.

In finding their own level, the students would progress from assignments that were just too easy for them, to assignments that were just too difficult, and in which they would be allowed to have the opportunity to experience stress in work, that is to say, to go through the experience of just being able to cope. The experience would be akin to what we ordinarily speak of as carrying responsibility and finding one's responsibilities too light or too easy, just right, or too heavy and overwhelming.

There are two major problems involved; first, the difficulty of designing such problems of creative application; second, the difficulty of introducing the experience of stress as part of the educational process. The first is a technical problem; the second – involving assessment of performance and experience of failure – is connected with the group dynamics in the classroom. Let us briefly consider each in turn.

VII

The problems of designing projects in creative application are manifold. In the first place, there must be room for the exercise of discretion by the pupil in the way he goes about tackling his assignment; he should not simply repeat someone else's method. Each assignment would have to some extent to be unique, in the sense that although the same ultimate object might be set, the conditions under which the problem was set would have to be able to vary sufficiently to call for the exercise of discretion afresh each time, so as to be a genuinely creative application. The problems would have to be able to be classed into grades of increasing difficulty. And they would have to be of such a kind as to make use of the knowledge which the pupil has been taught, but without going too far beyond it.

I cannot readily picture the form that such assignments in creative application would take in school. They are easy enough to arrange where professional education is concerned; for example, in clinical work in medical schools. But even in the ordinary University setting, there are difficulties. Thus, for example, in some Universities we achieve something of this end by the sandwich method of education in which students have three six-month work-training periods during their four-year course. They are actually in training at work, being paid, under conditions in which, ideally, the employing organization gives them work and opportunities in which they can use their acquired academic knowledge and take on as much responsibility as they are capable of.

VIII

But leaving aside the technical difficulties for the moment, are we justified in supposing that all would be straightforward if we were only able to think up definite assignments in creative application? Not at all. Let us look at the second problem, that of assessment of performance. The essence of a creative problem is that the result cannot be assessed objectively. Someone must judge the performance. It is like assessing the performance of a teacher. You cannot simply add up the marks made by his pupils, and take the total. Someone has to judge what he has done with the pupils he had working under the particular conditions of that moment.

This same problem occurs in assessing the work-training period of University students. The assessment is difficult, and no way has yet been found to get an effectual rating system which can enable work-training performance to be taken into account in deciding the final grade.

The problem is much the same as that of a manager rating the performance of a subordinate at work. This assessment has always been widely experienced as a great difficulty, although I believe that it is in fact fundamentally simple. The main reason that it is experienced as a problem is that everyone is so busy trying to discover objective criteria which will allow the performance to be measured, thus relieving the manager of the burden of using his own judgement.

Great effort and large sums of money are expended in designing accounting procedures and measurements of output which will throw up an index number, or perhaps a complex of index numbers, which will tell just how well each subordinate has done.

When I say that the problem is in fact simple, I do not mean that I know of any ready and easy method of making the judgements. What I mean is that it is simply a fact that the assessment of performance in work – whether in teaching, or in industry, or in a project problem – must remain basically a matter of judgement – a principal's judgement of a teacher, a manager's judgement of a subordinate, a teacher's judgement of a pupil. To seek a measuring yardstick that will give objectivity and strict comparability is only to complicate the issue and to steer attention away from the main issues.

These main issues in assessment I would see as twofold: first, to ensure satisfactory conditions of assessment; and second, to develop objective aids to assessment. Among the necessary conditions I would include that of continued assessment in many situations; and I would include also the building up of composite assessments based upon the judgements not of just one teacher, but of a series of teachers. These multiple judgements ought then to be processed by the departmental head to whom the teachers are responsible, so that a consolidated judgement may be reached.

Even with these safeguards, and with objective aids, the assessment nevertheless remains a matter of human judgement; and that always seems to give rise to anxiety. We tend to have a very ambivalent attitude towards such judgements. On the one hand everyone wants to be assessed by those above him – by his teachers, or managers, or headmaster. We need such assessment to help us to know where we stand. For the fact is that the assessments are made whether we like it or not. Mutual assessment is a basic element in all human relationships. If the assessment is a good one, of course we all like it, and would wish it to be taken into account in affecting our careers and our progress. It is when the assessment is below our expectations, lower than our own judgement of ourselves, that the difficulties arise. Why should someone else have got a higher rating? Why should my merits have been overlooked? Surely it is a matter of inadequate judgement, or of prejudice, or of personal dislike? Feelings of hurt, of resentment, of unjust treatment, enter the situation, and individuals may feel hard done by, or that others have forged ahead by currying favour. You will know the kind of feelings I mean if you have ever been passed over for some special duty that you wanted, or for promotion, in favour of someone whom you judged to be less competent than yourself for the work in question. When a place at a University, or the grade with which you graduate, is at stake, feelings can run high about assessments based on judgements about performance in project problems akin to work – where there is no objective or pre-set outcome to provide a base for objective comparability of results. That may be the reason why, in professional training when judgement of practical performance becomes a major element in the assessment of performance, grades are commonly not given, the student being either qualified or not.

IX

The third problem is that of introducing the experience of stress as part of the educational process. I am not speaking here of chronic failure, or of failure overall. I am speaking of the opportunity for the student to extend himself in project problems to the point where he begins to find it difficult to cope. By this means he would be able to test and to find the upper limits of his capacity. We are all familiar with individuals who, under the impact of stress or of changed or unusual circumstances, begin to manifest qualities which had previously laid dormant. Wartime, for example, often makes demands which stretch a man to the full, sometimes for the first time, so that his full capacities may be revealed.

The difficulty is that so long as a person is succeeding in his work, however difficult, it is not possible to know how effective he might be. The only way to know you have come to the upper limit is somehow to exceed it. To exceed it means for the student to experience failure – to experience the sense of the inability to cope.

Suppose then it were possible to design appropriate project problems to test the limits of capacity of students. Once again, anxieties would be aroused. Students would experience concern. So would their parents. And so, too, would their teachers. This concern readily turns to anxiety if the teachers themselves are not able to contain it, and if the school system is not geared to tolerate it.

X

Let us now consider some implications of these considerations. For purposes of exposition, I shall try to single out and magnify, so as to bring more sharply into focus, what I believe to be a factor of central importance in inhibiting the introduction of creative application into the teaching programme. I refer to the anxieties that are generated, two of which I have described; namely, the anxieties connected with assessment, and those connected with the stress of testing the limits of a student's creative capacity. These anxieties are ordinarily not apparent. They are not apparent because the educational process tends to be so solidly organized around the safety of the communication of knowledge. So long as we confine ourselves to this setting, we can produce relatively objective assessments. These assessments allow for comparison between one student and another, whether in the same or in different schools. No anxiety need be aroused, other than a concern that something is lacking, that somehow knowledge is not all, and that there remains a disjunction between formal education and the creative application required in work and in life.

The anxieties do become apparent, however, as soon as the question is raised of introducing exercises in creative application into the classroom as part of the assessed performance of the student. Then the neatness and tidiness of the arrangement is threatened. We have substituted for the assessment of the student's absorption of knowledge – his learning about the culturally available tools for work – the assessment of his capacity to do work. That is to say, we have shifted from concern only with certain cognitive capacities, to concern with appraisal of the creative capacity for work of the whole person. The reality of uncertainty is proclaimed, and anxiety is aroused. One expression of this anxiety is to argue that if practical work is introduced, then academic standards will be lowered. Practical work, however creative, is related to use, and the conjunction of academic knowledge and its use is so often felt somehow to tarnish the intellectual value of the academic work. Creative application therefore tends to be belittled as merely 'vocational' – a term of opprobrium.

I have seen this anxiety aroused in students in learning about work. If you create conditions in which they can experience the open-ended nature of the work situation and in which they have to rely upon their own judgement, they become uneasy. They demand more reading references. They want lectures or laboratory classes in which they can get back to the security of formulated knowledge. They want to know what they are expected to do, to observe, to record, to reproduce. They are made anxious by the experience of uncertainty.

Most teachers will have experienced this kind of anxiety among students. They are familiar with the way this anxiety can communicate itself to the teacher. It needs great will and perseverance to withstand it, especially in a setting in which it is not the policy of the school to provide the opportunity for creative application. Moreover, if the teacher has the task of assigning and assessing project problems without himself

supporting the general idea, his own anxieties in the situation
will ensure that his supervision will be unsatisfactory.

XI

One is led, therefore, to the conclusion that there is an unconscious collusive force operating as between teacher and student
to keep the academic situation pure, and free from the anxieties
of creative application. To put it another way, there is a strong
force unconsciously operating to ensure that the educational
situation is well structured, deals with formulated knowledge,
allows the student to know what to prepare for exams, and
enables him to do well and to get good grades so long as he has
learned the organized material. The fact that getting good
grades in the repetition of this knowledge gives little indication
of subsequent performance in real life, affects the dynamic of the
classroom group little if at all.

I use the term unconscious because the phenomena themselves are not consciously identified. Nothing much shows unless
there is the threat of introducing creative application and
uncertainty.

It may be noted that this unconscious collusion is not reality
based. As I indicated earlier, the reality of problem-solving as it
exists outside the school situation is very different from problem-
solving in school. It is something more than using well-tried
concepts to answer familiar questions by means of learned
techniques. Moreover, it overlooks the fact that however much
satisfaction high marks may give to students, their teachers and
their families, these high marks bear no necessary relationship
to eventual performance. There is an apparent enigma here –
that of collusion towards unreality in the group dynamic of the
classroom. Surely we might expect reality-testing to reign
supreme in the educational situation?

That the matter may, however, not be so simple, was suggested by Freud many years ago. It is not necessarily to be
assumed that the reality principle will inevitably dominate in
human affairs. At best there will always be some conflict
between the demands of reality-testing and the demands of
those more primitive qualities within us which seek for magical

solutions in accord with what Freud termed the pleasure principle. One particular expression of these magical impulses is in the power attached to words. Not only – as I have already mentioned – does the word become the thing, but to know the word is to possess control over outer concrete reality. To control the word is to control the thing. Thus it is that the educational process is constantly under human pressure to keep verbal knowledge and its transmission at the centre of the stage.

Verbal knowledge is, of course, important. But when it becomes elevated to the topmost position in education, then we may suspect that the dynamic of the classroom situation is being influenced by the pleasure principle to a greater extent than would be desirable. That is to say, to the extent that knowledge dominates the educational object and grading, and creative application takes a back seat, I would seek the reasons less in the technical difficulties of developing techniques for bringing opportunities for creative application into the classroom, than in the unconscious dynamic provided by avoidance of the anxiety and pain of reality-testing.

In short, how to bring creative application into the classroom, alongside knowledge, may be a technically difficult problem. But it is a problem worth tackling, for among other benefits are those of helping students to gain familiarity with the anxiety attendant upon work and creativity, and with the emotional difficulties of reality-testing, particularly the reality-testing of our own personal capacities. We shall never properly tackle the problem unless we get ourselves free from the unconscious collusion in the classroom to seek refuge in a word-dominated world – a world in which the word is the final secure and repeatable reality – as against the real world itself.

8

On Being a Manager

It is a fact of grave consequence that one of the difficulties in speaking about management or about managers is that the terms remain undefined. That is to say, it would be unwise to assume that everyone had the same idea of what the terms meant, even, for example, in a group of people who were all considered to be managers or part of management.

But is it really a matter to be taken seriously? Does it matter? Surely we all have a general idea of what is meant, and mean more or less the same sort of thing? For example, we talk about union–management negotiations, or about members of the management team: yes, but in the one case we refer only to the chief executive and his specialists, and in the second, we refer to everyone who might be a manager; and any assumption that might be made that all managers automatically feel involved in, or approve of, 'management's' policy for negotiation, would not always or necessarily be warranted.

Moreover, in the absence of definition of manager or management, it is impossible to know who all the managers are. For instance, are some or all foremen managers? Are some or all supervisors managers? An all too common situation is that some are considered to be, and some are not. For example, in several firms with which I have a close relationship, it is said that the foremen are managers and the supervisors are not, but it is complained that some foremen do not behave as though they are managers, whereas some supervisors do behave as though they were, by arrogating authority to themselves that they ought not to have, thus unbalancing the organization. But there's the rub. When it comes to the question of straightening the matter out, the firm finds itself unable to state quite how it has arrived at the opinion it has, and is certainly not able to state to the foremen and the supervisors concerned just what it expects them to do.

It is on this question of telling people what is expected of them that the matter of definition becomes so important. For if you cannot define a concept – in our case, define a manager – you cannot tell anyone what it is you are trying to achieve. What is so commonly done is to have recourse to descriptions in terms of attitudes; that is to say, a manager is a certain kind of person: he has qualities of leadership; he feels responsible for the company's interests; he is reliable; he gets things done; he has a certain intangible something that non-managers do not possess. But we are no further forward. Suppose you have a salesman or a research technologist working on his own without subordinates; must he not have most of the qualities described? Is he then a manager? Is he a member of management?

Or, suppose you wish to introduce managerial training. First of all, who do you train? Most companies have been plagued by that problem. And second, what do you teach? I know that that is an absolutely general problem, one met by everyone, including the British Institute of Management itself. I am not referring here to the so-called tool subjects – accountancy, production methods, use of computers, market analysis, and so on – but to that other and more difficult area, that of *being* a manager.

It is in this second respect that I can illustrate the significance of definition. For your definition *determines* your training pro-gramme. If you define managers in the terms set out above, then you organize training programmes calculated to inculcate the qualities of leadership and reliability, and the sense of responsibility that you consider so desirable. Then you run up against two things: first, that these qualities are desirable in everyone, whether manager or not, so that the training programme is not specifically managerial; and second, that you have undertaken the task of somehow changing the personalities of the people on the course – a change by no means easy to accomplish.

I would suggest that it is just this vagueness of definition of aim that is the cause of the weaknesses in the vast majority of management training programmes. These programmes may make people feel good. But there is little evidence that they have very much effect upon managerial efficiency or upon industrial morale. And is it not the case that the one main reason that the BIM, in concert with other management associations, is not able to arrange a professional qualification for managers, is that the concept of manager remains undefined? You cannot, for example, give a professional qualification on the grounds of a person's leadership qualities or his reliability!

Definition of Manager

The organization of managerial systems was discovered many thousands of years ago. It is part of the human heritage from our dim and distant past. We have always had executive hierarchies wherever there have been tasks calling for the united efforts of many men. That is the function of the executive hierarchy – to enable something to get done. It is to do work.

If we start out with the function of a managerial system in mind, we shall find it easier to define what a manager is. Manager-subordinate relations are to enable us to get work done. But how? When the work to be done gets beyond that which one man can expect to do, one way of coping with the situation is for him to hire someone to help him. When he does so he has become a manager. His employee works for him in return for payment, the manager being accountable for his employee's work. Let us call the manager A, and his subordinate B. If, in turn, the work that A wants to give to B becomes too much for one man, then A can either employ another subordinate besides B, or he can allow B to have a subordinate C to assist him. If he takes the second course, he has made B a manager, and we have a three-level system sufficient for our

purposes – we can note all the main properties of the concept
of a manager.

Let me first draw your attention to a simple but very important fact: namely, A should hold B accountable for C's work.
If things go wrong, for example, it ought to be no use for B to
say to A, 'Well, of course, everything would have been satisfactory if only C hadn't been so stupid.' For A ought justifiably
to reply, 'But it was your job to see that C did his work properly.
He is your subordinate.'

From this brief description we can note the essential characteristic of a manager, namely that he is someone who occupies
a particular kind of role in an executive system, a role in which
he has authority over people whom he employs in subordinate
roles and for whose work he is accountable. In short, we can
define a manager as *someone who is in a role in which he is authorized
to get work done through employed subordinates for whose work he is
held accountable.*

I would imagine that there is nothing untoward or unfamiliar
about this description so far. But let us look at the implications
for a moment. We wish to put B in the position where he can be
held accountable by A for C's work. What do we have to do to
achieve this aim? Do we not have to give him such authority
over C as will enable him truly to be accountable? What might
that authority be? The most general reply would be that C
must if possible be the kind of subordinate who is acceptable to
B in the sense of being likely to be able to do the work he
decides to delegate. Or to put it negatively, and more precisely,
C must not be unacceptable to B; for if C is unacceptable and B
is forced to take him, then B always has the justifiable excuse
that he cannot be held fully accountable for getting his work
done efficiently.

In order for B to have subordinates who are not unacceptable
to him, two steps are necessary: one, he must have the authority
to veto the appointment of any new subordinates; and two, he
must be able to have removed from his own team any immediate
subordinates who do become unacceptable to him.

On the first point, that of selection, we are saying not that
a manager should be entitled to have any subordinates he
chooses – that can lead to nepotism – but that neither should he
have unacceptable subordinates foisted upon him, for that

leads to inefficiency and trouble. What is required is for A to screen all applicants, and to allow B to select from all those who pass through the screening, that candidate whom he prefers.

On the second point, that of removal of unacceptable subordinates, I am not speaking of dismissal *ad lib*, but of what might be termed deselection. That is to say, the manager has the authority to remove the subordinate from his own team, but not from the company. The subordinate becomes available for employment elsewhere in the firm. Only if there is no alternative employment available does the subordinate leave the firm. But surely, you will ask, there must be some safeguard for the interests of the employee? Yes, there certainly must be; and there can be. I shall come to the safeguards for the employee in a moment.

In addition to veto on selection and the right to deselect, the manager must also have the responsibility and the authority to judge and assess his subordinates' performance. Not only must he assess performance, but he must have the authority to do something about his judgement, namely to determine the rewards relative to each other received by his subordinates within the policy set. By this means, the manager is experienced by his immediate subordinates as the person to whom they are in fact accountable and who can do something about their performance.

Given these conditions, it is possible to get some reality into the notion that subordinates must know where they stand. A subordinate can only know where he stands in the judgement of his manager if that manager has real authority in connection with him. Under the conditions described, a subordinate has the chance not only of knowing that he is acceptable to his manager, but also of knowing his manager's real judgement of him as compared with his colleagues.

Comparison with Civil Service and University
The fundamental importance of these conditions can be seen if we compare the industrial situation with that which obtains in the Civil Service and in Universities.

In the Civil Service under conditions which we refer to as permanent establishment, staff have security of employment in the Service. They are not guaranteed employment in any particular role, but they do know that so long as nothing goes radically wrong, they do have secure employment in the institution. They have institutional tenure, although not role tenure.

Under these conditions a superior (for they are not called managers in the Civil Service – rather superiors or administrators or supervisors) does not have the authority to deselect a subordinate. What he has to do if he finds he has an unsatisfactory subordinate is to seek to have him transferred elsewhere. Until such time as he can arrange such a transfer he retains that subordinate's services and does the best he can with him. If things are not going well, therefore, the superior is in a more difficult position than is the manager in industry.

The effect of this situation is that the superior in the Civil Service cannot be held as fully accountable for the work of his subordinates as can the manager under properly operating conditions in industry. He can be held only partly accountable, for his own superior must always take into account the quality of a member's immediate subordinates in judging that member's performance. Such judgements, as you will appreciate, are not always too easy to make.

On the other side, the subordinates themselves can never know as clearly where they stand as can the subordinates of managers in industry. The review of their pay comes pretty automatically and is not a subject for decision by the superior. In addition, when a subordinate is transferred he is never absolutely sure whether he is being transferred because he is needed elsewhere or because his own superior has tried to get rid of him. A report system is an essential component of the operation of such a system.

In Universities an even more striking situation obtains which highlights the nature of the employment contract and the manager-subordinate relationship in industry. All University academic staff, with the exception of assistant lecturers (the junior group), have what is called tenure of employment. That is to say, under all but the most extreme conditions, they have guaranteed employment for life, not only in the University but in the specific job to which they were appointed in the University. That is to say, they can neither be dismissed nor can they be transferred without their agreement. Merit review occurs automatically by annual increment, and the only points at which a University staff member really feels that he comes up

K

for review are those points where he comes either to the top of his existing role or to an efficiency bar in the salary bracket. At these points, if he is to get ahead, he will have to seek promotion or be judged satisfactory to move across the efficiency bar, and at that stage will find himself being assessed.

Under these conditions of appointment with tenure, it would be very much a misnomer to refer to the Head of a Department as a manager. The situation is rather that of academic colleagues, but with the Head of Department having certain authority in connection with his responsibilities for appointment of staff, assignment of teaching duty, and budgets. The relationship between Head of Department and teaching staff is thus very different from that in a manager-subordinate relationship. The Head of Department cannot in any real sense be held accountable for the teaching or research capacity or activities of his teaching staff. Nor can he really be held accountable for the way in which his department operates. He may be held partly accountable – but of course that is always difficult to define – to the extent that circumstances allow him to influence the departmental situation by new appointments.

The effects of these different types of relationship are very considerable. The University organization is one characterized by freedom to teach on the one hand, and high inertia to change on the other. In other words, the academic rights of teaching staff are protected, with the consequence that the institution is very slow to change.

By comparison, the Civil Service situation is one in which there is a moderate degree of inertia. The institution can be modified and changed only as rapidly as it is possible to effect staff transfers. This relative inertia has meaning in terms of the function of the Civil Service to carry out work for Ministers. It tends to have a dampening effect upon the rapid changes which might otherwise be introduced as a result of the sometimes very frequent turnover in Ministers. Indeed in this regard it is noteworthy that the stability of the Civil Service exists within the Ministries, balancing the relative instability in the tenure of the head of the organization, the Minister.

In industry, by contrast, the requirement is for organizational flexibility with stability in leadership. That result is, I believe, achieved by the industrial employment contract which not only allows but requires managers to change subordinates if they find that they cannot get their work done, especially under circumstances where sizeable changes have taken place either in markets or in technology.

Safeguards

There must of course be safeguards within the industrial situation for the rights of employees. The day is long past now when it was possible, or even thought right, for managers simply to be able to ride roughshod over their employees. There are three main safeguards which I believe are required, each of which can contribute significantly to industrial efficiency if properly implemented.

The first and prime condition is what I would call abundant employment. By abundant employment I mean an employment situation in which there is not only work for everybody (i.e. full employment), but available work for each person at a level consistent with his capacity. Given such conditions, it should always be possible for a member of society to find work at a level suitable for him, and thus with an income appropriate to his ability.

The great value of abundant employment is that it ensures that we use all the talent available to us. It avoids the wastage inherent in a national situation in which people may be working hard in terms of the amount of work they are doing but are nevertheless not being extended because the work they are doing is easier than that which they were capable of. This kind of marginal under-employment of those who are at work is one of the most serious dangers of a situation in which there may be marginal unemployment.

What happens is not only that, say, $1\frac{1}{2}$, 2, or 3 per cent of people are unemployed, but that everybody else tends to be marginally underemployed rather than put at full stretch by their work.

In addition, when there is less than a full employment situation, managers become extremely anxious about releasing subordinates, because of the disastrous consequences to them. People are therefore kept in their positions for the wrong reasons, with resulting inefficiency for the firm and inadequate work opportunity for the individual.

In addition to abundant employment, it is essential that the members of the company should have the opportunity to take part in the formulation of the policies which affect them. Such formulation of policy requires a very considerable extension of our procedures for consulting with employees. The ordinary kind of joint consultation committee or works council in which members of top management meet with elected representatives of hourly-rated members – or in some cases of staff – for discussions on an advisory basis, with payment questions kept out, is insufficient.

What are required are genuine policy-making meetings in which there is an opportunity for elected members of all levels of staff and hourly-rated workers to meet with a chief executive and to hammer out with him policy issues on all matters of differential entitlements and individual duties operating within the firm. By differential entitlements I mean such things as the total differential payment structure, premium payments such as night shift and overtime, holidays, sick benefit schemes, etc.

Given this kind of policy-making mechanism for agreeing on individual entitlements within the organization, it becomes possible for managerial authority to be more acceptable and more reasonable, precisely because it is sanctioned. Within such a setting, a framework is created within which managers can function effectively and within which each individual subordinate can be assured of his basic rights.

Such a policy-making mechanism as I have described provides a framework but still does not cope with the details of any particular individual's requirements. The big question is what happens if a manager judges one of his subordinates unfairly? What satisfaction can there be for the subordinate? In order to cope with such situations a third condition is necessary (i.e. in addition to abundant employment and policy-making mechanisms), namely a channel of individual appeal. Every subordinate must have the right to appeal against his manager's judgement of him to his manager's own superior and so on up the executive line, if necessary to the top.

The force of such an appeals structure is that if a subordinate has not been warned by his manager that his performance has been substandard, he is entitled to expect that his work has been acceptable. If then a manager, out of the blue, without warning, were to tell a subordinate that he is no longer acceptable to him, the subordinate would have grounds for appeal because he had not been told earlier that he was unacceptable, and had therefore not been given the chance to do anything about it. It ought to be a matter of policy for a manager who becomes increasingly dissatisfied with a subordinate's work, to warn that subordinate and discuss the matter with him in such a manner as to give the subordinate the opportunity to overcome the difficulties. Given such warning and adequate discussion, and given that the performance does not improve, the manager ought for a second time to take the matter up with the subordinate to give him yet another chance. It is only following this second stage, and in the event that the subordinate still proves unable to better his performance, that it becomes reasonable for the manager to decide that the subordinate is no longer acceptable to him, and to deselect him.

Given these three safeguards – namely: first, a situation of abundant employment which provides opportunity for work at a level consistent with the capacity of individuals; second, the right of all members to take part through their elected representatives in determining the broad policy within which managers will operate; and third, the right of appeal if a manager has not given the subordinate adequate opportunity to improve his work; then it may be agreed that the rights of the individual are well protected. The effect would be to reinforce the situation in which people find employment in jobs which they can do well and which employ them fully rather than stagnating in jobs which they are not doing well to the detriment of themselves, the employing organization and, in the final analysis, the country.

Characteristics of Manager–Subordinate Relationship
In the light of the above discussion, we can now consider what it means to be a manager. His first and prime responsibility is to be able to judge the performance of his immediate subordinates. Not only must he be able to judge their performance, but he must have the authority and responsibility for determining what work he allocates to them in the light of his judgement. Not only must he be able to allocate this work, but he must know enough about the work situation to plan and progress the

total programme for which he is accountable. I do not propose to go into these issues of programming and technology, however, since they are subjects from another field. I am going to assume that the manager is technically competent in the sense of being able to handle the necessary techniques of programming and knowing sufficient about the technology. This assumption allows me to pursue the theme of what is involved in manager–subordinate interrelations.

A manager must be able to judge applicants for subordinate positions, in the sense of knowing who, from a screened short list, he will choose to have. Managers in industry today are often protected from this responsibility by personnel departments who do most, if not all, of the recruitment and selection. When a manager is not accountable for selection, it is all too easy for him to say that he cannot be expected to perform as efficiently as his superior might wish, since after all he had no hand in choosing his own working team.

We must now ask, however, whether it is simply a matter of managerial personality that we are talking about in connection with carrying out these conditions. The person of the manager is certainly important, since if the individual does not have the capacity to carry the required responsibilities, then of course effective management will not result. But we can ask, nevertheless, whether there are any minimum conditions which must be satisfied in order to help to ensure that managers of the necessary capacity will be in charge of subordinates. I should like to describe one such condition that I consider to be of absolute importance. I call this condition optimum manager-subordinate distance.

By optimum manager-subordinate distance I mean the difference in capacity between a manager and a subordinate that would make it possible for the manager effectively to manage. Let me illustrate by two extreme examples. Consider first the situation where the manager and the subordinate are too close to each other in capacity. Many people will have experienced this situation in either or perhaps both of two ways. First, the situation where a subordinate feels that his capacity is either too close to, or equal to, or perhaps even above, that of his manager; or alternatively, where the manager feels that his subordinate is uncomfortably close to him in capacity, or perhaps even his equal. Under these conditions of manager and subordinate being too close to each other in capacity, the manager himself feels anxious because he cannot effectively assess his subordinate's work. The subordinate knows just as much or nearly as much about the task as the manager does, and is able to question the manager's plans and actions and his leadership.

The subordinate for his part feels too closely tied by his manager. There is not enough scope for his efforts. He feels that his manager does not know any more about the work than he himself does and is no more effective, when trouble occurs, in helping him get out of that trouble. That is to say, there is anxiety on the manager's part, and on the subordinate's part there is a feeling of constriction, of being held on too tight a lead.

At the other extreme, there is the case of subordinates who are too far removed from their manager in capacity. The subordinates seem ineffectual. They involve the manager in too much detail. He feels that he has to descend, to go down into their roles and to become too occupied with the details of the work that they are doing. The manager is never able to delegate to them the full-scale responsibilities that he would like to delegate, and therefore, being too occupied with their work, is unable to get on unhampered with the tasks that he has retained for himself.

The subordinates on their part feel that their manager is too far removed. They are made anxious by the ideas which he has. They often feel that he is taking too great risks, and begin to try to restrain him, and do not feel that he is as much help to them as he might be. They are often anxious about taking matters up with him because they feel he is likely to become impatient with their shortcomings. In short, the manager feels constrained and pulled down by his subordinates, and the subordinates feel anxious because their manager is too distant from them.

We can thus say that it is possible for a manager to be too close to his subordinates in capacity, or too far removed from them in capacity. The question is, what would be experienced as just right. It is possible to answer this question if you consider the quite universal feelings that exist with regard to optimum pay relationship between a manager and his subordinates. Thus, for example, ask any group of businessmen (whether they are in this country, France, Holland, the United States, Canada, or elsewhere) what is the most appropriate level of pay for subordinates having a manager whose capacity equivalent in terms of pay is represented by £2500 a year; they will not reply £700 or £2400, and this is because they feel that in the first case the difference is too large and that in the second case it is too small. It is quite a striking phenomenon that people generally name figures between £1500 and £1800 a year as being just about the right capacity level to match the capacity of a manager at £2500 a year. Using this line of questioning we discover that, expressed in financial terms, the capacity of a manager is usually rated at something like 50 to 60 per cent above that of his subordinates. This is confirmed by the fact that when this kind of relationship is not maintained, the subordinates feel either too close to or too far removed from their managers. In the case of their being too close – that is to say a £2500 a year manager with a £2300 a year subordinate – the subordinate tends to regard his manager only as a kind of administrative chief, whereas it is to his manager's own manager that he looks for leadership. A great deal of bypassing exists in this situation, with the manager-once-removed and the subordinate seemingly having to have a great deal of contact with each other.

Even more striking is the finding that there seem to be natural boundaries as you proceed upwards. That is to say, you have to get a level currently (1968) represented by about £1600 a year before you find anybody in a full-scale managerial role. At capacities below this, individuals do not appear to have the necessary capacity to manage subordinates. Then between £1600 and about £2410 a year, you find the first range of managerial roles, capable of managing shop and office floor personnel. It is not until you get above £2400 a year that you then find managers with the capacity themselves to manage the group in the £1600 to £2400 bracket, that is to say, to become managers of managers. This stratum extends to about £4700 a year. From data of this kind a series of strata has been found to exist, each stratum consisting of one level. That is to say, up to £1600, no managers; between £1600 and £2400, first-line managers; between £2400 and £4700, second-line managers; between £4700 and £9000, third-line managers; and so on.

It has been further discovered that if an executive structure contains more levels than are represented by these salary strata, then that executive structure becomes too crowded, in the sense that managers are too close to their subordinates. This situation of *too close* tends to be very common, indeed almost universal, in industrial organizations. There are reasons for this, which I cannot go into here. Let me illustrate, however, by saying that if you have an organization whose chief executive role is worth, say, £12000 a year, then that organization ought to be able to be effectively managed with five executive strata including the shop floor. That is, the chief executive, say, at £12000, who ought to be able to manage his own immediate team of subordinates at, say, around £5–6000 a year, who in turn ought to be able to manage managerial subordinates at around £2700 a year, who in turn would have first-line managerial staff in the £1600–2400 bracket, who in turn would have operator or office floor subordinates. In practice, however, in companies of this kind with the chief executive role at the level I have mentioned (£12000) you will usually find not five executive strata, but six or seven, or possibly even eight or nine. That is to say, at a number of points in the executive line you will find managers and subordinates who are crowded too close together.

In these conditions of too many executive levels resulting in too close a relationship between managers and subordinates, the minimum managerial conditions which we have been describing simply cannot apply. When a manager is too close to his subordinate, as I have indicated, he cannot effectively judge that subordinate, since the subordinate's capacity is too much like his own. He will therefore inevitably be weak in selection. He will also have shortcomings in assessing the subordinate's performance, and in determining the relative rewards of his subordinates, since, again, they are all too much like him. He will also feel greater anxiety about deselecting a subordinate, because his subordinates have more of a feeling of being his colleagues than his subordinates. The managerial structure tends, therefore, to be weakened, since the managers do not and cannot feel accountable for the work of their subordinates, nor do the subordinates feel fully accountable to their immediate superiors.

Conclusion

I said at the beginning that I proposed to consider the minimum conditions to allow of effective management. In attempting to follow this course, I have frequently made reference to what ought to be the case, to what managers should do. In order to make it as clear as I possibly can that I have not been speaking in the ethical sense of 'what a good thing it would be if only managers did what they ought to do', nor in the sense of exhorting managers to do something, nor in the pessimistic sense of wishing or hoping that managers would behave in certain ways, let me explain what I have meant in saying what managers ought to do. I have tried to define what must requisitely happen *if* managers are to be defined as accountable for the work of subordinates – and I assume that that definition is unexceptionable. By requisite I mean demanded by the nature of things – by the nature of work, and of people, and of accountability.

From these considerations we can then conclude not only what responsibilities a manager must requisitely discharge, but what minimal policies the enterprise must accept if it is to have effective managers. May I repeat this formulation in another way, for I believe it to be the most neglected feature of management considerations today – or perhaps more accurately, the most *avoided* issue. I repeat: before any company can expect to have an adequate management structure, with good managers using their authority to bring about efficiency, competitiveness, and imaginative development in the operation of the enterprise, that company must establish, as a matter of policy, certain minimum conditions to enable each and every manager to be held accountable in actual fact for his own work and that of his subordinates, and to give each manager in actual fact, and again as a matter of explicit policy, that authority requisite to the discharge of his accountability.

I have discussed some of these main conditions. Let me summarize them:

    (*a*) the establishment of explicit and therefore readily identifiable managerial roles, with the assignment explicitly to each role of the following minimum authority:
        (i) authority to veto an appointment;

    (ii) authority to decide allocation of work;

   (iii) authority to assess performance and determine the relative reward pattern among immediate subordinates, within policy;

   (iv) the authority to deselect;

(b) an explicit policy of holding managers accountable for the work of their subordinates;

(c) maintaining an executive structure in which the number of managerial levels is kept down to that number which allows sufficient capacity distance between managers and subordinates;

(d) the provision of institutions through which employees may influence company policies, and through which felt injustice may be made a matter for appeal;

(e) the allocation of resources consistent with getting the assigned work done.

When you have established these minimum conditions, it then becomes realistic to ask your managers to behave like managers. It becomes possible to sharpen your managerial selection because the specification for a manager is clearer and more precise. And finally, it becomes feasible to construct more soundly-based management training and development programmes.

With respect to management training, the core of the programme can become concrete and specific teaching and instruction by the company itself in the company's policies and procedures. Those managers who cannot cope too well may be assisted by the currently more common forms of personally oriented training. Such methods are made more effective when they can be used in relation to a policy which is actually in operation, thus avoiding the fish out of water feeling on return from training.

The establishment of minimum conditions for effective management throughout industry is a worthy aim, an aim whose achievement would at one and the same time give a foundation for qualification of managers, enhance the prestige of management, and give a spur to national efficiency.

9

Stress

Our relationship with our work is one of the several important areas of life. It is important for at least two main reasons, both obvious but easily lost sight of. The first is the simple matter of existence: through our work we provide ourselves with the primitive requirements of food and shelter. The second is the fact that in our work we test in reality our ideas about our personal capacity. This second reason links with the fact that in our society, by and large, we pick up our social and economic status via our capacity as exercised in our work.

It would seem then, that there ought to be some readily observable connections between stress disorders in the individual and stresses in the work situation. In stresses in the work situation we might include such factors as: lack of outlet for a person's interests or experience; absence of sufficient challenge to his capacity, or an excessive challenge; inadequate financial reward or other recognition – or, perhaps, an excess of reward; or too much or too little work; difficulties in relationships with managers or colleagues; or, in extremes, forced unemployment.

For at work, there is certainly an apparent abundance of opportunity for insecurity, dissatisfaction and anxiety. Gastric or duodenal ulcer, or coronary thrombosis for example, are commonly stated to be occupational hazards of higher executive work. Certainly ulceration occurs frequently enough for those sections of modern office buildings housing the senior executive group to be referred to as 'the milk bar'!

Yet the problem may not be so straightforward as it is often made out to be. The human being is capable of prodigious feats of hard work, and over large periods of time, during which we certainly become tired, but with periods of rest we are able to revive and continue, without necessarily developing pathological symptoms of fatigue or stress. If we are to examine the possible relationship between work and stress symptoms, we must find ways of discriminating between genuine stress on the one hand, and hard difficult work or heavy responsibility on the other. Moreover, it will be useful to be able to distinguish between a stressful situation and symptoms of stress in the individual. I shall use what I hope is a simple enough terminology. Let us speak of stress-inducing situations to refer to external circumstances which may give rise to symptoms of stress in the individual. Let us also confine our use of the term stress to states of pathology in the individual, and let us avoid using it loosely in speaking about the ordinary feelings of worry and concern that we all experience in our work and which from time to time can become very severe.

Our first problem then becomes that of identifying the differences, if any, between stress-inducing situations and ordinary hard work or heavy responsibility.

II

I have had the occasion during the past eighteen years to collaborate with members of the Glacier Metal Company – an engineering concern employing some four thousand people – in an extended research into executive organization, management, and industrial relations. During that time I have had daily contact, in the capacity of social consultant, with many hundreds of members of the Company, always at their own request, from

Board level to and including the shop and office floor, in a wide range of social problems. Examples include: helping to work through difficulties resulting from inconsistencies between the work to be done and the organization for getting it done, or between the responsibilities borne by an individual and the authority and resources he is assigned – in short, difficulties arising from non-requisite organization; or problems of the balance between a person's capacity, the level of work he is carrying, his financial reward for that work, and his rate of career progress; or circumstances of sharp conflict and strife between managers and shop stewards, in situations verging on strike.

In the course of these many years I have had a peculiarly favourable opportunity for extended contact with individuals and for access in depth to their strivings and uncertainties, their successes and failures, during periods of advancement or stagnation, and to their attitudes, their reasons for joining or leaving, their sense of achievement and satisfaction or of strain, worry and anxiety – all of this in a setting where I was concurrently involved in work with these same individuals in committees, in executive meetings and in other events giving first-hand access to the work situations.

I wish to set before you some of the main conclusions from the Glacier Project, relevant to the theme of this article. You will see that these findings are equivocal and uncertain. For being forced to observe the interaction between an individual, his work, and his work situation, over periods of years, all possibility is lost of making neat generalizations which can so often be based upon short term observations of chance concurrence between the development of somatic stress symptoms and difficult work situations. This open-minded view of the matter is underscored by the common psycho-analytic experience that psychopathology in the individual has but a tenuous and uncertain connection with external events.

III

The first conclusion I would present, is to confirm that hard work, responsible work, a lot of work with long hours, and over long periods of time (by which I mean months and years) is not by itself a sufficient condition for inducing stress symptoms. This finding is obvious enough, but it may nevertheless be worth stating, so that it can be set to one side and allow us to move closer to the heart of the problem. To put it another way, to work at full stretch, on work that is nevertheless achievable in the sense that it is just within the capacity of the individual and under circumstances and with resources that allow results to be obtained within the standards set, can be a psychologically invigorating experience just as easily as a psychological strain, however intense the effort, however fine the judgement required, and however tantalizing and uncertainty-provoking the decisions to be made.

The stress-inducing situations are more likely to be those in which a person finds himself operating under non-requisite conditions. These conditions may be either:

(a) being held accountable for the completion of tasks which are non-feasible because of inadequate resources or inconsistencies in organization, or are too easy because of excess resources; or

(b) being held accountable for tasks which are too difficult because the level of the work is too much beyond the capacity of the individual, or too easy because the level of the work is much too far below his capacity.

That is to say stress is caused by work which is too easy or too difficult, either for organizational reasons or because of discrepencies between level of work and capacity. And of these two situations it is discrepancies between a person's level of work and his capacity which in my experience cause the most trouble. The typical manifestation of work that is beyond a person's capacity is that the person becomes either anxiously indecisive, or unwise and precipitate in decision, or paralysed.

The reason why difficulties arising through organizational shortcomings may be less traumatic than those arising through inadequate personal capacity may be that you can always argue for organizational change or for increased resources. Your personal reputation is not necessarily at stake in so doing. You are challenging your manager or company policy. The shortcoming is outside you.

But when the cause of difficulty is your own inability to cope, the shortcoming is inside you. To do badly, or to fail, is to expose the fact that your level of capacity is lower than it has been adjudged in terms of the level of responsibility you have been deemed worthy of assignment. It is your own personal reputation that is now very much at stake. To try to hang on is to put yourself under strain, and that is where the trouble begins from the point of view of inducing stress.

IV

Let me give two brief examples, to illustrate the much greater seriousness of having a job that is too big for you.

First, an example of a person big enough for the job, but working under difficult circumstances. Mr X found himself in a very difficult position over a period of some years. He was held accountable for certain crucial activities, but without the authority appropriate to their discharge. He had to wheedle and cajole his colleagues, use personal persuasion, or throw his weight around, to get his work done. And if he fell short of his targeted tasks, it would become immediately apparent in the sensitive area of customer complaints. But he did not develop ulcers, nor did he become ill at all. He was aware of his difficult position. It was a position very characteristic of his type of work. Countless others were in the same position, and it was widely recognized as a very difficult organizational problem to do anything about.

In the event, the problem was tackled and eventually resolved. That was some ten years ago. Very extensive reorganization of many sections of the firm was involved. The new organization has been experienced as more satisfactory. It would be interesting to have been able to report that Mr X and many others had had stress symptoms, and that they then gave evidence of a diminution or disappearance of these stress symptoms. But that is not the case. The improvement of the external conditions made it possible to get more done, and led to greater satisfaction in work. But dissatisfaction is a very different matter from being ill.

By way of contrast, we can take a case where the conditions for work were excellent but the person was not big enough for the job. Mr Y was encouraged by his manager to accept promotion and take on the responsibility for a large department. His authority was clear enough, and resources were appropriate. But he himself turned out, in the event, not to have a high enough level of capacity. He was well liked, and no one wanted to see him fail. He was bolstered up in his position for a period of over three years. The strain finally told, and he developed a severe gastric ulcer, necessitating surgical intervention. After convalescence, he returned, and was put on so-called light duties at lower pay where he has been now for some five years, and doing very well indeed as gauged by his own feelings of satisfaction and by his manager's satisfaction with his performance.

These two cases will, I would think, seem very ordinary and familiar. But there is one aspect that is readily overlooked because it is so familiar. That is, the meaning of Mr Y, of the gastric ulcer, being put on light duties. Did he have shorter hours? For a few months yes, but then he went on to the same hours as everyone else. Was there less physically exacting work? No. One was a managerial and the other an office specialist role, both involving the same physical conditions. Was the pace slower? I can assure you it was not. Were the outside pressures less? Again, no. The sole difference was that there was a lower level of work in the new role. Mr Y's responsibilities were now within his capabilities. He felt he was earning his salary, and was on top of his job, rather than having his job on top of him. The critical difference lies in the fact that the level of the work was now within his capacity.

V

From data of this kind, we may conclude that the relationship between a person's capacity and the level of work he is assigned to carry, is one of the central factors in determining whether that work is experienced as easy or difficult, light or heavy, satisfying or stress-inducing. We may express this relationship in terms of

$$C - W = \text{equilibrium}$$

$$\begin{array}{l} C \\ | \\ W \end{array} = \text{capacity too great for work}$$

$$\begin{array}{l} W \\ | \\ C \end{array} = \text{work too great for capacity}$$

L

If now we introduce the factor of payment, a group of thirteen possible patterns is obtained, the reaction to each of which may be found to be readily predictable.

(i) $C-W-P$

Pay is just right for the work, and work just right for capacity.

(ii)

$$P$$
$$|$$
$$C-W$$

Payment above equity, but work just right for capacity.

(iii) $C-W$
$$|$$
$$P$$

Payment below equity, but work just right for capacity.

(iv)

$$P$$
$$|$$
$$W$$
$$|$$
$$C$$

Payment above equity, but work too high for capacity.

(v) $W-P$
$$|$$
$$C$$

Equitable payment, but work too high for capacity.

(vi)

$$W$$
$$|-P$$
$$C$$

Payment below equity, but higher than would be equitable for work consistent with his capacity.

(vii)

$$W$$
$$|$$
$$C-P$$

Payment that would be equitable for work consistent with his capacity.

(viii)

$$W$$
$$|$$
$$C$$
$$|$$
$$P$$

Payment that is below equity for work that would be consistent with his capacity.

(ix)

$$P$$
$$|$$
$$C$$
$$|$$
$$W$$

Payment above equity for the work level consistent with his capacity.

(x) $C-P$
$$|$$
$$W$$

Payment that is equitable for the work level consistent with his capacity.

(xi)

$$C$$
$$|-P$$
$$W$$

Payment that is below equity for the work level consistent with his capacity, but above equity for his current work level.

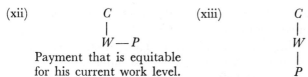

(xii)

$$C$$
$$|$$
$$W — P$$

Payment that is equitable for his current work level.

(xiii)

$$C$$
$$|$$
$$W$$
$$|$$
$$P$$

Payment below equity for his current work level. which is too low for his current capacity.

From these we may pick up case (iv) as a strong stress-inducing situation. The work is beyond the person's capacity, but the financial reward is enticingly high. It is a circumstance compulsively attractive to some people, and one to be found often enough, for example, at higher executive level, or in the newer fields like market research and advertising. A person who attempts to cling to such a situation will in due course exhibit the symptoms of stress.

Equally, case (ix) (that is, a too easy job, accompanied by overpayment – a featherbed situation) may be associated with stress of another kind – if indeed, we are to call it stress. It is the stress placed upon character by too easy gain. I do not propose to pursue this topic because I have had little opportunity for first-hand observation. But you may not be surprised to learn that, in one firm whose medical officer I know well, this circumstance had come to be identified by him as the 'gout situation'.

VI

But there still remains an important unanswered question, even if it is the case that $W P C$ disequilibrium is stress-inducing. That question is why does the person stay in the situation? Why, for instance, did Mr Y persist in hanging on to the managerial role that he was well aware would eventually break him? Is it a matter of saving face? I think not. The situation is more complex than that. For Mr Y's manager had also decided explicitly that Y would not be able to keep a grip on his job for much longer. And yet neither acted until the breakdown precipitated its own solution.

One is aware of other forces in the situation, exposed in the form of an unconscious collusive relationship between Y and his manager leading on to breakdown. These destructive forces, familiar enough to those engaged in psycho-analytical work, inhibit positive action before breakdown. One of the effects of these inhibiting forces is that perhaps the most common method of dealing with subordinates who are not up to a job, is to allow stress to pile up to the point of manifest symptom formation and breakdown, and to clear up the mess at that point. The demoting of an inadequate subordinate proves to be one of the most difficult managerial situations to cope with – especially in the higher executive echelons. If the subordinate obsessionally hangs on, then there is psychological trouble in store.

We are led, then, to conclude that external situations, even discrepancies between level of work and capacity, cannot by themselves induce stress symptoms. There must also be a destructive compulsion at work in the individual which causes the seduction into the stress-inducing situation. It might be described as a kind of stress-proneness, akin to accident proneness.

The creation of stress symptoms is thus not a simple matter. To be retained in a situation of unbalance between level of work and capacity, with or without excessive financial reward, requires a combination of an individual unconsciously working towards breakdown, and a stress-inducing opportunity to collude unconsciously with a manager. It may be worth repeating that there are also individuals with sufficient internal conflict for stress symptoms to arise pretty much independently of the external situation. Modern industrial society does not necessarily, therefore, in and of itself produce more stressful occupations. It may, however, provide greater opportunities through the greater mobility it offers in work, for neurotic disjunctions between an individual's capacity and his work.

IO

Social Organization
and Individual Adjustment

I

It has long been assumed – and surely with some reason – that adjusting to the organizations in society in which we live affects our behaviour and our mental well-being. But the actual nature of this connection between the individual and the roles he occupies in his society has been difficult to establish – and it is not clear yet whether we can determine that connection with any exactitude. During the past twenty years, however, very considerable advances have been made in detailed exploration of this problem. These advances have a not inconsiderable importance for psychiatry and for the general alleviation of mental disorder and stress.

In particular, I should like to illustrate the kind of evidence now becoming available in the following main areas:

(a) the possible connection between social structure and mental illness – in particular, the significance of differences in the incidence of various types of mental illness in different social classes;

(*b*) the effects upon the behaviour of individuals and the stresses to which they are subjected, of the social institutions, organization and groups of which they are members;

(*c*) the implications of these findings for the organization of psychiatric hospitals for treatment; and

(*d*) the development of healthy social institutions – that is to say, institutions which are organized so as to minimize unnecessary stress upon individuals.

I shall use the phrase requisite organization to refer to the healthy type of organization – requisite in the sense of conforming both to the individual and to the institutional requirements of the situation.

II

The most obvious connection between social relationships and mental illness is to be seen in the family. Psychodynamic studies show up sharply the impact, for example, of the mother's behaviour upon the mental development of the child. We know the effects upon infant development when these relationships go astray – through neglect by the mother, or through emotional inability of the parents to cope with the demands of the child either by providing adequate love and security or by taking and coping with the child's hate and aggression.

I do not, however, propose here to dwell upon these family relationships. I do not propose to do so for one main reason, a reason that may help to outline more precisely the nature of my object. For, even though it may be the case that families and their behaviour affect – and seriously affect – the mental development of their members, it is equally the case that improving the mental climate within families is not much easier than improving the mental health of the individual.

Psychological treatment of individuals, and of families, is a profoundly important endeavour – for the individual, for the family, for knowledge, and for society. But this type of work, as we are all well aware, pecks only at the fringe of the problem of mental illness from society's point of view. We must provide treatment for willing individuals and for willing families, but doing so does not relieve the mass of illness and emotional stress that exists all around us. To tackle this larger-scale problem, we require methods that are informed by work with individuals and families, but larger in scope and in scale.

Educational methods directed at the individual and his own behaviour are usually the first to be thought of when we talk about mental health programmes on any scale. Such educational programmes are, however, notoriously ineffective when it comes to changing behaviour. In saying this, I am not taking up a pessimistic theme. For I wish to go further, and to suggest that we may be able to grasp this large-scale problem, and to reduce it significantly, by paying adequate attention to the organization of our society and of the institutions within our society. This particular path is not an easy one. There are great technical obstacles in the way – we must, in the first place, extend our knowledge far beyond what we presently know about what makes requisite institutions. And, even if we knew more, there are always powerful forces and resistances counterpoised against change. But given the development of the required knowledge, our society and general social institutions – unlike the family – are amenable to conscious organization and control by means of agreed policies. We can decide how we are going to organize them, and do it. We can thereby lay the foundation for tangible and significant changes in individual behaviour, not by exhortation or hopeful education, but by the practical and explicable step of changing the setting in which each one behaves. In this context, education itself can take on a new and practical meaning, that of conveying information about the organization and administration of any institutions, and the expected modes of behaviour in them.

I am going to suggest, therefore, that attention to our social institutions and the way they are organized and administered, is an essential, practical, hard-headed exercise in community mental health – that sound organization and administration of our institutions is an essential component for the improvement of mental health.

III

Allow me first of all to talk about my experience in a social consultancy role with an engineering company – the Glacier Metal Company. Our work there has come to be known as the Glacier Project. It has been possible for me in the course of this project to help bring about extensive changes in organization. I was on the spot, and during the years following the changes I was involved in follow-up work. I have thus had the opportunity to observe what happened to individuals as a result of these changes. What has impressed me is the radical nature of the changes in behaviour of many individuals. It is not all black and white. But by and large there is an easier atmosphere.

Let me illustrate the kind of problem we had to face, and the solution we proposed.

A works manager was in charge of a factory employing about a thousand people. He was supposed to be responsible for the quantity and quality of the work done, and for seeing that completion was on schedule. He had to do this within the various limitations imposed upon him by his equipment and tooling, the quality and availability of supplies, the efficacy of permitted methods, and the quality of the labour to hand. The manifest content of his responsibility showed him completely in charge.

The extant or actual situation, once you looked beneath the surface, was quite different. The general manager to whom the works manager was responsible had a number of other direct subordinates: a chief production engineer in charge of methods, a chief production controller in charge of scheduling and deliveries, a chief inspector responsible for quality, a chief accountant, a personnel manager, and a chief buyer. Each of these had a considerable staff under him with duties that took them on to the shop floor in contact with the works manager's command at several levels removed.

What actually took place at supervisory and operating levels? Methods engineers, layout engineers, and time-study engineers fixed and altered methods and times and did development work; scheduling officers responsible to the chief production controller routed work, loaded machines, and revised schedules as required; and, without going into detail, the staff of the chief inspector, chief accountant, personnel manager, and chief buyer also had their duties to carry out at shop-floor level. In fact (the extant situation), the production managers shared responsibility for methods with the production engineers, for delivery with the production controllers, for quality with the inspectors, and so forth.

Now move back up to the works manager. He was bypassed by a network of instructions from these specialist colleagues to his subordinates. According to the manifest organization he was in charge of production – except for methods, quality, cost, delivery, personnel, and budgets! Was he in fact in charge, as was manifestly described to be the case? The answer is clearly no!

It may be thought that this example of inconsistency between the manifest and the extant situations is a special one. That is not so. The particular example is a common pattern of organization in industry, one which is the cause of a great deal of stress and inefficiency. In the instance given, the effect was frustration accompanied by susceptibility to fatigue and a chronic sense of overwork, in a series of four works managers who succeeded each other in the job over a period of eight years. Moreover, the members carrying responsibility in the specialist positions I have described were similarly affected.

An extensive analysis of the work situation led to the recognition that the organization requisitely demanded by the type of work carried in the works manager role was different from either the manifest or the extant. By requisite organization, I mean the establishment of jobs whose stated responsibilities are consistent with the assigned authority and with the pattern of responsibilities assigned to colleague positions. Examination of the actual situation showed that the works manager role required to be taken out of the direct line of command and explicitly established as an administrative position. The shops were reorganized into units of 200–400 operators, divided into sections of 10 to 50 members under a section manager. Each unit manager was allocated his own specialist staff of production engineers and production controllers, and was soon to have his own personnel specialist. The net effect was an organization in which responsibility and authority were not out of line with each other, as was previously the case.

Is it not my purpose to go into details of this new organization.[1] The point to emphasize, however, is that it was built up in relation to the work to be done, the essential principle being that of building an organization and establishing mechanisms whereby members actually were accountable for what they were stated to be, in the sense of their responsibilities being consistent with each other, and of their having the authority that went with the responsibilities for which they were being called to account.

The effect of the change upon individuals – and I have been able to observe it for over twelve years now – was to make it possible to behave with greater decisiveness. Complaints about stress and fatigue due to overlapping responsibilities correspondingly diminished – diminished that is, in all but a few instances of individuals who had been enabled to play out neuroses in the previous situation, and who now had to find other ways to deal with their personal disturbances.

Production controllers no longer had to beat their way around the shops, using the 'iron fist in the velvet glove' to fulfil a responsibility for which they had not been given the requisite authority. The methods engineers were no longer treated as outsiders, the 'strangers from upstairs'. And it was possible for operational managers realistically to be held accountable for their work.

In similar vein, requisite institutions have been developed which allow for all employees at all levels to interact through elected representatives with the Managing Director, in agreeing or modifying the policies governing their individual duties and entitlements. The methods are not in terms of irrelevant concepts of industrial democracy, or of group decision, but of social institutions that take into account the actualities of the power situation, and therefore can succeed in mediating power. Every employee also has the absolute right of appeal against any decision of his manager that affects him. The effect of these institutions on the outlook and behaviour of both managers and militant representatives has been dramatic. Industrial tension

[1] Brown, Wilfred, *Exploration in Management* (London: Heinemann, 1960, and Penguin Books, 1960).

has been markedly reduced. As managers, shop stewards, and staff representatives put it, they have explicit and agreed constitutional means for resolving disputes. It is not that they do not have arguments. But they have more telling and fruitful arguments. And the arguments can take place when the problem occurs, rather than simmering under cover, combining with other unresolved stresses and eventually erupting with a bang. These constitutional procedures were developed out of social analyses and modifications conducted from 1948 to 1955. They have been fairly stable for the past twelve years, despite considerable changes in personnel, and are therefore, I would say, entitled to be thought of as fairly tested.

I believe that by means of detailed and painstaking social-analysis, we may even have discovered a fundamental solution to the vexed national problem of arranging for equitable payment – that is to say, payment related to the level of responsibility that a person is called upon to carry. If that is true, and I think we have got far enough at least to demonstrate that the problem is resolvable, then think how much social tension based upon economic rivalry, envy, jealousy, suspicion and class hatred might be alleviated.

Requisite social organization and procedures related to the realities of the social situation as revealed by analysis, can provide a setting for extensive behavioural change. That is the lesson for me from the Glacier Project. But the question still remains, how far can it be said that these changes in behaviour are connected with improvements in mental health? Do they, for instance, lead to changes in family relationships that are conducive to mentally healthy atmospheres? My data here fall far short of what one would like to know. But I should like to turn to the evidence of another research project, suggesting that what happens at the work place in fact may profoundly affect marital and family relationships for the better or for the worse.

V

In a study of families and work in the Detroit area, Miller and Swanson[1] have shown how the switch from an entrepreneurial

[1] *The Changing American Parent* (New York: Wiley, 1958).

situation to a bureaucratic situation by the head of the family can have radical effects upon the patterns of individual relationships within the family. When the father works in an entrepreneurial role, his own concern for resources and for the people he serves affects his own outlook in such a manner as to cause him to inculcate into the family mores that are usually thought of in terms of the protestant ethic. When the father is employed, however, in the relative security of the bureaucratic situation, where he himself no longer risks personal loss as the result of his decisions, a loosening of his concern for others and for resources occurs, with effects upon the moral standards which he inculcates in the family, resulting in a loosening of moral standards with an increase in social deviance and emotional disturbance. Interactions between individual behaviour in a social setting of the kind teased out in the Miller–Swanson study require to be carried on much more extensively if we are to be able to help society organize its affairs on a more rational basis.

VI

The Miller and Swanson study gives some idea of the significance of the results that can be obtained from carefully conducted large-scale social analyses. Such studies have become more frequent recently in the field of epidemiology of mental illness, and some data from that area can help to extend our present analysis of the interaction between the individual and his social environment to the level of society as a whole.

For many years now, it has been assumed that the more severe mental illnesses occurred among the economically and socially most distressed sections of our urban populations. This assumed relationship has been established pretty conclusively in a series of studies, notably in the United States. During the 1950s in Chicago, for instance, Faris and Dunham showed that schizophrenia was significantly more frequent in occurrence among the working classes, and depressive illnesses more frequent among the middle classes. It might be argued, of course, that such studies merely demonstrate that schizophrenics and schizophrenic families fall to the bottom of the social scale and there reproduce themselves. But that this explanation is perhaps too simple was suggested by a unique feature of the follow-up study.

The social structure of Chicago is peculiarly related to its geography. The city is like a great half-circle with the flat diameter stretching along the front of Lake Michigan. It was populated by successive waves of immigrants, each landing and settling first in the loop – the central area of the city, at the lake front. As each new wave of immigrants came in, the already settled group, now prospering, moved outwards forming a concentric half-circle around the loop. Thus as time went by, the city came to be composed of different ethnic groups, situated in a series of concentric bands with the loop at their centre, with the groups becoming increasingly prosperous the farther you got from the centre of the city.

Taking a sample from the ethnic groups in each of these concentric rings, it was again found that schizophrenia was significantly more frequent in the loop, and became less frequent as you moved into the more prosperous outlying areas. That is to say, as each ethnic group adapted, and became more prosperous, the incidence of schizophrenia decreased.

These findings were more recently duplicated, on a much larger scale, by Hollinghead and Redlich in Newhaven, Connecticut. There the population of one district of the city, called Yorkville, was studied in toto. Every family was investigated psychiatrically. The findings were in many respects startling; for example, some 25 per cent of the population were assessed as being urgently in need of psychiatric treatment. But for our present interest, the finding was again clear, namely, that schizophrenia was an illness that occurred to a significantly higher degree among working-class families, while depression and neurosis had a relatively higher incidence among middle-class families.

These studies, and related findings, are highly suggestive of the fact that poor economic circumstances in modern industrial urban conditions are conducive of severe psychiatric disturbance of schizophrenic character. What might be the reason? In my view, the most likely explanation that has been propounded is that of the simple neglect that can and does occur in urban poverty. Not necessarily lack of love, but physical neglect of infants and children through mothers working, or economic harassment. Not all working-class mothers neglect their children. But consistent emotional and physiological care is not so readily possible under conditions of crowded working-class family life and lack of facilities, so often made worse by economic uncertainty and despair.

The presumptive conclusion, therefore, is that there is increasing evidence from epidemiological studies that improved economic conditions in urban industrial society may in time reduce the incidence of development of the more severe forms of mental illness, as manifested in schizophrenia, by means of the effect upon the structure and content of relationships within families.

VII

I have tried to illustrate some connections between social organization and behaviour – moving from the micro-social region of industrial work, through the relation between work and family life, to the impact of the macro-social structure upon human relations and emotional development. These considerations, it may be apparent, might have implications that are very close to home for those of us who are concerned with the care and treatment of psychiatric patients in mental hospitals. For hospital organization itself can, and does, suffer from some of the same unclarities in organization found in industry. To take the problem equivalent to that of the works manager I described earlier, who is accountable for the effective running of a hospital? What is the authority of the consultants? Of the nurses? Of the administrators? And for what are they held accountable? And by whom? And what are the criteria of assessment – is it a matter of good housekeeping? tidiness? well-behaved patients? discharge rate? or lack of trouble? These questions do not have ready and easy answers.

But it may also be asked if it really matters whether or no the authority and accountability, the organization and administration, are all that explicit. And the answer to that question is fairly clear. We are familiar, for example, with the Stanton and Schwarz studies, which describe so vividly the manipulations that are open to patients when the relationships between doctors and nurses and orderlies are disturbed by lack of explicitness about how far the accountability and authority of each extends. The attendant stresses in the professional sphere may be capitalized on by patients, and not always to their betterment.

And not only is the question of the role of the doctors and nurses important. We have to ask also, what is the role of the patient in a well-run psychiatric hospital? Studies such as those by Goffman[1] and by Caudill[2] show the extent to which the proper role of the patient is so often either to be a patient or to be well by spontaneous remission. As a patient, there are certain required forms of behaviour *vis-à-vis* doctors, nurses, orderlies and other patients – and in many situations this expected form of behaviour is to be mentally ill. How far behaviour can be changed when we change the organizational structure and role expectations is shown by what happens when wards are organized in such a manner that patients become active participants, rewarded if they work and deprived if they do not. So-called deteriorated patients show themselves to be capable of very lively behaviour, much more in contrast. But of course, life in the ward does not so smoothly follow the former settled routines.

We have a long way to go in sorting out the optimum organizational requirements of all hospitals, including mental hospitals. It is likely to be a difficult task, since hospitals with their multiplicity of interacting professional and administrative groups, are among the most complex of social institutions. But the problem has begun to be tackled, and when optimum types of organization have been formulated, I believe that a major contribution will have been made to mental hospital treatment.

VIII

In general terms then, the problem of mental illness must be tackled on many fronts: individual treatment; treatment of

[1] Goffman, E., *Asylums* (Anchor Books, Doubleday, 1961).
[2] Caudill, W., *The Psychiatric Hospital as a Small Society* (Harvard University Press, 1958).

families; educational programmes; and by the elucidation and establishment of requisite social institutions to provide a supportive social frame within which sound behaviour patterns can be encouraged and reinforced. Widespread mental health calls for a healthy social surround. But in fact, society is in turmoil, and still has to learn to live in large groups. We are only at the beginning of an understanding of how individuals interact with each other and with their broader social environment.

The nature of a healthy society and requisite social institutions tends to be a matter for political debate. As human scientists, we can no longer let the matter rest there. Psychiatric and social research combined may have much to say about how society ought to organize itself, in terms of the requirements of the mental life of the individual, upon which ultimately the good of that society will depend. In short, it is to be hoped that we are entering an era in which social policy and organization will be determined not by political debate and negotiation alone, but by political debate informed and reinforced by the hard findings, concepts and formulations from research into the actualities of the relationship between the individual and the social institutions we inhabit.

I I

Guilt, Conscience, and Social Behaviour

I

What makes civilized social behaviour possible? Here is a
question that has engaged the interest of men through countless
centuries. How is it that it is possible to have laws to which
people on the whole will conform? Why do most conform?
Why do some break the laws? And most particularly, why do
most of us not break the law, even when we might gain con-
siderably from doing so and there is no apparent risk of being
caught?

It is this question that I wish to consider in this article. For
contained within it is the intriguing question of the sense of
morality, of conscience, of justice, which we all have, and which
causes us to behave in accord with externally prescribed modes
of conduct and behaviour. To understand the nature of this
inner sense of conscience is of the greatest importance. It is the
key to an understanding of the process whereby we learn to live
in our families, among our friends, and in society at large, the
process of the socialization of the individual. In order to
understand it, we should have to understand where our social

M

awareness and conscience came from; how it develops; why it is very strong in some and weak in others; why it is sometimes felt as harsh and oppressive; and why it is sometimes accompanied by rejection and rebelliousness.

To these questions, psycho-analysis has certain solutions to offer. These solutions stem from Freud's profound and original insight into the nature of human guilt, an insight which marked a great step forward in our understanding of human behaviour. It set the stage, as we shall see, for understanding that social relations, and concern for law and order, are not just imposed upon the individual, but result from active needs and strivings whose roots are established in earlier infancy.

Before proceeding further, let me first make clear the sense in which I shall be using the term guilt, for there are two main meanings and I wish to focus only upon one. The use with which many of you will be most familiar is that in which some-one is held guilty of having done something wrong: he is pro-nounced guilty by a judge, or by some other authority, or by his parents, or friends, in short a judgement of guilt from outside the person. The second use is that of guilt in the sense of how someone feels, that of personal guilt. You will know that these two uses are not the same, for it is possible, and indeed not un-common, to be held to be guilty of some misdeed but not to feel guilty about it. And, psychologically even more interesting, it is possible to feel guilty without having done anything which others would declare you to be guilty of, and yet to feel intensely guilty for some reason or other which may be vague – perhaps for thoughts we might have – or even for reasons which may be entirely out of the reach of our conscious minds.

It is upon this latter sense of the feeling of guilt that psycho-analysis has concentrated its attention. It is this feeling of guilt, or conscience, that is so fundamental to our capacity to become social beings. It is the mental process that Freud attributed to the mental structure which he named the super-ego, but I shall return to that in a moment.

Everyone knows what it is like to feel guilty. In its mildest form it is that sense of having done wrong, of something inside you speaking to you and telling yourself that it was wrong. In more intense form, it is that inner voice criticizing and castigating. It can be ceaseless and unrelenting, taking over our thoughts completely, until it seems that everyone must know what is going on in our minds. Our expression may change and become suffused with the guilt we feel within. We are forced, in order to assuage the guilt, to do something about our wrongdoing – to make reparation in some way and so gain relief from inner judgement. In still more extreme form, guilt may reach pathological proportion, leaving the person abject and depressed, a prey to unconscious feelings of having harmed or damaged or destroyed others, of being worthless and of meriting only the severest punishment and retribution.

II

Freud's first big breakthrough to an understanding of the norms which control our behaviour from inside, came from his analysis of the Oedipus complex. The theme is well known. The young child, between the ages of four and six, deeply attached to his mother with a strong unconscious sexual bond, finds himself in an unconscious rivalry situation with his father. Jealous of his mother, envious of his father, he unconsciously wishes his father dead. Overwhelmed by anxiety, and seized by guilt, he suffers acute disturbance. How is the conflict to be resolved? In Freud's terms the boy, suffering severely from the threat of being castrated, turns to his father and identifies with him. He takes over his father's standards for his own – in other words internalizes these standards, and takes over the responsibility for the control of his own behaviour.

By this process, the resolution of the Oedipus complex results in a situation in which standards of conduct that previously existed in the form of external parental remonstrance and control, now become the boy's own internal standards, by virtue of which he tries to control his own behaviour. The father's voice from without becomes the voice from within. As Freud has put it, the super-ego is the inheritor of the Oedipus complex.

By the super-ego, Freud refers to a mental organization, a structural concept, which differentiates out from the ego. Super-ego formation takes place as a result of identification with outer figures – or, in more general terms, with external objects. This identification occurs by means of introjection, the process of taking in and establishing the object inside. The super-ego thus built up acts as though above the ego, scrutinizing our thoughts and impulses and exercising a moralistic censorship and control.

These identification processes, as Freud has shown, are fundamental to all group formations. Thus, for example, in religious groups, identification takes place with the religious figure – God, or Christ, or Buddha, or Mohammed – so that all followers of the particular faith introject or contain a common set of precepts or controls and can behave in common ways through this identification. By the same means we can learn to obey common laws.

But to describe this process is to raise numberless additional questions. How is it that external standards become internalized? What does internalized mean? What kind of mental structure must be assumed when we speak of internalized parents? To put it into more technical language, what is the nature of the process by which we identify with another person and not only accept his standards but internalize or introject them; that is to say, how does introjective identification come about?

Moreover, what are the factors which determine the nature of the Oedipus complex and its resolution? Why is it more intense in some children than in others? Why does it lead to constructive identification and super-ego formation in some, and why to a restrictive super-ego in others?

The answers to some of these questions were indicated by Karl Abraham. Abraham picked up Freud's formulations and considered them in terms of the earlier developmental stages in the life of the child. He differentiated out the more primitive aspects of development, and laid the foundation for our understanding of infant mental life. Three main features of his theories are of particular interest to our present theme. First, his hypothesis of an early oral phase of development followed by an anal phase; second, the emphasis he placed upon the psychological processes of expulsion and incorporation, or projection and introjection; and third, his recognition of the great importance of Freud's double instinct theory – the interaction between love and hate.

In short, Abraham, before his untimely death in the mid-1920s, was actively concerned with unfolding the picture of development in infancy and the first few years of life. In that period he sought the sources of character formation and of psychological disturbance. The infant he perceived as torn by conflict between its loving impulses and powerful forces of hate and sadism. Its earliest relations were lived in terms of active fantasies of taking into itself the mother and breast upon which it suckled, either lovingly establishing them inside or sadistically biting and attacking them. This phase he saw as succeeded by one in which the primary emotional zone moved from the mouth to the anus, with the infant's external objects related to in terms of loving or sadistic incorporation or expulsion.

The significance of Abraham's formulations in terms of zones need not here concern us. The important thing is his description of the way the infant makes relations with the people in his outside world in terms of fantasies of taking them in and forcing them out; it is as though psychological relationships in the primitive recesses of the mind are carried out in terms of digestive processes – a process not unfamiliar to those of you who work with the problems of psychosis.

III

Upon these foundations has been constructed the particular picture of infant and early child development with which many British psycho-analysts have been associated, and which has come to be identified as the British school. The central figure in these developments has been Melanie Klein, and certain of her formulations may help to throw some further light upon the question of how moral standards and social behaviour come about.

Taking as her starting-point Freud's formulation of the Oedipus complex and its significance for the child's social relationships, Klein through her direct analysis of children from the age of three, observed the existence of much earlier processes akin to those hypothesized by Abraham. She noted especially the way in which these very young children, and infants, are in fact tied up in social relationships from the very beginning. The infant is actively concerned about its objects. It loves, and its love is intensified and supported when it is satisfied. It hates, and its hate is aroused and expressed when it feels frustrated. It responds in the very early months not only to parental handling and fondling and feeding, but also to parental expression.

The central point, however, is that the infant is an active agent. It feels and reacts. This active mental life of the infant is carried out in terms of very primitive fantasies akin to those suggested by Freud and elaborated by Abraham. I should like to try to outline these to you, so that those of you who have not had the good fortune to have direct experience of working with small children may get some feeling for what I am talking about. When I say that the infant is active, I mean that its reactions are not just the product of stimuli from its environment. It is not limited in its behaviour simply to responding to whatever happens to it – feeling satiated and content when fed, angry when frustrated, disturbed when ill. On the contrary, the infant (and certainly the young child) reaches out to its environment. It colours its environment with its own feelings. It makes assumptions about its environment, and its responses are duly influenced by those assumptions.

One of the infant's earliest tasks is to learn to sort out the difference between what is going on in reality in its environment, and what it unconsciously supposes to be going on as a result of its own fantasies and impulses. This task, described by Freud in terms of the process of reality-testing, is one that is never completed. Is there anyone of us who can lay claim to that perfection of understanding of himself and his world, that allows him to say that his perceptions and his judgements are unclouded by his own unconscious prejudices or by his impulses, wishes or desires? There is always the struggle, and reality is not always the victor, between the command of the reality principle on the one hand, and on the other hand, the pleasure principle dictating that we treat the world as though it is in fact taken up with nothing other than meeting our own needs, or at least ought to be.

It is out of this struggle to get through to reality that the early foundation of the super-ego, and thus of our capacity for social behaviour, is laid down. For, let us note, there is a very real sense in which ideas of good and bad exist from the very beginning. I say 'ideas' of good and bad, where perhaps I really mean feelings. It is that sense of satisfaction and love, or of frustration and hate and rage, that constitutes the primitive emotional substrate of the idea of goodness and badness.

It is in finding a formulation of how the mental life of the infant goes on that one of the greatest difficulties arises. How are we to describe in words that which occurs in feeling and behaviour but is not expressed in words? Moreover, the moment we try to put into words how an infant thinks and feels, it is all too easy to assume that we are attributing to the infant the selfsame words and ideas. With this difficulty in mind, let us attempt the task of outlining what in Melanie Klein's theory is the critical stage in child development prior to the Oedipus complex – that stage occurring during the second six months of life.

The infant is in a situation in which maturation has occurred to the point where conscious experience is becoming a significant part of total experience. The infant is aware of his relationship with his mother as a whole intact object, a person with continuity. The use of language is looming on the horizon. Under these circumstances, there is a problem of a special kind encountered, head-on and unavoidable – the problem of mixed feelings, of conflict, of ambivalence. The difficulty of this problem for human beings of all ages cannot be over-estimated. It is the problem of enduring shortcomings in those we love, of recognizing good features in those we dislike or oppose, of being capable of experiencing conflict, that simultaneity of positive and negative feelings, without turning away from conflict by emphasizing the good and denying the bad, or vice versa.

In the infant, the problem of handling conflict is a major one. To hate the one you love, because you are frustrated, can be a catastrophically frightening feeling when you are so dependent; to love the one you hate, exceedingly difficult when explosive fits of rage have taken over the whole of experience for the time being. But the main difficulty centres on the problems attendant upon ambivalence itself. Love and hate, simultaneously, for the same person, is the prime producer of feelings of guilt. Perhaps you yourselves may have no difficulty in recalling situations in which this kind of conflict resulted in guilt. In the infant, much more at the mercy of feeling, because feelings are so much less controlled, the conflict and the guilt are incomparably greater.

In order to appreciate the problem of the infant in its first encounter with the exigencies of the depressive position (the term used by Klein to refer to the complex of impulses, conflicts, anxieties and defences in the period under consideration) we must consider, however briefly, the situation that existed before, in the very earliest stages of development. Here evidence from child analysis, child observation, and the treatment of psychosis, and of psychotic phenomena in the neurotic and the so-called normal, suggests the following picture.

The infant is from birth impelled by very strong impulses of love and hate, the hating or destructive impulses being at the high point of the whole of the individual's life. Ambivalence, conflict, and guilt are avoided by splitting mechanisms. That is to say, the infant experiences either his good or bad impulses, his good or bad objects, separately and not together. He hates the bad, and loves the good, and deals with the opposite feelings in each case by denial and by projection. In essence when enraged, he puts his love and the parts of himself he loves, into his good objects (in the earliest phases into his mother and the feeding breast), and is able to hate the bad or frustrating mother and breast in an uncomplicated and fulsome manner. Or, vice versa, he splits off his hate and the parts of himself that he hates, and projects them into his bad objects, leaving himself free to love without reservation or conflict.

The price to be paid for this freedom from conflict is considerable. The good objects become idealized: and as such they are demanding of care. The bad objects become persecuting: they threaten and harass, and the persecution cannot be mitigated by love and reassurance, because of the splitting that has occurred.

Under these conditions, our first relationships with the world are established, and the precursors of the super-ego and of social relationships are formed. For along with the projection of its own impulses, the infant identifies with its objects, and introjects and incorporates them. With the concrete fantasies characteristic of this stage of development, the idealized objects in the surrounding world, with all their bountiful but demanding characteristics, are experienced as being inside as well as outside the infant. So too are the bad frightening objects into which the infant has projected his hate and destructiveness, and which are then experienced as internal persecuting and terrifying things.

So an internal world is built up in which good is good and bad is bad, and the groundwork of morality, the primitive sense of good and bad is fixed. The very earliest super-ego precursors are thus built up from a mixture of threatening internal bad objects, and of idealized demanding objects. The nature and strength of these processes will be much influenced by the infant's experiences, and by the strength of his own impulses. If he experiences normally good care and love, and if his own loving impulses are sufficiently strong and his hate of manageable proportion, these primitive social processes will not be too difficult. If, however, hate is strong, and frustration high, then the external and the internal world will be deeply split into highly idealized objects making strong demands, and very frightening persecutors. The resulting internal situation is nightmarish; and a foundation is laid for social relationships being experienced as harsh, and persecuting. This latter condition is important in criminality, where one of the main features is the failure to advance significantly past this state of splitting and projection mechanisms. The lovelessness so characteristic of the psychopathic criminal is not so much a matter of lovelessness, as the inability to bring loving impulses to bear upon his own hostility and destructiveness. By maintaining the separation, the capacity for guilt does not develop, for he remains totally unconcerned about the objects of his hate. His love is split off and denied, or directed elsewhere.

IV

Given an adequate balance between love and hate, the infant is able to advance towards the depressive position. His growing capacities and skills strengthen the reality sense, and make him more aware of the wholeness of his objects. Splitting mechanisms are weakened; and he begins to recognize that the objects he hates and those he loves are the same. As ambivalence and conflict enter the mental scene extremes of pain are experienced. For under the influence of the primitive processes we have described, the infant's hate is experienced as destructive of the very things he loves. When hate takes over, the infant has fantasies of having injured and damaged his loved objects.

Anxiety characterized by depression and feelings of loss set in. The depressive reaction encountered is to set the scene for every subsequent experience of loss. Where the experience of the infant has been such that the internal situation is not too threatening, then love and sadness can be felt when conflict occurs. The sense of guilt can develop, not too harshly, but enough to help the infant to want to make reparation to the object he has in fantasy so miserably treated and damaged. The function of guilt expressed by the emerging super-ego is to allow of concern for the object, without having to deny love, and the reassurance that the infant's own hate and destructiveness can be mitigated by love.

If the conditions are not so good, then refuge is sought in various defences. Reality is denied, and manic activity and playfulness take the place of guilt and concern. Or depression takes over, with inaction and immobility. Or there is a retreat, a regression, to the more primitive processes that I have described – with a return to splitting, projection and denial mechanisms, and the elimination once again of ambivalent feelings and conflict.

This kind of regression to primitive splitting mechanisms may occur at any time in life when a person is threatened by conflict and guilt, and does occur, at least to some extent, every time we experience loss and mourning. For the infant to move forward, to make progress towards an enhanced sense of reality, it must learn to cope with conflict and guilt. In order to do that, it must have sufficient confidence in its capacity to love to enable it to tolerate the pain of guilty or depressive anxiety. This pain reaches its peak at the time of weaning. The feeding breast is lost. Its loss is mourned – a process in which, as Freud has described, the fullness of love is gradually detached from the lost object, and life can go on. To the extent that the loss is experienced in unconscious fantasy as the result of the infant's own sadistic aggressiveness, mourning is warded off and inhibited, because to that extent the pain is too unbearable. 'I have destroyed what I love, I have lost it through my own hate' is the emotional experience. It is an experience that in later life when once we can talk, we express poignantly in terms of 'if only – if only I hadn't . . . if only I could have another chance'.

But time goes on. The infant becomes the young child. It can walk, and talk, and get about. The early stages of the oedipal situation begin. We can pick up the thread of our earlier theme and ask once again, what are the conditions under which conscious norms of conduct are established.

If the earlier depressive position has been successfully worked through, then the oedipal situation will be experienced as less threatening than it would otherwise be. For the child is less persecuted by its super-ego, and therefore is not subjected to such harsh treatment internally for its jealousy, and rivalry and hatred. At the same time, it has less need to project into its parents its own destructiveness and hate, and thus they are not experienced as persecuting disciplinarians, however firm or rigorous their handling. Under such conditions, parental admonition can be perceived in perspective, in proportion, for what it is, without too much of a persecutory increment from the child – that is, without the child unconsciously perceiving it as frightening and hostile.

If, however, there has been a less successful working through of the depressive position, the child through its own projections of hate and badness into its parents, will be subject to an oedipal situation which will be experienced as more harsh and persecuting than it would otherwise be.

Thus, in short, under moderately good conditions, the full-scale super-ego, with its norms of behaviour, will precipitate out, and parental norms identified with and internalized in a constructive way. Codes of conduct can be accepted and conformed to, in an understanding way. Under unconscious persecuting conditions, the parental norms become yet a further harsh admonishing voice added to the super-ego.

V

From these considerations it would appear that our ability to conform to the norms and codes and laws that make human relationships possible is not just something forced upon us from outside. We start out in a situation of primitive object relations – social relations – and with an endowment of conflicting love and hate that takes us into active relationships with our objects. As a result of ambivalence and conflict, we develop early on a primitive sense of concern for our objects, and for what we do to them. In short, the live human being *is* concerned about others, and does not have to wait to be taught through outside pressure to be concerned about them.

The basis of social concern lies in the capacity for guilt which results from internal conflict. By virtue of guilt and concern we seek for external support for our good and constructive social impulses. Such support, to be found initially in early maternal care, is later sought from both parents, and then from teachers, the law, and other parental surrogates.

The existence of deeply rooted norms of justice and social cohesion has been borne in upon me by my experience in research in social and industrial relations. Here, underneath the turmoil and conflict on the surface, one finds underlying norms of equity, justice and fairness, even, for example, in such conflict areas as payment. The problem is to formulate policies that express these deep and primitive norms, so that justice can be seen to be done. Indeed, one of the conclusions to which we are led, is that if a sound mental health programme must include not only treatment but prevention, then prevention must include attention to our modes of social organization and our laws – the way we organize and run our schools, our industries, and our government; the way we construct our laws; the way in which every institution which mediates social relations is established.

To take but one example, I cite the inability of our society to control inflation without unemployment, and our growing acceptance of the notion that 3 per cent unemployment may have to be tolerated. We cannot afford to tolerate this notion for there is nothing that society can arrange that is so calculated to bring the primitive anxieties we have described so forcibly into play. And these primitive anxieties are not allayed by unemployment benefits, for in addition to the threat of financial deprivation there is also the threat of role-deprivation, i.e. deprivation of the right to participate in a social relationship with others, in creating our economic security. And unconsciously the full impact is felt in terms of deprivation of an effective social relationship in the early care and feeding situation. Paranoid anxieties are added to objective economic fears, and the mixture is intensely disruptive for the mental health of the individual.

Sound social relationships and soundly constructed law are thus immensely important for the psychological health and well-being of the members of society. They support the constructive impulses in individuals and reduce the amount of projection of hate and destructiveness. For when our laws and codes are not soundly based (as, for example, they are not where differential payment and reward are concerned) not only are they perceived as manifestly unfair, but they attract masses of projected guilt and persecution. The effect is that society itself, or its leaders, are experienced not just as bad or inadequate, but as persecuting and beyond repair. Paranoid attitudes are reinforced and expressed in such ways as political splits, prejudices, xenophobia, and in social withdrawal, strife and chaos.

One point, however, perhaps needs mentioning before I finish. In all that I have described, I have assumed that in the connections between the adult and his laws and social behaviour, there are also still in play the more primitive processes which so markedly colour the quality of an individual's perception of and relation to his society. I tried to illustrate this process in showing how the child's development in the depressive position, and in the oedipal situation, could readily regress or throw back to the earlier and more primitive processes of splitting and projection. It would appear that I am suggesting that the adult carries with him the whole of his past. And, of course, that is what I am suggesting. For that is one of the basic tenets of the psycho-analytic model of human behaviour. The accretions of experience are piled on layer after layer, and, as Freud has described, can be observed in the same way that archaeological findings are exposed layer after layer, deeper and deeper into the past.

Unlike archaeological remains, however, the earlier psychological layers remain active. They are dynamic, and affect the on-going psychological field. As we work out our current social relationships, we are influenced by the extent to which our more primitive conflicts and reactions are aroused and come unconsciously into our perceptions and responses.

Thus it is that a healthy society, like good psychotherapy, helps to support the healthy side of human behaviour. As we work out our social relationships, so too do we work through again and again the more primitive conflicts, anxieties and guilt that we carry with us from our infant and our childhood days. And most important, our reality sense, and our concern for others which we ought never to take for granted, is thereby reinforced and extended.

I 2

Psychotic Anxieties and the Sense of Justice

I

The aspiration towards the discovery of inherent norms of justice in mankind has been a recurring theme in the theories of law propounded by jurists for the past two thousand years – through Aristotle, Cicero, St Augustine, Aquinas, Locke, Hume and Kant. It is the theme of natural law. Because, however, the concept of natural law has been founded upon moral, ethical, political and religious imperatives, it has fallen into lesser repute among present-day thinkers.

Psycho-analytical experience and theory strongly support the intuitive basis of the theory of natural law, even if they differ radically from any of the philosophically derived arguments propounded to establish the theory. This comes especially from Freud's conception of super-ego development and function. The sense of what is right and wrong, just and unjust, fair and unfair develops in early childhood, and sets the groundwork for what appear later as the more sophisticated judgements of justice and of culpability.

The further developments of Freud's work which are associated with Melanie Klein have served to strengthen the bond between psycho-analytical theory and the conception of natural law. I refer particularly to her concepts of the early infantile development of the experience or sense of good and bad objects, good and bad impulses, and of the primordial super-ego and primal guilt; and her discovery of the unconscious psychotic anxieties and processes, deriving from early infancy, which disturb and distort normal adult behaviour. These conceptions reinforce the implication of Freud's theories that there is a normal sense of morality and justice which would emerge and express itself were human behaviour not so commonly and intensely influenced by personality disorders stemming from the force of those psychotic anxieties. The possibility thus emerges of laying a basis for making objective judgements about human values and norms of justice.

I propose to combine these leading notions from psycho-analysis with certain data from my social-analytic work to establish that in fact an empirical science of human law may be a practical endeavour. In order to preclude any possible confusion between this scientific approach to human behaviour, and the moral, ethical, religious or political approach of the natural law theorists and philosophers, I shall use the concept of requisite law rather than that of natural law. By requisite, I mean reality-determined, required by the real properties of the situation, or, as the dictionary has it, required by the nature of things. By the phrase requisite law, I shall refer to law which is required to facilitate psychic equilibrium in the individual members of a society and social equilibrium within the society as a whole. I shall hope to show that the establishment of such equilibrium in individuals and in the social groups they compose is entirely possible, so long as their behaviour is not too much under the domination of unconscious psychotic anxieties and processes.

II

We each have a sense of when we are being treated fairly or unfairly. Equally, we know, or feel, when we are behaving fairly or unfairly towards others. How we come to have these feelings, or make our judgements on these questions of the justice or injustice of others or of ourselves, may not be immediately apparent. Our sense of right or wrong, of grievance or gratitude, of self-righteousness or guilt, is not usually a thought-out reaction. It is a spontaneous response. And if the issue is one which seems important to us, our response is not only spontaneous but very strong.

Thus when a person does something which he considers to be deserving of some reward or recognition, he has a strong and definite sense of whether the reward he receives is an appropriate one. He is aggrieved if it is less than he deems fair. I will suggest that he is also chagrined or uneasy in some part of his mind if it is more than he feels is fair. Similarly, he has an aggrieved sense if he receives too great a punishment for a misdemeanour; and, I will suggest, he will somehow feel over-indulged and guilty if he gets off too lightly.

When we ourselves do the rewarding or punishing, we equally have an intuitive sense of whether we are being mean or over-generous with our praise or other reward, and of whether we are being cruel and sadistic or faint-hearted and indulgent in taking someone to task.

In considering these questions of right and wrong, fair and unfair, just and unjust, there are two points worth noting. First, we are dealing with relationships between people – with the differential entitlements of people under given circumstances. It is a question of what is fair, or right, or just, relative to someone else or to some others. What is fair for A depends on the entitlements of B, C and D. Whether it is a case of children assessing the fairness of parents or teachers, or employees assessing the fairness of their pay, or a citizen evaluating the fairness of his treatment by a magistrate or by the tax laws – there is a common thread: 'Why should I get only this much, when he got that?', or 'Why should he have forfeited only that, when I suffered so heavily?'.

The second point is that we are dealing not only with differential entitlements – with comparative treatment – but with a sense of balance or equilibrium. For something to be fair or just connotes that it is just right; neither too much nor yet too little. There is a point at which the amount of gratification or obligation of reward or punishment, just balances the act to which it is

N

connected. If the amount is any more or less then there is an imbalance, a disequilibrium. It is this disequilibrium which is experienced as a grievance or a feeling of persecution if the punishment is too great or the reward too small; and as guilt or fear of the envy of others if the punishment is too little or the reward too great.

III

It is a matter of common experience and common expectation that the expressed judgements of individuals on what is fair or unfair tend to be pretty unreliable – especially when their own interests are at stake. Two persons in conflict with each other over a question of their respective rights are hardly likely to be good judges of the merits of their own argument on the matter at issue. It would appear that we simply do not have any common individual standards or norms of justice which can be relied upon. We each apparently differ in our standards – our judgement being distorted by the operation of such mental processes as jealousy or envy, pride or vanity, omnipotent self-justification and aggrandisement or masochistic self-punishment. More, our needs and desires differ, as do our backgrounds, our experiences, our outlook on life. It would hardly be surprising, therefore, if we had widely varying notions about what constitutes justice.

And yet, our views cannot be all that fortuitous and individually determined. We do have laws to which we all conform, many of which are pretty universally held to be fair and just. The fact that law based on equity is possible as well as common law, suggests that deep inside us there are at least some common standards of justice. Both consciously and unconsciously we have a strong desire for law and order in our social relations, and we shun chaos and disorder, whatever unconscious impulses there may be to the contrary. However much the play of the pleasure principle may distort our desires and judgement, the reality principle demands that we bring reason into our relationships with one another.

The possibility that in the reality-bound conscious and unconscious areas of the mind we may have standards of equity which are the product of our psychological make-up, and which we share in common with each other, was brought home to me in the course of studying the reactions of employed people to the wage or salary they received for their work. This subject of payment is an explosive one. The levels of payment appear to be determined pretty exclusively by power bargaining. Actions based on principle do not appear to have much of a part in the process. Employers are assumed solely to want to buy labour at the lowest possible rate; and every employed person is assumed solely to be out to get for himself just as much as he can. The balance is thought to be held by the labour supply and demand situation, which strongly influences the power positions and thereby affects the precise level at which the bargain will finally be struck.

That these competitive and self-seeking motives operate there is little reason to doubt. They are revealed in the actual conduct of negotiations. And they are to be expected from the destructive impulses – the unconscious hate, greed, envy, omnipotence – which influence human behaviour. The question is whether there are not other motives and judgements which play a part as well. In particular, what part do the loving impulses – reflecting the operation of the life instinct – play? My evidence is that they have a most important influence, which is usually unrecognized.

I have had considerable opportunity to collect information about people's reactions to their pay. This information was gathered under the special conditions of a method of measuring the level of responsibility in individual jobs, so that each person's feelings about his payment for his work could be matched against the size of responsibility he was carrying in his job. What may at first sight seem a very surprising result was obtained. People carrying the same level of responsibility in their jobs stated the same level of payment as fair for the work they were being given to do. Regardless of their occupation – manual worker, clerk, engineer, chemist, factory manager, accountant managing director – regardless of what they were actually getting paid, and regardless of their income tax levels, each person carries a private opinion of what his job is worth – and these private opinions of individuals match – as though each person, without knowing it, is using precisely the same

standards in judging what he considers to be fair pay for his
work.

This pattern of felt-fair payment I have termed the equitable
work-payment scale. I have data (1958) from persons with
incomes of 4s. 6d. an hour at the bottom level, to £11000 per
annum at the top.

IV

When reactions of individuals to their payment are considered
in the light of their level of work, a characteristic pattern of
responses can be found. Payment at the equitable level is
intuitively experienced as fair relative to others, although there
may be a simultaneously held view that the economy as a whole
ought to provide a generally higher standard of living for all.
Deviations in payment below the equitable level are accompanied by feelings of dissatisfaction which become stronger the
greater the deviation. Deviations at the 10 per cent level lead
to an active sense of grievance, complaints or the desire to
complain, and, if no redress is given, an active desire to change
jobs, or to take collective action if an organized group is involved; these reactions become very strong at the 15 to 20 per
cent level of deviation.

Deviations above the equitable level (rare in the recent
inflationary situation) are accompanied by feelings of being
relatively well off as compared with others; at the 10 to 15 per
cent level of deviation there is a strong sense of receiving prefer-
ential treatment, which may harden into bravado. There is
an underlying feeling of unease about the arousal of jealous
resentment and envy in others and therefore uncertainty
about how long the relatively advantageous position can be
maintained.

The results suggest that it is not necessarily the case that each
one is solely out to get as much as he can for himself for his
work. There appear to be equally strong desires that each one
should earn the right amount – a fair and reasonable amount
relative to others.

At the same time, results were obtained which indicate that
each person has an intuitive judgement both of his level of

capacity and of the rate of progress of his capacity. Without presenting the results in detail, I can say that they show that we have a sharp intuitive judgement not only of whether our work is above or below our capacity, but also of just what the equitable level of payment is for work that would be consistent with our capacity.

In short, the upshot of these findings is that we each have an accurate intuitive judgement of:

(*a*) the level of work we are capable of doing;
(*b*) the actual level of work in our job;
(*c*) the payment that would be equitable for our job;
(*d*) the payment that would be equitable for work consistent with our capacity.

Most striking of all, however, were those findings connected with our intuitive comparisons of differentials. In the first place, the differential distribution of the equitable work-payment scale was felt to be fair. Suppose for example, £1000 a year is the equitable rate for the level of work A, and £5000 a year is the equitable rate for level of work B. And suppose that one person is working, say, as a designer in a job with level of work A, while another person is working in a job as a factory manager, with a level of work B. Then they will each feel they are being paid fairly relative to each other, if in fact the first is receiving £1000 and the second £5000. We feel that differential reward should go with differential responsibility carried.

Second, we have a strong intuitive sense of how we are faring relative to each other with respect to the equity of our pay. If our own payment is equitable, and others also are in receipt of equitable payment and not over-equity, then ferment over payment dies down to a low level. If, in addition, the conditions are such that there is opportunity for individuals to be employed at a level consistent with their capacity and to be progressed in work and payment at a rate consistent with their rate of progress in capacity, a state of equilibrium is created, with the induction of feelings of incentive towards work.

V

These findings and conclusions about our unconscious awareness of the degree of consistency between our capacity, work, earnings and consumption, and of the sense of balance and peace of mind which we tend to experience when we judge all to be in line with each other, may be at variance with everyday notions and with customary ways of talking about these matters. Work and money are so commonly the source of fantasies and day-dreams of wealth and creativity, comfort and security, greatness and power – or, in contrast, of masochistic fantasies of failure, impotence, and destructiveness. Our conscious self-evaluation and ambitions may be subject to gross fluctuation from depressed self-contempt to omnipotent aggrandizement, according to our mood as affected by our unconscious fantasies.

There is an apparent paradox in our outlook. Our unconscious awareness appears on the one hand to be unexpectedly realistic, and on the other hand and at the same time, to be irrational and emotionally unstable. This paradox is resolved once it is recognized that both processes – reality-tested awareness, and fantasy-dominated wish-fulfilment – may go on simultaneously in different parts of the unconscious mind. In the neurotic parts of our unconscious minds – and indeed in the psychotic-dominated pockets which are a part of the mental make-up of even the most normal persons – the picture we may have of ourselves and our economic condition may be totally at variance with that outlined in the foregoing assumptions.

It is likely that anyone who is capable of earning his own living has developed a sufficient degree of inner reality to be able to make the unconscious judgements about himself and his work of which I am speaking. But the existence of an unconscious assessment of our real capacity does not necessarily mean that this assessment is consciously accepted. Quite the contrary. Very few of us are capable of tolerating consciously an accurate and stable self-appraisal of our capacities and limitations. Some of our deepest unconscious defences against anxiety would be threatened – fantasy gratification and omnipotence, or, by contrast, self-effacement. We repress our knowledge of our true capacity, and retain it repressed and split-off in our unconscious mind. This splitting and repression makes for emotional oscillations in our conscious self-evaluation, while at the same time we may maintain our unconscious awareness of our adjustment to work reality. It is only in the exceptional mature and integrated person that the unconscious awareness of work and capacity becomes the sole or even the major determinant of conscious self-appraisal.

At the same time, just because our conscious picture of ourselves and our capacities may be heavily influenced by unrealistic unconscious fantasies, this does not necessarily imply that we will behave unrealistically in our work and economic life. The unconscious reality sense has an extremely powerful influence on behaviour in the real world, particularly in that area of the real world where behaviour is reality-tested by economic satisfaction or dissatisfaction, and, in the final analysis, by economic survival. We are always dealing, therefore, with a typically human situation of conflict in each person between the demands of fantasy satisfaction and the demands of reality.

VI

The existence of such powerful and consistently experienced norms as I have described may seem to make it difficult to explain why there is so much trouble about payment differentials and wage negotiations. How is it that the norms do not simply dominate the social scene and impose a pattern on the economic relationships between individuals such that the demands of equity are met? This question raises the fundamental issue of the difference in the effect on behaviour between unconscious intuitively comprehended norms and comparisons, and those norms when they are made explicit and consciously recognized and applied by appropriate objective social mechanisms.

In fact, the unconscious norms of equity play a larger part in wage and salary negotiations than is usually recognized or assumed. Notions of what is fair figure very prominently in these discussions and negotiations, and in the feelings of unrest which stimulate demands for increase. It is not possible for one group to get too great an increase without stimulating demands all round precisely on grounds of fairness and justice, mixed with jealousy, envy and hostility, which are also aroused. Thus considerations of what is fair and equitable play a considerable part in determining the general pattern of differentials in distribution of incomes in the country at large. But, in the absence of explicit and conscious control, there is room for sufficient uncertainty and unclarity to allow for trouble, but without the whole system necessarily breaking down.

The extent to which unconscious motivations enter into the continuing troubles over payment differentials may be observed if we consider for a moment what the situation would be if there existed requisite procedures for regulating payment in an equitable way.

Given requisite law controlling the actual relations between individuals, each one is more exposed in himself to his own unconscious destructive impulses and the anxieties which arise from them. The opportunity to express greed, envy, hate, jealousy, and dissatisfaction, by unconscious participation in social relations which in reality contain some economic inequity, is lost. To the extent, therefore, that we are influenced in our behaviour by unconscious psychotic processes, requisitely controlled social relations externally appear to threaten our inner psychic equilibrium. To demonstrate this point, I shall turn for a moment to consider the general question of psychic gratification and equilibrium.

VII

The gratifications we receive, and frustrations to which we are subjected, have two main aspects: the requisite, and the psychotic. The requisite gratifications are both physiological and symbolic. They include sexual gratification and the taking in and putting out of water, food and air necessary for the material maintenance of life. The symbolic gratifications include the intake and output of love and affection, the emotional aspect of material things, language and ideas, arts, competition and recognition – and all the activities which we think of as human activities, concerned with the psychological satisfaction of the individual and the carrying on of social relations.

As against the requisite content of gratification, the psychotic content of gratification and frustration is that which is based upon unconscious psychotic processes – upon unconscious magical fantasies – in which the gratification is disconnected from the reality of either the material or the symbolic content of the object which is taken in or given out.

The distinction I am making is one aspect of the distinction made by Freud in terms of the operation of the pleasure principle and the reality principle. In the deep unconscious mind, instinctual gratification gained under the dominance of the pleasure principle is connected with the hallucinatory gratification of the young infant.

It is to the work of Melanie Klein that we owe a much clearer understanding of these psychotic processes in the normal personality. According to her theories derived from her clinical experiences, unresolved psychotic anxieties – both persecutory and depressive – from earliest infancy, persist into adult life. The operation of these anxieties, and of the defences against them, influence our behaviour in a decisive manner. The most fundamental of these influences is the use unconsciously of violent splitting and fragmentation of objects, impulses and parts of the self as a defence against persecutory anxiety and internal persecutors. This violent splitting is accompanied by a type of projective and introjective identification which gives an unconscious hallucinoid aspect to all of our perceptions and experiences. That is to say, in addition to the normal requisite and symbolic content of our perceptions, in the deepest layers of our unconscious minds we deal with our objects in a quasi-psychotic manner. We concretely expel the products of our internal violent splitting and fragmentation into external objects, and partially behave towards those objects as though they really are the projected bits with which we are identified. Simultaneously, we violently introject the projectively modified object, and experience it inside as though it were concretely there.

These processes of violent projective and introjective identification based on unconscious splitting and fragmentation, must be distinguished from the normal processes of projection and introjection which lead to symbol formation and symbolic relationships. In symbolism, the external objects are perceived in their own right, the split-off and projected objects being experienced as in the external object, but not engulfing it.

According to the view outlined, every experience of gratification – material and symbolic – always contains an element of unconscious giving out and taking in of parts of our selves, our impulses and our internal objects. And we unconsciously experience similar processes of projection and introjection on the part of those to whom we are related in connection with the gratification. The hallucinoid content of the process, however, distorts our relation to the event, so that unconscious elements enter into our response based on our identification of the gratification or frustration with our own unconscious psychotic projections. It is these last elements which are responsible for the most intractable forms of personal disequilibrium, and which contribute heavily to the persistence of motivated injustice in human affairs.

VIII

If we were motivated only by loving impulses, our psychological processes would by implication be requisite ones, and there would be a certain balance or equilibrium in our material and symbolic gratifications and frustrations. Thus, for example, the intuitively equitable norms and standards which I have described would be free to operate unhampered. We would be in a state of quasi-stable equilibrium – that is to say, a state not of perfect equilibrium, but of ups and downs, in which we would seek requisite gratification, and accept requisite obligations, and experience satisfaction when we had had enough. Moreover, frustrations would be more effectively withstood. Frustration, indeed severe frustration – arising from real external difficulties or catastrophe, can be tolerated so long as it can be felt that everyone is suffering to the same relative degree; i.e. so long as it is experienced as equitably shared.

From the very earliest days, genuine gratification is derived from the experience and taking in of feeding and maternal care, and the putting out of excreta and love under the dominance of loving impulses. There is a minimum of greed and demandingness. The healthy ego knows when it has had enough. Sucking is followed by loving play and reparation, followed by sleep. Under these conditions the groundwork of the healthy super-ego is constructed – and the basis for healthy self-restraint and due regard for the needs of others is laid – through the introjection of the satisfying breast and mother, and identification with these objects and loving impulses.

But we are not simply under the influence of libidinal impulses. The death instinct, and its reflections in our destructiveness – in hate, greed, envy, jealousy, omnipotence – powerfully influences our behaviour. In the infant in the paranoid-schizoid position, it distorts gratification by threatening to destroy good objects and the self. Violent splitting and fragmentation, and projective and introjective identification, are used as defence against the resulting unconscious threat of annihilation. These defences lead to the establishment in the deep layers of the unconscious mind of primordial persecuting objects split off from primordial idealized objects. These objects disturb the formation of the super-ego, and adversely distort its functioning. In the depressive position, when whole objects are created, under the impact of greater integration and capacity for reparation, the ability to achieve symbolic along with material gratification is strengthened. But the deeper-lying unconscious relationship with the primordial idealized and persecuting objects remains. Gratification is always tinged with a degree of disappointment, either through shortcomings in the idealized content of the object, or unconscious fantasies of annihilation by its persecuting contents. Both frustration and punishment are experienced as intensely persecuting. At this level of mental functioning there is no differential justice. There is either persecutory injustice threatening the self, or guilt-provoking favouritism depriving one's good objects of their due share, and stimulating their hatred and envy.

The strength of these psychotic processes determines how much we fall short of a genuine quasi-stable equilibrium in our psychic life and limits our capacity to tolerate justice and law and order. Superimposed upon the requisite and genuine quasi-stable equilibrium is the pseudo-equilibrium of successful defences against psychotic anxiety. This equilibrium is a pseudo-equilibrium because it is not based upon positive satisfaction. It arises rather from schizoid and manic defences which wall off and segregate persecutory and depressive anxiety, but do not resolve them. The individual is therefore constantly threatened by recrudescence of anxiety, and the pseudo-equilibrium likely to be broken.

Our defences against psychotic anxiety – other than by retreat into psychosis – are markedly enhanced by evidence of the existence of external injustice, and by internal evidence of resulting unfair frustration produced by the greed, cunning, dishonesty, selfishness, and deceit of others. Such external conditions constitute a projection screen which support splitting and denial mechanisms. The basic psychological mechanism is that of nursing a grievance.

Nursing a grievance for purposes of self-justification is an everyday phenomenon. Children often refuse to be humoured when they feel persecuted or guilty. Adults harbour grievances against each other. In the clinical situation, patients frequently develop and harbour grievances, in the transference relationship, as for example in the following case of Mrs X, a forty-five-year-old divorced woman. She re-experienced her oedipal conflicts in her resentment of my being married. She envied my wife for enjoying what the patient perceived as an ideally good marriage, and was jealous of me for giving my wife such ideally good care and attention. She was equally grudging of the analysis she received from me. On one occasion, for example, when she consciously thought my interpretations were especially accurate and good, she became hostile and spiteful. She hated everyone, she said, and felt I was trying to get her to be nice, and to like everyone.

From previous sessions, I was able to analyse this material in terms of her nursing a grievance against me representing her mother, and particularly against the feeding breast. She felt she had destroyed her mother's peace of mind and sanity, and at a deeper level, the creativeness and goodness of the breast. She, therefore, projected her destructive impulses, her envy, her greed, her unfairness, into me representing her mother and the breast. I was then unfair and mad, and good to my wife in order to make the patient jealous and envious. She in turn was therefore justifiably aggrieved. But if I appeared to give her good analysis, much of the justification for her grievance was removed. She was then more exposed to her own guilt-ridden anxieties, and thus begrudged and resisted the analysis – a typical negative therapeutic reaction.

She then recalled occasions when she was a very small child, when her mother would tickle her tummy in order to get her out of severe temper tantrums. She responded to this treatment overtly with glowering rejection, but inwardly with delight. From this and subsequent material, we were able to explore how she introjected her good mother and good breast, and tried to get rid of her own bad impulses, parts of herself, and persecuting objects, by projection into external objects. Being aggrieved and nursing the grievance thereby took on a double function, which I think is probably present to some extent in all grievances. She was aggrieved, in the sense of *having a grievance against* the split off and projected bad objects; and she was aggrieved, in the sense of being *grief-stricken about* her destroyed good objects, towards which she tried to make reparation by internally nursing them.

When anxiety, guilt and despair became unbearable, she would become confused, resort to drugs and alcohol, and precipitate her affairs into a chaotic state. She blamed all the people she attacked, for her troubles, and was aggrieved by her unconsciously motivated perception of their hostility. She had little capacity to enjoy gratification, and accept obligations, without feeling guilty and persecuted. A certain amount of external chaos was essential to her defences against her anxieties. Without this chaos, her self-justification was weakened. To the extent that ideas of justice entered into her world, it was the obsession of a harsh and severe super-ego. Real ideas of justice were displaced by chronic grievance.

IX

I have illustrated the nursing of grievances, and unconscious need for external chaos, because I consider these mechanisms to be the paradigm for the psychological forces which inhibit and distort the play of equity in social life. Self-justification swamps justice. Or, contrariwise, equity and justice are unconsciously perceived as threatening to the denial by means of self-justification which is used as a defence against persecutory and depressive anxiety.

Where payment questions are concerned, the reflection can be observed in social processes of the defences against psychotic anxiety I have mentioned in the brief case illustration. A prominent feature is the chaos and confusion, which can be blamed on 'the other side'. Splitting is complete. Our side is right. Their side is wrong. 'They' are accused of being greedy. Everyone is seen as out for all he can get. Denial of reality is very strong, as witness the internal inconsistency of the majority of the arguments and counter-arguments put forward in favour of one case or another.

Triumph and the exercise of power, and the attribution of omnipotence to one's own arguments and of omniscience to one's leaders, are prominent features. Unprincipled cunning in bargaining, and mutual vilification, are accepted as a part of the game.

This social situation gives full scope for the concealed and socially sanctioned play of greed and envy, including, on occasions, carrying chaos to the point where there is likelihood of spoiling it for everyone – the natural fruit of envy. Hostility is rife, and open aggression often occurs. Genuine exploitation is in fact carried out by the most powerful side. There is the fullest opportunity for idealization of one's cause, grievances against the exploiting persecutor, self-justification, and a general playing out of schizoid and manic defences in mass social processes which effectively obscure the unconsciously collusive participation of each individual person composing the mass.

But all the time, balancing these psychotically dominated social processes, are the reality dominated forces, and the strong impulses in individuals towards genuine gratification and equilibrium. The effective operation of these forces is partially blocked by the fact that conscious intellectual clarification of the problem is inhibited by the psychotic anxieties and processes. The development of principle and law is therefore held back, so that the constructive strivings get little or no support from externally established requisite knowledge and social institutions.

Nevertheless, as the findings on equity in payment demonstrate, the unconscious intuitive awareness of individuals about differential entitlement and equity set a frame, a limit, to the play of psychotic anxieties in social relations.

These norms of equity are a part of healthy super-ego functioning. If, for example, the members of one group go too far in blackening the character of members of the opposing group, projecting into them their own malice, greed and destructiveness, then the sense of requisite guilt, derived from the healthy areas of the super-ego, becomes too powerful, and inhibits further irrational behaviour.

It is thus in connection with the healthy areas of the ego and the super-ego that social life, justice and law have their effect. The sense of justice in the individual is most actively tapped by laws and regulations which conform to our unconscious norms of right and wrong and which thus contribute to genuine equilibrium in the individual. The explicit formulation of law allows the healthy parts of the super-ego to be projected into the institutions which mediate the law, and to be reintrojected and reinforced by contact with the consciously recognized and accepted social consensus. The good law symbolizes the good conscience; and the scales of justice symbolize genuine equilibrium in the individual as much as they do the act of weighing the evidence.

X

Because the concept of natural law has been founded upon moral, ethical and political imperatives, it is not of use for our present purposes. In its place, I would substitute the concept of requisite law – that is to say, law based upon scientifically discovered and objectively demonstrable, generally occurring, human norms. It is law which springs from the inherently orderly parts of the mind of men, and which, when correctly understood, is as immutable as is our basic psychological make-up.

The discovery by Melanie Klein of the unconscious psychotic anxieties and processes in normal adult behaviour, makes it possible to distinguish between requisite and non-requisite law, in terms of the extent to which these psychotic processes and unconscious collusions are involved. This discrimination between right and wrong, in terms of the intensity of psychotic gratification, is one example of what is likely to be one of her fundamental contributions – her extension of the work begun by Freud, to lay a basis for making objective judgements about human values.

One of the main tasks of law and of legal procedures and institutions is to establish in a manifest and external form the conditions governing the duties and entitlements of individuals and corporate bodies in relation to each other and to the state, when interests overlap and encroach upon each other. In its fullest sense, requisite law should not only express what we might consciously consider reasonable and just in the sorting out of conflicting needs and requirements were we not ourselves personally involved in the matter. It ought to express the deep unconscious sense of order and norms of fairness which, given unfettered outlets, would suffuse our conscious awareness with the impulse to achieve what is sane and balanced in human relations, and would provide the solid intuitive foundation for that conscious achievement.

Side by side with the unconscious constructive and balanced sense of individuals, occur the psychotic processes which we have considered. It is these processes, based on anxiety and conflict, which cause such profound distortion of the way we see things in practice, and sway our judgement away from balanced and equitable conclusions towards unconscious collusive involvement in psychotic group processes designed to relieve anxiety and personal confusion and chaos, regardless of the cost in social injustice and strife. In our minds, a sense of natural law and order coexists with the impulse towards lawlessness and chaos. It is the function of the externalized statement of requisite law to reify the internal sense of law and order we possess, so that we can exert conscious effort and employ our intellect in negating the effects of the outpouring of unconscious and disruptive forces into our social relationships.

The equitable society, then, is a lawful society in the deepest sense of lawful. Its laws bolster the rational strivings of its members. And they inhibit the dumping into its social relationships of the irrational hate, envy, greed and omnipotence which undermine those relationships and the institutions which mediate them.

To the extent that requisite laws exist, we are gripped more firmly in contact with our inner selves. These conditions are among those essential to psychological health and integration. They support the strengthening of character and the growth of moral courage. To achieve and maintain these conditions we must understand the reality of the power of our unconscious destructiveness, and equally learn to trust the power of our unconscious striving towards psychic equilibrium and to express those strivings in the form of conscious and explicit norms and requisite social institutions.

13
Psycho-Analysis and the Current Economic Crisis

The centenary of Sigmund Freud comes at a time of perplexing economic uncertainty. We have the spectacle of apparently irrational and self-destructive economic impulses at work causing inflation. This state of affairs would surely have attracted Freud's scientific attention. Despite government exhortation, wage spiralling continues. And despite the fact that each wage increase no longer means any very real consequent gain in standard of living, there is no immediate sign of abatement of wage pressure.

One of the very important factors causing self-control of our economic relations to elude us is the perpetual conflict between rival wage-earning groups and between economic classes. The outcome of this conflict is to restore an unrecognized and unspecified, but nevertheless very delicate, balance in the level of our money-incomes relative to each other. The potency of this rivalry between us, arising in one region after another because of repeated disturbances in the pattern of real money differentials between groups, has become a menace to our economic survival.

This paper aims to show how the work of Freud – and the

scientific development he set in train through his successors – is directly and urgently relevant to the resolution of our current economic and industrial dilemma. The attempt to apply Freud's work in this way need occasion no surprise. In his wide-ranging studies, Freud went well beyond the subject of emotional disturbance in the individual, applying himself to the analysis and understanding of the play of unconscious factors in group psychology. Group rivalry on a scale approaching self-destructiveness is a theme at the heart of psycho-analytic endeavour. And when this group rivalry is concerned with economic and material security and gain, then it may seem self-evident that powerful unconscious forces are likely to be at work.

Our Unconscious Evaluation of our Work

It is a bitter paradox that our recent years of peace-time full employment – the first such years in the modern history of our nation – have been attended by calamitous disputes over payment.

What is required for balance and self-control to be regained is a structure of payment which would assure to each of us a return for our work in line with the responsibility we carry. So long as we each received comparable payment for comparable responsibility, the problem of differentials would be diminished and possibly resolved. Such a view is widely accepted in theory. Agreement upon this goal of economic fairness and equity is, however, much easier to realize than agreement upon the means of achieving the goal.

The problem of resolving the acute rivalries stimulated by payment differentials is commonly regarded as intractable. We are each of us prone to regard the other as out to get just as much as he can. Greedy self-interest is supposed to have supplanted a responsible giving of fair work in return for one's pay. Interest and satisfaction in doing a good job are presumed to have been lost. Supply and demand are held to rule the labour market – shortages of some types of skill supposedly allowing those in possession of such skills to hold the community to ransom for excessive incomes solely because of scarcity.

Our psycho-analytic experience would warn us, however, not to accord too ready acceptance to these commonly held views. I propose the suggestion that an orderly pattern of behaviour can be scientifically observed within the apparent disarray and jumble of our procedures for regulating payment and work in industry; that there is, in fact, a systematic national wage and salary scale which is unconsciously perceived, understood, and, most important, put to use; and that we are each well aware, unconsciously, not only of our own true level of capacity for work, but also to what extent we are being accorded responsibility consistent with our capacity, and payment consistent with that responsibility within the national scale of earning. This is not to say that we always behave in accord with our unconscious awareness of this reality, and that we never behave irrationally or neurotically.

At the same time, I shall endeavour to show how a gross denial, constituting a sort of psycho-pathology on a national scale – a mass psychotic process in which we all unconsciously participate – inhibits scientific recognition of these realities of work relationships and of individual motivation. It may, then, be possible to demonstrate that some of our general conceptions about economic behaviour are themselves the projection of our own unconscious motives – a projection caused by unconscious anxieties which make us blind to the most commonplace and ubiquitous characteristics of everyday social and economic relationships.

Capacity Growth Curves

As I have shown elsewhere,[1] if we study the pattern of real earnings of individuals, a certain regularity may be observed. A curve of earnings can be found for each person (employed in industry) which commonly shows a regular progression. If we take a large number of such individual curves and examine their general pattern, they arrange themselves in a regular pattern in accord with a family of biological growth curves.

The most striking and, perhaps, unexpected regularities are found when we consider our intuitive and unerring judgement of our own capacity growth curves. Conformance of our earnings to a normal curve is accompanied by the sense that we are getting a proper income within the current payment levels.

[1] Jaques, Elliott. *Equitable Payment* (London: Heinemann Educational Books, 1961, and Penguin Books, 1967).

More may be desired, but nevertheless we experience a sense of fair pay for our worth relative to others.

Deviations from this regular progression are experienced as follows. Deviation upwards feels like being overpaid relative to others. When overpayment of this kind is experienced for any length of time, guilt and anxiety set in. Compulsive expenditure with purchasing characterized by waste and ugliness ensues – expenditure described by the economist as naïve ostentation beyond the norm of conspicuous consumption. Or an equally compulsive hoarding may occur.

Deviation downwards (the most common circumstance in an inflationary economy) is accompanied by a sense of underpayment. Poor morale is to be found under these circumstances, with symptoms ranging from anger and disaffection with pressure for increase in pay, to depressed acceptance of the situation and feelings of worthlessness.

Our intuitive response to deviations from our expected earning level can be precisely observed. Deviations of 2 per cent are just noticed. Deviations above 10 per cent evoke strong feelings and the impulse to leave one's job. And if a man is asked to state what he thinks he will be earning in, say, five years' time, he will name a figure remarkably close to that to be concluded by extrapolating his capacity growth curve. His prediction is unaffected by whether or not he might be considered financially ambitious. The same conformance appears in the man who says he needs to gain more money and in the man who says money is not of much importance to him.

The Conflict between Unconscious and Conscious Evaluations of Work
This statement of our unconscious knowledge of the degree of consistency between our capacity, work, and earnings, and of the sense of balance and of peace of mind with respect to them we tend to experience when we judge all three to be in line with each other, may be at variance with everyday notions and with customary ways of talking about these matters. Work and money are so commonly the source of fantasies and daydreams of wealth and creativity, comfort and security, greatness and power – or, in contrast, of masochistic fantasies of failure, impotence, and destructiveness. Our conscious self-evaluation and ambitions may be subject to gross fluctuation

from depressed self-contempt to omnipotent aggrandizement, according to our mood as affected by our unconscious fantasies. Thus we may all have experience of individuals whose thinking was dominated by fantasy – consciously and unconsciously – for greater or shorter periods in their careers, and who made a failure of it.

There is an apparent paradox in our outlook. Our unconscious knowledge of our capacity is realistic and stable. Our conscious self-evaluation – connected with unconscious fantasy as well as with unconscious knowledge – may be irrational and emotionally unstable. Unconscious knowledge and the dictates of fantasy may be at odds. These conflicts between the demands of reality and of fantasy have been elaborated by Freud into one of the keystones of his thoughts on the ultimate problems of life – his theory of the conflict between the pleasure principle and the reality principle in human behaviour.[1] This theory can be applied with benefit to the analysis of behaviour at work.

Freud has described how under the influence of the pleasure principle, adjusted to a primary mode of operation, pain is evaded and immediate gratification of impulses is sought. The demands of self-preservation, however, lead to the partial replacement of the pleasure principle by the reality principle. We give up our striving for immediate gratification of whatever impulse happens to feel most urgent. The limitations of what is possible in reality are recognized and accepted, and temporary pain and frustration are endured. Eventual satisfaction is by this means assured – satisfaction within the limits afforded by reality, but real satisfaction and not the substitute gratification of fantasy which in the end cannot satisfy genuine material needs.

At work especially the requirements of reality have to be subserved – continued employment and survival depend upon it. If anyone takes on work at a level above his capacity, he eventually fails in his work. If he accepts a level of work below his capacity, he meets the resistance of his innate need to express his creativity and to avoid impotence. He also meets the external resistance of his colleagues, his superiors, and his subordinates (if any), who will not tolerate the disequilibrium in organization and in payment structure caused by someone

[1] Freud, S. *Beyond the Pleasure Principle* (London: Hogarth Press, 1922).

occupying a position at a level below the capacity he can exercise. In short, each one is subject to a strong field of force tending to keep him in a position at a level of work consistent with his capacity.

It is our reality sense responding to this external field of force which produces our unconscious knowledge of the level of work we can successfully carry. For external reality to be accurately perceived and retained even unconsciously requires that there has been a sufficient working-through of what Melanie Klein has termed infantile paranoid and depressive anxieties. (I shall have more to say in a moment about this topic.) With sufficient reduction of these anxieties integration of the ego becomes sufficiently well established for the reality principle to operate, and appreciation of experience at work is possible.

It would appear that anyone who is capable of earning his own living has developed a sufficient degree of inner reality to be able to make the unconscious judgement of his work-capacity about which I am speaking. But this does not mean that the assessment of our real capacity is consciously accepted. Quite the contrary. Very few of us are capable of tolerating consciously an accurate and stable self-appraisal of our capacities and limitations. Some of our deepest unconscious defences against anxiety would be threatened – phantasy gratification, omnipotence, self-effacement. We repress our knowledge of our true capacity, and retain it repressed in our unconscious mind. This repression allows emotional oscillations in our conscious self-evaluation, while at the same time maintaining our unconscious knowledge of our adjustment to work reality. It is only in the exceptional naturally mature and integrated person that much of the unconscious knowledge of capacity becomes conscious. Consciously realistic self-appraisal is also a condition to be hoped for in a successful personal analysis.

With respect to payment for capacity and level of work, similar forces come into play. Payment above or below the level of work carried means that greater or lesser relative payment is being received by others – by colleagues, by superiors, by subordinates, or by those working in other parts of the establishment or in other establishments. These deviations inevitably become public – through positions falling vacant and having to be advertised, through newcomers bringing standards from elsewhere, or simply through comparisons of earning with colleagues and friends. Overpayment stimulates pressure from others to regain a situation of equilibrium. Underpayment stimulates pressure in oneself.

If the above observations are accurate, then much of the upheaval and disturbance about differentials (including economically devastating strikes) would appear to be resolvable if we could tap the unconscious knowledge of individuals. If we were each allocated increasing responsibility according to the unconsciously perceived growth in our own capacity, much heart-burning and disaffection might be avoided. And if we were each paid on the basis of the correct wage or salary for the level of work we carried, then much of the acute social disequilibrium and greed provoked by invidious rivalries over differentials could be obviated. Such a move might mean planned and foreseen changes in occupation if a person outran the level of work available in his existing job; but our full-employment economy has provided plenty of opportunity for our making changes of this kind.

The solution, however, is far from being so easy – as is readily appreciated from our actual experience of industrial strife. Our behaviour is not solely determined by such rational considerations. Unconscious phantasies and impulses seek gratification as well. And unconscious conflicts and anxieties produce pain and suffering. Because these processes are unconscious, they cannot be brought under the dominion of the reality-principle in mental functioning. The unconscious needs for gratification and for avoidance of frustration and pain, expressed under the code of the pleasure-principle, do not tolerate delay. They provoke immediate and compulsive forms of behaviour which, because they are unconsciously admixed with our more rational and controlled objectives, may often be self-defeating in their effect.

Working and striving for a particular standard of living, revive and reactivate some of the most primitive and deep-lying of these unconscious phantasies. These primitive phantasies, at work in the adult mind, are now much more clearly understood as a result of work stemming from Freud – notably the work in this country of Melanie Klein.[1] I shall combine some of

[1] See, for example, Klein, M. (Ed.), *New Directions in Psycho-Analysis* (London: Tavistock Publications, 1955).

the broad outlines of their conclusions with examples from industry which I have had the opportunity frequently to observe in order to illustrate the revival of these primitive phantasies in our work relationships.

Unconscious Anxieties Affecting our Behaviour at Work

In the unconscious mind, work, ambition, and desire for material gain and security revive unconscious phantasies of infantile activities and the primitive relationships with parental figures. When employment is satisfactory – when it is interesting and fairly remunerated, and when opportunity exists for progress at a rate compatible with personal development – it will tend to revive the satisfactions and unconscious constructive and creative impulses established in infancy under the influence of good feeding and experiences, and good loving impulses. The extent to which good morale may be created when work is satisfactory will depend on the strength of the primitive feelings of love and co-operativeness in the unconscious mind. In the absence or near absence of any such positive unconscious feelings, psychotic or severe psychopathic personality development occurs of a kind which reduces the capacity to work to zero or near zero – and consideration of such conditions is outside our present scope.

But even when work is experienced as good, it may not revive good unconscious memories alone. It may also revive unconscious feelings of guilt and of depressive anxiety – the residues of infantile fantasies of the destruction and loss of the good aspects of primitive objects as a result of aggressive and sadistic attacks upon these objects. Added to these depressive anxieties are the deep and strong paranoid anxieties which may be revived in the unconscious mind by the unsatisfactory features – and these are always present – in our work. These paranoid anxieties are established in the deep layers of the unconscious as a result of the projection into external objects of the young infant's greedy and destructive impulses – the external objects seeming the more dangerous and persecuting the stronger the infant's impulses and the more frustrating its external circumstances.

These very deep-lying paranoid and depressive anxieties are present to some extent in each of us, constituting a vaguely felt threat to our sanity, and indeed to our existence. They show themselves in our work for example, in the unconscious response of managers and subordinates to the fact that they are mutually dependent. This dependence readily invokes unconscious feelings of hostility and persecution, such that victimization and unfair practices are commonly anticipated to an extent which may be out of all proportion to the real situation. The giving and receiving of instructions, consciously accepted and desired as necessary for getting work out, nevertheless creates conflict at the unconscious level. Receiving an instruction is experienced as being subjected to persecuting omnipotence on the part of one's manager. Giving an instruction is experienced as wielding destructive and sadistic power. Paranoid anxiety in the receiver of orders, and depressive anxiety in the giver of them, are important reasons why the exercise of authority is chronically experienced as difficult.

In like vein, deep-lying passions of envy may be expressed. In the infantile unconscious, as Mrs Klein has recently shown[1], envy is directed against the parent's possession of creativity and adult peace of mind; it arouses intense impulses to spoil that creativity and peace of mind. In adult work, envy may manifest itself as envy of the person in the superior position who is perceived as creative and free. It may also be manifest as envy of those in subordinate positions who are perceived as having peace of mind because of lesser responsibility. In either case, unconscious envy is provocative of wrangling and perturbation in the relationship between superiors and subordinates.

Unconscious rivalry also plays its part as well as conscious rivalry. In omnipotent fantasy, parents are surpassed, their positions and their possessions are usurped; sibling rivals – the unborn ones as well as the living – are defeated and destroyed; and a state of complete gratification is achieved. At work these fantasies express themselves in omnipotent feelings (operating at all levels in executive systems) that one could do the other's job so much better, or warrants the higher job if only ability were what counted. More concretely, they are observable in the notorious difficulties which surround promotion and advancement procedures.

[1] Klein, M., *Envy and Gratitude* (London: Tavistock Publications, 1957).

Unconscious Collusion in Group Relationships

Such, then, are examples of the unconscious impulses and conflicts which coexist with the more reality-determined components of our behaviour. How, then, do we get control of the
anxieties which accompany these unconscious processes? To
some extent we counteract the anxieties by repression, and by a
variety of psychological mechanisms within the individual, as,
for example, sublimation. But they are rarely to be completely
coped with in such a manner. Attempts to reduce the pain and
anxiety of these unconscious phantasies may result in neurotic
behaviour under the influence of the pleasure principle. In our
work, such influences may not only provoke phantasies of greater
success or failure, but may provoke the actual seeking of
employment, or of payment, out of keeping with the unconsciously known limits of our capacity.

But of greater importance for our immediate purpose is the
fact that these anxieties and impulses may be externalized and
played out in group life. It was Freud, in his great studies of
group psychology,[1] who showed how we unconsciously identify
with each other, live parts of our lives by identification with the
behaviour of others and by taking these others and their
behaviour as parts of ourselves. We enter into what I would
term unconscious collusion with each other so as to pool unwanted and painful parts of our unconscious lives in group
relationships. The operation of unconscious influences in
economic life has long been familiar to economic and political
scientists – Keynes, for example, making frequent reference to
the unconscious instinctive reactions influencing the expectation
of income, the propensity to consume, and the inducement to
invest.

At workshop level, the unconscious collusive relationships
can be observed, for example, in exaggerated 'flaps' and crises
about production, or in objectively uncalled for stresses between
groups and between individuals, such as those I described earlier.

Or there may be unconscious denial and concealment of
actual difficulties. The collusive element shows in the manner in
which aspects of reality are denied all round, the resulting confused situation, for example, enabling managers and workers

[1] Freud, S. *Group Psychology and the Analysis of the Ego* (London: Hogarth
Press, 1940).

alike – directly and through their representatives – to see each other as persecuting and persecuted, guilty and injured.

But it is the larger-scale aspects of economic organization which provide the farthest removed and the most impersonal screen for the projection of paranoid and depressive phantasies and anxieties. Socially sanctioned and well-established stereotypes of groups and of individuals, however inaccurate these stereotypes may be, serve admirably to represent figures of the unconscious mind – whether idealized or persecuting. There is full scope, for instance, justifiably to take sides for or against, when group conflict exists, and by this means to live out one's internal conflicts through identification with a conflict which can be observed to exist outside.

This kind of projection of internal conflict by individuals in the mass has the most disturbing effect on the stability and sanity of our economic and industrial arrangements. It plays havoc with any basis of reality-assessment in these arrangements. It is quite incredible, for example, to what extent the reality of level of work is ignored in wage negotiations, despite the fact that agreements are supposedly made on the basis of what is referred to as the 'rate for the job'. The great railway strike of 1955 is a good example of what commonly happens. The payment differential between the footplatemen and the porters had lessened – the payment gap had closed. And so it was argued that the footplatemen had been losing. But there was no evidence considered as to what had happened to the relative levels of work of these two classes of worker. Had their work changed over the years? For, if the differential in level of work between the footplatemen and the porters had dropped in the same proportion as the differential in payment, then there was no real change in the situation. In the absence of evidence about level of work, the argument about payment could not be resolved in principle. It was resolved finally by intuitive judgement about level of work, whatever the supposed basis of the discussions.

The extent to which phantasy can override reality was also shown in the widely used and accepted argument that locomotive drivers were responsible for the safety of hundreds of passengers and for countless thousands of pounds' worth of property. The reward for this supposed responsibility was to be an increase to a minimum wage of some £10 per week. The

disjunction in thought needs only to be pointed out to be self-evident. A moment's reflection makes it clear that in fact no discretion which could affect lives is left to the driver. The safety system works according to a set of prescribed rules, non-conformance to these rules constituting negligence. Objective examination of any work situation will demonstrate that we simply do not make payment relative to the possible consequences of negligence. Yet in the heat of conflict we readily and publicly discuss and argue the ludicrous as though it were fact.

Comparisons for negotiation purposes are usually made in terms of people and not of work – the value of miners as against machinists, of typographers as against unskilled workers, and (recently) the value of those in the so-called middle-class occupations as against the value of the skilled artisan working-classes. These methods of negotiation are well-suited to the unconscious need for having invidious and, inevitably, destructive comparisons publicly made between individuals, between occupational groups, and between classes of society.

In the absence of any objective yardstick for comparing responsibilities, executive leadership is inverted. Waiting for dissatisfaction to arise becomes a basic technique for adjusting and regulating payment. When employees become sufficiently dissatisfied with their pay, they are expected to ask for more. Initiative is expected from below rather than from above. And the various groups are left to fight out their own differentials, with the employers sitting by, apparently helpless, but unconsciously taking part in the shambles through having relinquished their initiative. The consequence is a discrediting of authority, and an enfeeblement of leadership – a familiar problem in contemporary society.

It will be noted in all our examples that the maintenance of the unconsciously motivated difficulties depends upon the constant repression of the unconsciously grasped relationship between level of work, level of capacity, and a national scale of earnings. Without this unconsciously collusive repression and denial, the more chaotic, compulsive, and confused aspects of our economic relationships would be lost. But their loss would also mean the loss by the individual of a great defence against psychotic anxiety – for it is precisely these seemingly irrational and chaotic features which contain and reflect the mass

projections from our unconscious minds. I say seemingly
irrational, for their logic is the logic of the unconscious.

The Control of Unconscious Social Collusions

How, then, are these social processes akin to mass psychotic
phenomena to be kept under control? They are limited by two
factors: the coexistence of processes operating under the reality
principle; and the fact that the chaos induced to relieve unconscious pain itself becomes too painful to endure. The demands of
reality and of economic survival, of the individual and of the
group, eventually force compromise and resolution, and a
return to temporary states of equilibrium. The individual cannot
make a living if he indulges in wholesale neurotic behaviour in
his work. In the workshop and the office, for any enterprise to
survive, a minimum good working relationship is necessary in
the day-to-day work situation between managers and workers,
and between colleagues. At national level, the impact of
economic and work reality, intuitively perceived and understood, forces eventual solutions despite the emotional and
irrational impulses at work in all parties to the dispute.

But it is fast becoming apparent that the reality principle
operating at the unconscious level cannot necessarily be
counted upon to take effect quickly enough to avoid serious
disturbance to our industrial economy while disputes are in
progress. The final results of wage negotiations are too often
achieved in spite of, rather than because of, the manifest
content of the arguments brought to bear and the methods of
negotiation used. A distorted and unrealistic perception of
economic motivation, work, and payment has become established in the public mind. And the fabric of leadership is torn,
managers and workers alike finding themselves at a loss to
discover those principles on which challenging and acceptable
leadership and initiative can be exerted with respect to work
and payment.

But our analysis suggests that there are unexpectedly profound difficulties in the way of change. Unless we individually
become better able to deal with our unconscious anxieties, any
decrease in the use of unconscious collusions in industry will
only cause a displacement of projection and of chaos into other
group situations. Yet widespread change in individuals is

clearly too much to be hoped for. Such change means each one achieving a deeper relationship with himself, an increased awareness and understanding of his internal reality. And it is precisely this contact with our inner world which has always proved difficult; the threat of madness from the unconscious psychotic anxieties we bear causes us to recoil from too much personal insight and sense of reality. Nevertheless, a growth in insight and understanding in those who presume to positions of leadership and high responsibility would be of great practical value. They at least might come to grips within themselves with the forces which distort their sense of reality and, without their being aware of it, cause them to take part in the collusive arrangements to deny reality at the social level, and, indeed, unwittingly to lead such collusion.

A change to reality-based leadership means the application of methods for arranging payments in a manner precisely consistent with the level of work we are each given to carry, and work consistent with our capacity. (Our evidence suggests that the development and use of these methods is not too difficult – if we can get away from our unconscious anxiety-distorted social conception of the economic world.) Such leadership would make contact with our unconscious knowledge and inner reality. It would encourage a sense of satisfaction and peace of mind. This is not to say that any such arrangement would automatically eliminate unhappiness and neurosis. But it would mean that our work would not be one more force in itself stimulating emotional disturbance. It would at least act in the direction of stimulating in each of us as much satisfaction and peace of mind as our personality make-up and other life circumstances can allow.

Furthermore, such arrangements might enable us to find our way out of the spur to inflation caused by not having any objective standard of level of work against which to pitch, and hold firm, a satisfactory pattern of payment differentials. The alleviation of problems of differentials could effect a lessening of the destructive rivalries between groups and between classes. Publicly sanctioned acceptance of reality as a basis for considering work could allow for more satisfactory and constructive leadership. It could add to our national store of sanity. It could strengthen our national morale.

In concluding, I recognize that this analysis may be felt to lead to an essentially pessimistic outcome. But this view is not necessarily warranted. By the discovery of his techniques, Freud has made it a practical matter to gain genuine and conscious insight into the deeper recesses of our own minds. Through the theories which he and his successors have elaborated by the use of these techniques, a conscious intellectual and scientific understanding of social problems may become possible. To fail to direct our social endeavours towards greater reality based on insight is to encourage the burgeoning of the psychotic state, a state which readily calls forth its psychotic leaders. As against such a cataclysm, increasing social sanity can gradually be gained – but only if we recognize mass unconscious social collusions for what they are and bring them under the control of conscious and mature insight.

14

A Contribution to a
Discussion of Freud's
'Group Psychology and
the Analysis of the Ego'

Freud showed the possibility of reasoning about psychological
processes by the examination of group life. I should like to
consider the present-day position by looking at group behaviour
in the light of analytic devlopments since 1920 in the understanding of psychotic areas in neurotic and normal personalities
as well as in psychotics.

Let me start by inquiring why it is that psychotics cannot form
groups? For example, if you try to get them to play football or
otherwise co-operate in groups, they tend to wander aimlessly
about. Severely disturbed neurotics do form groups, but the
tendency is to form groups that are rather unstable or inflexibly
rigid; in such a way that the individuals become embedded in
the group. The more normal the personalities in individuals, the
more effective the groups that they can form. Why should this
be so?

Freud recognized that groups can have both a constructive
effect and an inhibiting effect on the individuals who compose
them. He tended to confine his considerations, however, to the
inhibiting effect of groups. I would like to reverse the process
and look first of all at the constructive side.

P

Life, in fact, begins and goes on in a group situation, despite the fact that the infant has only rudimentary ego-function and cannot consciously differentiate itself into self and other.

With individual development, however, and the independence which goes along with more mature ego development and formation which allows for symbol formation, and the recognition of the difference between self and others, constructive group relationships become possible.

Thus, for example, in committee work, and in work groups and work organizations, individuals are able to work co-operatively in such a manner as to reinforce each other's effectiveness. Group decisions become possible that are better decisions than those that might have been taken by any of the individuals concerned. Or there is the spontaneous structuring of leaderless groups in such a way that different individuals take up the lead depending upon the problem being tackled and their own individual skills for tackling them. Or again, in what Freud calls artificial groups, a hierarchy of decision taking becomes possible, calling for greater capacity the higher in the system one goes, with individuals opting into roles in these systems at a level consistent with their capacity.

These examples show that under certain group conditions, individuals are capable of publicly manifesting their own capacity level as a matter of social reality.

The constructive role-taking described requires that relationships are to some extent inhibited; in order for such inhibition and sublimation to occur, the individuals must be operating under the dominance of libido with fusion of hate transformed to constructive aggression. These psychic conditions are the same as those required for the acceptance of the reality principle and reality-testing, as against the pleasure principle.

In this connection it can be noted that it is by membership of the group that the individual achieves an important aspect of his reality-testing, for it is the group which records the socially verified results of reality testing and transmits these results from one person to another and from one generation to another. Thus it is the group which communicates the conceptualization of reality, that is to say, reality expressed in symbolic form.

But why is it that groups do not always function in this constructive manner?

Freud sets the stage for analysing this problem by establishing the identification processes by which group formation occurs. In *Group Psychology and the Analysis of the Ego*, he establishes both processes of identification – that is to say identification by introjection of the object, and identification by projection into the object. Indeed it is in that book that the process later called 'projective identification' by Melanie Klein is first described.

If now we look at Melanie Klein's development of these concepts, she makes a distinction which is germane to an understanding of group processes. That is the distinction between normal and pathological projection and introjection.

Her view is that when anxiety is strong then a great deal of splitting and possibly fragmentation takes place in the ego, with the result that projective and introjective identifications take on a fixed or psychotic quality; that is to say, the introjected object is felt concretely as inside in either split or fragmented form. Equally, when parts of the self, impulses and objects, are projected into the external object, the external object is concretely experienced as controlled or dominated by the bits that have been projected into it.

When pathological projective and introjective identifications are being made, then the experience tends to be that of the ghostly or the uncanny in the sense of being penetrated or controlled by objects or having omnipotent control over them. I think it is this quality which Freud remarks on when he points out that one of the outstanding characteristics of hypnosis is its uncanny quality.

Practical experience suggests that in ordinary social life or group processes, normal processes tend to exist side by side with processes that give the appearance of being psychotic and which I think are most accurately identified as being psychotic in fact. Let me give an example from industry. It has to do with setting prices.

What commonly happens is that the cost per unit is estimated, and a percentage profit added. This estimating procedure is complex and costly. And the results are not really used. For if Sales say the estimated price is too high, the job is usually re-estimated. Or if too low, then a higher price is set; i.e. the price is set in relation to what it is known the market will pay – and this fact is known before the estimate is drawn up.

Moreover, the estimating procedures are based upon unrealistic costing procedures, which I do not propose to go into here.[1]

The point I want to illustrate is that the price is fixed by means of the reality-based procedure of assessing the market. But not without going through the costly and troublesome unreality-based estimating procedure.

The striking thing is the way in which the unreal procedure is embedded in and coexists with the realistic perception, and is corrected by it.

The unreality-based perceptions I think are dependent mainly upon the play of unconscious omnipotence – the fantasy that whatever one creates must be good and must be valuable. There is a denial, indulged in by all the group, of the fact that it is quite possible to create valueless goods unwanted by others.

Another example is that given by Freud of the girls and their movie idol, in which there is a denial of jealousy and they become the equals of each other. There is a group-supported denial of the reality of differences among them.

There are dozens of examples that one can give all the way from the mixed picture which tends to be characteristic of reality-based work groups, through to group formations whose sole purpose seems to be to act as vehicles for the expression of psychotic processes in the individuals. Religious groups for religious observances, for example, tend to be at this latter end of the scale.

Or to take another example, although in hierarchically structured groups the reality principle requires the recognition of differences in status and capacity, and individuals are able to work to some extent on this basis, there exists side by side with reality the expression of unconscious pride or arrogance and omnipotence in these groups. These occur in the endowment of 'higher-ups' with magical power and the resentment and fear of that power; and in the split between the idealization of those at the top and the disparagement of those in intermediate groups.

Now what purpose does this participation in group psychotic

[1] See Brown, Wilfred and Jaques, Elliott. *Product Analysis Pricing* (London: Heinemann, 1964).

processes play in the psychic economy of the individual? I would suggest that we are dealing with a fundamental defence against anxiety in the so-called normal individual; I say 'so-called normal' because if any of us were in fact genuinely and deeply normal in the sense of having full insight into the psychotic content of our anxieties, then this kind of group formation would no longer serve any purpose.

By unconscious collusive relations with other individuals, it is possible for us to play out and externalize – get outside of ourselves – conflicts and anxieties which would otherwise be experienced at the deeper levels of the mind in terms of overwhelming anxiety or unendurable psychic pain and torment.

By anxiety and psychic pain I am referring to the unconscious fantasies of persecution internally by objects experienced as hostile and destructive, and to the intense unendurable psychic pain for good objects which have been experienced as damaged or injured and which may be the source of the most horrific guilt and remorse.

We can deal with these conflicts and impulses to some extent by collusive interplay in groups. Manic denial of envy and jealousy, for example, can be reinforced in the group as in Freud's example of the girls and the movie idol. Destructive impulses, hate, death wishes, can be split off and projected into members of the out-group: with the attendant development of idealization and of whitewashing of the good in-group, and paranoid attitude towards the bad out-group. Destructive impulses and paranoid impulses can then be coped with externally, to some extent by active public hate and paranoia and by psychological and, in the final analysis physical, violence. These forms are vividly observable, for example, in political debate, where the most violent slanging of the opposite camp is used as a means of exposing concealed anxieties.

One of the features about the group which is both consoling and provocative of anxiety is the fact that groups – especially corporate groups – are in fact immortal; individuals may die but the group goes on. Thus it is that by achieving his individuality within a group an individual also becomes aware of the fact of his own personal death.

As a result of the play of psychotic processes, he seeks immortality by identification with the group which is idealized;

by being a member of a powerful and ideal group, he becomes powerful and ideal as well as immortal. The most effective of such groups from the point of view of allaying anxiety, but in a pathological way, are groups which establish deities representing in a concrete way the group's sense of its own immortality.

These projections into group life are the main cause of the diminution of the effectiveness in individuals and a noteworthy characteristic of many groups.

In short, since our knowledge of reality is limited at any given time, group relationships allow for the collusive avowal of a wide range of psychotic or unreal fantasies. These fantasies then become highly structured, they allow for a variety of idealization processes: splitting and fragmentation; paranoid denigration and a cutting of the existence of omnipotent external persons and deities; denial of envy, hate, jealousy, rage, murderousness, all expressed in socially sanctioned and therefore concealed and denied ways, side by side with, and fused with, reality-based processes.

The fact that these impulses and conflicts are externally projected and built into social structures becomes clear when they are challenged by observations of reality. Resentment and fury are engendered and intense denial occurs.

In other words, resistance to new ideas is directly dependent upon how far the ideas which they would replace are the subject of unconscious collusive processes in which the individuals are involved in order to avoid anxiety and psychic pain.

The behaviour of the townsfolk in the story of the Emperor's new clothes is the myth which best embodies the psychic processes which I am trying to describe.

Coming back now to the individual, the following conclusions present themselves.

The way in which psychotic and non-psychotic processes appear side by side in a quasi-integrated manner in groups, suggest that in the so-called normal personality these psychic processes are integrated in the same way.

Following the kind of sequence described by Freud in the postscript in which he tries to discriminate between the states of being in love, hypnosis and neurosis, the following list suggests itself:

(*a*) the psychotic individual is one in whom the psychotic parts of personality are overwhelmingly strong, split off from the rest of the personality, unmitigated by normal processes, and with independence of action for longer or shorter periods of time; psychotic individuals are unable to form groups because their projections and introjections are so overwhelmingly concrete and intense that relationships with others are experienced as too persecuting and painful; they aimlessly wander about if presented with group tasks or games;

(*b*) neurosis is a process in which the psychotic and the reality-based processes are more evenly balanced and intermingled, with psychotic processes from time to time gaining the upper hand;

(*c*) the so-called normal individual is one in whom psychotic processes are fused with reality-based psychic processes and mitigated by them, making it possible to take part in reality-based group activities, but still using group life to play out in a psychotic way his deeper lying conflicts;

(*d*) the model of the genuinely normal individual is that of a person with conscious and unconscious insight into the psychotic contents of his mental processes, so that a more complete mitigation of these by reality-based processes is achieved, with reduced necessity to play out psychotic contents in unconscious collusive behaviour with other individuals in group life. He can form effective working relationships without unconscious group collusion because of the tolerance and resignation made possible by insight.

As a side issue, it may be of interest to note that with the development of society the independent individual comes more prominently to the fore. In primitive society the group is dominated by the family, and the individual tends to remain embedded in his family throughout his life. Primitive law is based on this fact and tends to be the law of the family rather than a law of the individual in his society. Modern industrial society requires a greater independence in the individual in the sense that it requires the individual to relate himself more to the large social unit unprotected by the family group in which he has grown up.

The observation of group processes and the interplay between individual and group life can give a particular perspective on primitive pre-verbal infant impulses and conflicts, and relationships; it gives a kind of magnified picture of these processes, and as such can complement both analysis and infant observation.

Index

Abercrombie, 118
Abraham, Karl, 170, 171–2
Abundant employment, 137, 138, 139
Academic freedom, 22, 25, 30, 36, 37
Academic rights, 136
Academic staff
  assessment of, 135–6
  employment tenure of, 135
Academic standards and practical work, 127
Acceptability of subordinate to manager, 6, 133, 134, 139
Access
  to data, gaining, 31
  in natural sciences, 31
Accountability (*and see* Responsibility)
  inconsistency with authority, 29, 148, 160
  in Civil Service, 135
  in hospitals, 164
  left vague, 21
  of managers, 6, 15, 133, 134, 135, 143, 144, 145
  mental models showing, 129
  nature of, in management and administration, 25
  of union leaders, 23
  in universities, 21, 30, 136
Action
  decision and, 70, 75, 92–3
  and knowledge, 68, 71
  symbolic work, 69, 71
Activity, mental: *see* Mental activity
Administration
  authority and accountability in, 25
  and behaviour, 157
  of hospitals, 18, 164
  of institutions, 157
  scientific method in, 19
Administrative work
  effort in, 118
Administrators

education for, 33, 34
educational, 33
hospital, 164
and uncertainty, 114
Adolescent crisis, 41
Adult
  behaviour, and infant psychotic anxieties, 182
  carries past with him, 179
  and laws and behaviour, 179
Adulthood, early: *see* Early adulthood
Adulthood, mature: *see* Mature adulthood
Aeneas, 74
Ageing, 57, 59
Aggression (Aggressiveness)
  of child, 156, 176
  constructive, 216
  in payment negotiations, 196
  in role-taking, 196
  and work, 70, 73, 76
Allocation of mental capacity (apparatus)
  to task, 85, 87–8
  and of time, 88
Ambition(s), 27, 76, 77, 79, 112, 188, 207
Ambivalence, 10, 62, 173, 178
  in infant, 173, 175, 176
  in process of work, 86, 88
Analysis (*and see* Psycho-analysis; Social-analysis)
  of behaviour at work, 204
  criteria for termination of, 12
  and group observation, 222
  of nature of man, 16
  by social scientists, 32
Anatomy of Judgement, 118 fn.
Annihilation, 69, 77, 193
Anxiety (Anxieties)
  about assessment, 125, 126, 127
  about capacity, 126, 127, 188, 205, 206
  about creative application, 122, 126, 127, 128

and requisite social institutions, 199

in resolution of economic questions, 212

striving towards, 199

and work, payment and capacity, 187, 203

Equitable (fair) payment (and reward) (*and see* Payment)

  arranging for, 161

  intuitive sense of, 202–3

  reactions to, 187

    to deviations from, 186, 203

  right to, 11, 15

  social-analysis and, 161

Equitable Payment, 16 fn., 108 fn., 202 fn.

Equitable society (*and see* Society), 198

Equitable work-payment scale, 79, 186, 187

Equity

  achieving, 201

  law based on, 184

  and loving impulses, 185, 192

  norms (standards) of, 178, 197

    in payment, 8, 178, 189, 196

    shared, 184–5, 197

    and super-ego, 197

  in pattern of differentials, 15, 189, 201

  psychological forces affecting, 195

  and self-justification, 195

Estimating, 217, 218

Ethics, 23

Etymological appendix, 99–102

Evaluation of our work

  unconscious, 201–2

  and conscious, 203–7

Examinations

  and aim of education, 115

  and creative application, 113–14

  essay-type, 118

  judging teacher by results of, 23

  judgement in marking, 118

  and knowledge, 114, 115, 118, 128

  for learning to work, 121

Examples

  Analysis of organization problem, 158–61

  Analysis of works manager role, 158–61

  Disturbance in capacity to work; clinical illustration, 96–8

  Girls and movie idol, 218, 219

  Inconsistency between level of work and capacity, 149–51, 153

Inconsistency between manifest and extant organization, 158–61

Mid-life crisis case histories, 48–9, 50, 51–6

Patient nursing grievance in transference situation, 194–5

Payment negotiation ignoring level of work, 210–11

Price setting in industry, 217–18

Executive hierarchy (hierarchies) (and structure and system) (*and see* Organization), 5–8, 15

  and capacity distance, 145

  defined, 5

  and four major needs of man, 15

  function of, 132

  manager-subordinate relations (*q.v.*) in, 7, 15

  and nature of society, 15

  number of levels in, 5, 143, 145

    too many, 143

  and requisite organization, 17

  role of manager in, 133

  and salary strata, 142, 143

  setting policies in, 15

  size of, 5

  stress at higher levels in, 147, 154

  work in, 15

Executive organization(s) (*and see* Executive hierarchy; Organization)

  analysis of, 16

  and effective (social) institutions, 16

  research into at Glacier Metal Company, 147–8

Expenditure, compulsive, 203

Experience, 119, 179

Experiments, 24, 29, 121

Exploitation, 78, 79

Exploration in Management, 16 fn., 160 fn.

External working (*and see* Work; Symbolic work), 42, 75–7

Facts

  and concepts, 26

  and observation, 26

Factory, mental model of, 28

Failure

  etymology of, 101

  in work, 65, 70, 75, 77, 78, 87, 92, 99

Fair pay (*and see* Equitable payment), sense of, 7

Fairness

  and equilibrium, 183

Judgement *(cont.)*
of performance, 13, 23, 116, 124, 125
in creative application projects, 123–5
gives rise to anxiety, 123–5
of students, 124
pleasure principle and, 184
and psycho-analysis, 4
quality of, 116
reality principle and, 184
and sensation of work, 119
of size of task, 88
verbalizing, 116–17
Jurisprudence, 34
Justice
capacity to tolerate, 193
and depressive position, 193
and ego, 197
norms (standards) of, 178, 181, 184, 193
and self-justification, 195–6
sense of, 167, 183, 197
and differential entitlements, 183
and equilibrium, 197
individual differences, 184
psychotic anxieties and, 181–99
and super-ego, 197

Keats, 41
Keynes, 209
Klein, Melanie, 9, 49, 50, 54 fn., 57, 82, 83, 84, 93, 94 fn., 171, 173, 174, 182, 191, 197, 205, 208
Knowledge
acquisition of (acquiring): *see below*
and certainty, 114, 117, 122
and creative application, 114, 122, 127, 129
defining, 116
and education, 113, 114, 115, 120, 121, 127, 129
and ego, 68, 74
etymology of, 100, 116
and examinations, 114, 115, 118, 128, 129
experienced as persecuting, restrictive, 69, 74, 94
function of, 67–9, 74
and psychopathology of work, 34
and judgement, 115–16
is man-made, 117
and percepts, 117
and principles and law, 196

and problem-solving, 113
and reality, 68, 213
rewards for, 114
and super-ego, 67, 68, 74
and symbol formation, 69
and symbolic work, 68
and work, 67–9, 74, 81, 90, 94, 115, 116, 118, 119, 127
difference between 116, 120
Knowledge, acquisition of (acquiring) *(and see* Knowledge), 113, 115, 116, 117
and ability to learn, 115
and aim of education, 113, 115
assessment of, 127
and creative work, 115, 127
and examinations, 115, 118, 128
grades and, 115, 128
rewards for, 114
brings security, 117
and sense of closure, 118
work and, 115

Labour
and standard of living, 66
value of, 66
Labour supply and demand, and payment levels, 185, 201
Language
careful use of, 28
and concepts, 24, 34, 47
Lantos, Barbara, 80 fn.
Law(s) *(and see* Legislation)
capacity to tolerate, 193
and collusion, 197, 198
and conscience, 197
and differential payment, 179
and duties, 198
and education, 34, 120
and ego, 197
and entitlements, 198
and equilibrium, 182, 197
and equity, 184
expressed as legislation, 30
and knowledge, 196
main task of, 198
and morality, 26
natural, theory of, 181, 182, 197
and requisite, 182, 197
supported by psycho-analytical experience, 181
and order, 193, 198
in prescribed content of work, 81

Index 247

economic, 4, 210
made explicit, 35
extant, example of in consistency with
    manifest, 158–61
in government, 178
in hospitals, 164–5
inconsistencies in, 148
    making tasks non-feasible, 149
and individual behaviour, 4, 155, 157,
    158
in industry, 136, 158
informal, 20, 22
of institutions (in society), 4, 157
in the intermediate zone, 3, 5, 12
manifest, example of inconsistency with
    extant, 158–61
    in hospital administration
    and non-feasible tasks, 149
non-requisite, 148
policies, 156, 166
political, 4
precision in description of, 22, 35
requisite, 4, 12, 156
    defined, 4, 156
    establishing, 12
    in the intermediate zone of society,
        12, 17
    social, 4, 155
    of society, 157
    of trade unions, 18
    of Universities, 18
    vagueness in, 20, 22
    and work, inconsistencies between,
        148, 149
'Organization and Science', 28 fn.
Over-employment (beyond capacity)
    (and see Employment), 78, 209
Over-payment (and see Payment), 78,
    203, 205–6
Overtime, 138

Pain, psychic, 219, 220
Painters, 43
Painting, 43
'Paradiso', 47, 63
Paranoid anxieties (and attitudes)
    and economic organization, 210
    in receiver of orders, 208
    and work, 205, 207, 207–8
Paranoid attitude to out-group, 219
Paranoid-schizoid position, 10, 16, 76,
    83, 84, 193
Paranoid-schizoid regression, 78, 79

R

Parental figures, 207
Parents, 172, 176, 177
    and child, 156, 169, 183
    envy of, 208
    and infant, 172, 208
    internalizing of, 170
    and parental norms, 169, 177
    and psychopathology of work, 73
    rivalry with, 208
    and uncertainty, 114
Participation, 3, 7, 9, 15, 16
    development of effective institutions
        for, 17
    effect of absence of, 6
    in policy-making, 8, 11, 13, 15
Passivity, and industrial society, 13
Patient(s)
    manipulations open to, 165
    nursing grievance, 194–5
    role, 165
Pattern of earnings, 202
Payment (and Pay, Reward) (and see
    Equitable Payment; Payment
    Differentials)
    in accord with ability, 79, 137, 186
    bargaining for, 11, 185, 196
    beyond capacity limits, 209
    capacity and level of work and,
        relationship between, 14, 79,
        151–3, 154, 187, 203, 205, 213
    cross-comparisons about, 8
    differential, 138
    disputes over, 201, 212
    dissatisfaction with, 211
    and equilibrium, 187, 197
    and equitable work-payment scale, 79,
        186
    reactions to deviations from, 186
    and exercise of power, 196
    and gratification, 196
    inconsistencies in arguments about, 196
    individual views about, 79, 185–6, 187,
        201
    level(s) of
        determining, 7, 185
        and power bargaining, 11, 185, 196
        and supply and demand, 185, 201
        unconscious impulses in, 185
    and level of responsibility, 7–8, 161,
        185, 201, 202
    individual views about, 79, 185, 186,
        187, 202
    of manager and subordinate, 141–2

Reality principle (*cont.*)
  psychic conditions required for acceptance, 216
  and recognition of status and capacity differences, 218
  and relationships, 184, 212, 216
  and work, 80, 205, 212
Reality sense
  in adult, 180, 188
  and behaviour, 189, 206, 209, 212
  in infant, 175
Reality-testing
  and awareness of death, 60, 61, 62, 63
  of capacity, 129, 146
  in classroom group, 128, 129
  and depressive position, 60
  and economic survival, 189
  and ego boundary region, 68
  and external world, 68, 129, 172, 188
  in infant, 172
  and point of decision, 75, 93
  in process of work, 61, 70, 71, 75, 82
  completion of, 72
  and role-taking, 216
Recruitment and selection, 140
Redlich, Hollingshead and, 163
Regression, 78, 176
Regulations
  and equilibrium, 197
  in work, 66, 74, 81
Reincarnation, 49
Relationship(s) (and Relation(s)) (*and see* Social Relationships)
  collaborative, 32
  defining qualities of, 27
  and differential entitlements, 183
  economic, 202, 211
  to employer, 67
  ethics in, 26
  family, 162
    and changing behaviour, 162
    and economic circumstances, 164
    individual, within family, 162
    and mental health, 164
    and work, 162
  group, 216, 220
    collusion in, 209–12, 219
  between infant and mother, 156, 171, 173
  between infant and outside world, 171
  sense of justice about, 183
  norms, codes and laws for, 177, 190, 198
  to object in work, 65, 66–7

a challenge, 66
  and to employer, 67
  between observer and field, 32
  with parental figures, 207
  pre-verbal, 222
  psychological, 171
  and reality principle, 184, 212, 216
  regulating (mediating), 31, 178, 190, 198
  and role-taking, 216
  with self, 213
  social: *see* Social relationships
  causing stress, 146
  between superior and subordinate (*and see* Manager-subordinate relations), 3, 7
  working, good, 212
Religious groups, 218
Religious mysticism, 58
Reparation
  to assuage guilt, 169
  and awareness of death, 58
  and balance between love and hate, 58–9, 60
  and depressive position, 49, 60, 84, 87, 176
  and meaning of death, 49
  and object in work, 65–6, 77, 87, 93
  and symbol formation, 84, 87
Representatives, elected
  analysis of role of, 16
  formulating policies, 138, 139, 160
  meeting with chief executive (managing director), 138, 160
  and requisite (and effective) social institutions, 16–17, 160
Repression
  to counteract anxiety, 209
  and economic relationships, 211
  and knowledge of own capacity, 188–9, 205, 211
Requisite, defined, 182
Requisite law: *see* Law
Research
  effort in work, 118
  into industrial relations, 147, 178
Research and development, 33, 37
Resignation, 45, 56, 62
Resistance
  to change, 157
  to new ideas, 220
Resources
  allocation (and committal) of, 86, 92, 145

and responsibility, relationship between, 149
and tasks, 86, 149
Responsibility *(and see* Accountability;
Work, level of)
and authority, consistent with, 148,
160
and capacity, 202, 206
in commercial enterprises, 18–19
and differentials, consistency between,
206
and equitable work-payment scale
(*q.v.*), 186
experience by students, 122, 123
between Government and nationalized
industries, 18
in industrial enterprises, 18
leaving unspecified, 20
level (weight) of, 8, 12, 81, 98, 109,
110, 185
and capacity, 12
experience of, 81, 109, 110
measuring, 81, 109, 110, 185
and payment, 8, 161, 185, 200, 202,
206
individual views about, 185, 202
and stress, 147, 160,
and time-span of discretion, 98, 109,
110
variations, in, 109, 110
and managers, 133, 134, 139, 144–5
and payment, 8, 147, 160, 161, 185,
200, 201, 202, 206
precision in description (definition) of,
28, 29
and resources, consistency between,
148, 160
and stress, 147, 160
yardstick for comparing, 211
Results, reporting and checking, 32
Reward(s) *(and see* Payment)
for acquisition of knowledge, 114
in education, 115
sense of appropriateness of, 183
and equilibrium, 183–4
and stress, 146
for subordinates (employees), 6, 7, 8,
134
Rights
academic, 136
of employees, 11, 15, 139
Rimbaud, 39
Rivalry

and depressive position, 177
and income (payment) levels, 78, 200
206, 213
group, 201
and payment differentials, 201
at work, 208
Riviere, 40
Robbins Report, 21, 22, 30
Role(s)
behaviour in, 31, 33, 36
concept of, 26
disciplined descriptions of, 19
of elected representatives, 16
imprecisely defined, 22
and individual, connection between,
155
level of work in, 103
measuring, 103
managerial: *see* Managerial role
of social scientist, 32
Role expectations in hospital, 165
Role-taking, constructive, 216
Role tenure, 135
Rossini, 39
Rule of thumb in management, 19
Rules
and examinations, 117
and knowledge and concepts, 117
in prescribed content of work, 66, 81
Rycroft, Charles, 82

Sadism, 73, 87, 171
Safeguards for employees, 134, 137–9, 160
Salary strata and executive structure
(*and see* Payment), 142, 143, 145
Sandwich mode of education, 35, 36, 123
Sanity and work, 99
Satisfaction
and equilibrium, 193–4
and ideas of good and bad, 172–3
and loving impulses, 192
and reality, 204
in work, 86, 148, 201, 207, 213
Scale of measurement
length, 107
mass, 108
time, 108
Scanning, 86, 90–1, 91, 95, 100
Scarcity value, 201
Schizoid defences
and collusive participation, 196
and payment negotiations, 196
and pseudo-equilibrium, 194

Standard(s) (*cont.*)
  moral, 171
  of performance, 29
  in society, 16
  of work, 65, 67, 72
Stanton and Schwarz studies, 164
Status
  differences in, in groups, 218
  equitable distribution of, 15
Stereotypes, 20, 210
Stress
  and capacity, 126, 149, 150
  in educational process, 125
  and group collusion, 209
  at higher executive levels, 147, 153
  individual, 156, 160
    and stress-inducing situations, 147
  minimized by healthy (requisite)
    social institutions, 156, 160
  and personal reputation, 150
  and work, 60, 146, 147, 148, 149
    factors in, 146
    relationship between, 147
Stress-inducing situations, 147, 154
  caused by non-requisite conditions, 149
  collusion in, 154
  and hard work, 147
  and heavy responsibility, 147
  and stress in individual, 147, 154
  in work-payment-capacity relation-
    ships, 153
Stress symptoms, creation of, 154
Strike(s), 148
  about differentials, 206
  railway, 210–11
  and representation of management's
    views to workers, 23
Structure
  of institutions, 33
  executive: *see* Executive hierarchy
Students (and pupils)
  adapting to change, 121
  anxiety of, 126, 127
  assessment of performance, 36, 116,
    122, 123, 124, 126
    in creative application projects,
      123–5, 126
    main issues in, 124
  assignments for, 122
  capacity of, 116, 126
    anxiety about, 126
  and certainty, 114
  collusion with teachers, 122, 128

creativity of, 114
and examinations, 23, 36, 115
exercise of discretion by, 122, 123
experiencing stress in work, 122, 124,
  125
initiative of, 114
and knowledge, 114, 115, 121, 122, 123
and open-ended problems, 122, 127
project work for, 122, 123, 123–5
relationship with teacher, 115
and responsibility, 123
rewards, 114, 115
of social sciences, 33
and teachers, 115, 122, 128
and uncertainty, 113, 114
and work-training period, 123
Sublimation, 58, 84, 92, 93, 98, 209, 216
Subordinate (employee) (*and see* Manager; Manager-subordinate relations)
  acceptability to manager, 6, 133, 134,
    139
  accountable to manager, 6, 134, 143
  assessment (judgement) of performance
    of, 6, 8, 9, 13, 15, 16, 66, 124, 134,
    135, 139, 141, 143, 145
  authority over, 6, 15, 133
  capacity of, and of manager, 140–1,
    145
    too close, 140, 141, 142, 143
    too far removed, 141, 142
    in financial terms, 141–3
  capacity levels of, 142, 154
  in Civil Service, 134–5
  in collusion with manager in stress-
    inducing situations, 151, 154
  demotion of, 154
  deselection of, 134, 139, 143, 145
  envy of manager, 208
  institutional tenure of, 135
  not up to job, 154
  manager accountable for work of, 6,
    133, 135, 136, 143, 144, 145
  and manager, mutually dependent, 6,
    208
  optimum distance from manager, 140,
    145
  pay relationship with manager, 141–2
  relationship with manager, 3, 6,
  removal from team, 6, 133, 134, 135,
    137, 139
  rewards of, 6, 7, 15, 134, 143, 144
  right of appeal of, 15, 138, 139
  role, tenure of, 135

Task(s) *(cont.)*
lysis and scanning in, 90–1
and mental effort and strain, 88–9, 90, 92
non-feasible, 149
objective (goal), and objective of work, 66, 67, 86
and organization, 149
as persecutor, 74
and resources, 149
and reward, 86
in running a business, 65
and symbol formation, 69
in symbolic terms, 66
and symbolic work, 70
target completion time of, 108, 109, 110
and time-span of discretion, 110, 111
Teacher(s)
assessing (judging) performance of, 23, 36, 124, 135–6
assessing students, 36, 116, 122, 124, 125, 127
and students' concern (anxiety), 126, 127
and creative application projects, 124–6, 127
and certainty, 114
collusion with students, 127, 128, 129
and knowledge, 114, 115, 119
and pay comparisons, 8
and pupils (children), 31, 115, 121, 183
and uncertainty, 114, 127
Teaching
effort in, 119
modes (methods) of, 18, 36
Technology, 25, 31
social, 32
Temperature
concept of, 104
measurement, 102, 103, 104, 107, 109
and thermometer, 106
Tenacity, 112
Tenants' associations, 31
Tenure
in Civil Service, 135, 136
employment, 135
in industry, 134, 136
institutional, 135
role, 135
of Ministers, 136
in University, 135
Termination of analysis, criteria for, 12

Theory of natural law *(and see* Law), 181
'Theory of Symbolism', 82 fn.
Thermometer, 103, 107, 110
development of, 103–8
and thermoscope, 105
Thermoscope, development of, 105
and thermometer, 105
Thinking
concrete and abstract, 83 fn.
conscious and unconscious, 120
convergent and divergent, 120
preconceptual and conceptual, 120
Thomson, 43
'Thoughts for the Times on War and Death', 48
Time
allocated to task, 88
and human activity, 110–12
limits on, 66
and the measurement of human attributes, 103–12
Time-scale
of human attributes, 110, 111
and measurement, 112
of tasks, 109, 110
Time-span (of discretion)
and anxiety, 98
and capacity, 111
of children, 111
and feelings about pay, 109
and genius, 111
and level of responsibility, 98, 109, 110
to measure level of work, 108
an objective datum, 110
and sensation of responsibility, 98, 109, 110
and target completion time, 108, 109
variations in, 110
Time-Span Handbook, 108 fn.
Touch, 89
Trade union(s)
mental model of, 28
and negotiations with management, 23, 130
leaders' accountability during, 23
organization of, 18
Trade union leaders, representing Management's views to workers, 23
Training: *see* Managerial training
Transference situation, example of grievance in, 194–5